NEW DEVELOPMENTS IN
ARCHAEOLOGICAL SCIENCE

NEW DEVELOPMENTS IN ARCHAEOLOGICAL SCIENCE

A Joint Symposium of
the Royal Society and the British Academy
February 1991

Edited by
A. M. POLLARD

Published for THE BRITISH ACADEMY
by OXFORD UNIVERSITY PRESS

28208

Oxford University Press, Walton Street, Oxford OX2 6DP

Oxford New York Toronto
Delhi Bombay Calcutta Madras Karachi
Petaling Jaya Singapore Hong Kong Tokyo
Nairobi Dar es Salaam Cape Town
Melbourne Auckland
and associated companies in
Berlin Ibadan

Published in the United States
by Oxford University Press, New York

British Library Cataloguing in Publication Data
New Developments in Archaeological
Science: Joint Symposium of the Royal
Society and the British Academy, February
1991 – (Proceedings of the British
Academy; v. 77)
I. Pollard, A. M. II. Series
930.1
ISBN 0–19–726118–3
ISSN 0068–1202

Typeset by Alden Multimedia Ltd

Printed in Great Britain at
The Alden Press, Oxford

Contents

List of Plates   vii

Preface   viii
   A. M. POLLARD

Introduction   1
   M. J. AITKEN

I. PAST HUMAN ENVIRONMENTS

Dendrochronology and Past Environmental Change   5
   M. G. L. BAILLIE

Landscape Reconstructions in South Sweden for the Past 6000   25
   Years
   B. E. BERGLUND

Soil Micromorphology in Archaeology   39
   M.-A. COURTY

II. ARTEFACT STUDIES

Lead Isotope Studies in the Aegean (The British Academy   63
   Project)
   N. H. GALE & Z. A. STOS-GALE

New Views of Early Mining and Extractive Metallurgy [summary]   109
   P. T. CRADDOCK

The Impact of Electron Microscopy on Ceramic Studies   111
   M. S. TITE

Geochemistry, Sources and Transport of the Stonehenge   133
   Bluestones
   O. WILLIAMS-THORPE & R. S. THORPE

Counting Broken Objects: The Statistics of Ceramic Assemblages   163
   C. R. ORTON & P. A. TYERS

III. ARCHAEOLOGICAL EVIDENCE FOR FOOD

The Survival of Food Residues: New Methods of Analysis, Inter-   187
   pretation and Application
   R. P. EVERSHED, C. HERON, S. CHARTERS & L. J. GOAD

Food Remains, Food Webs and Ecosystems   209
   M. K. JONES

IV. NEW SITE SURVEY TECHNIQUES

Remote Sensing in Archaeological Research   223
   I. SHENNAN & D. N. M. DONOGHUE

New Developments in Geophysical Prospection   233
   A. ASPINALL

V. THE STUDY OF HUMAN REMAINS

Light Stable Isotopes and the Reconstruction of Prehistoric Diets   247
   N. J. VAN DER MERWE

Carbon and Nitrogen Isotopes and the Amino Acid Biogeoche-   265
   mistry of Fossil Bone and Teeth [summary]
   P. E. HARE

Biomolecular Archaeology: Past, Present and Future   267
   R. E. M. HEDGES & B. C. SYKES

Meeting Summary: The Identity and Future of Archaeological   285
   Science
   A. C. RENFREW

Appendix: List of Poster Presentations on Dating Techniques   295

List of Plates

Landscape Reconstructions in South Sweden for the Past 6000 Years

following p. 24

1. Landscape reconstruction of the Ystad area for the Late Mesolithic Age.

2. Landscape reconstruction of the Ystad area for the Late Viking Age.

Remote Sensing in Archaeological Research

following p. 232

3. (a) Crop marks indicating a settlement site, and associated artificial and natural water courses. The data are from band 7 of the NERC ATM Daedalus scanner, Table 1, with a nominal ground resolution of 2 m, and have undergone an edge enhancing procedure. (b) SPOT Image panchromatic image of Morton Fen, after edge enhancement. A series of features are visible, some of which are enlarged. The pixel resolution is 10 m and the Plate shows an area *ca.* 10.2 km by 10.2 km. (c) SPOT Image panchromatic image of Morton Fen showing a medieval field boundary (T. Lane, pers. comm.), the dark horizontal line; a part of the 'Bourne-Morton Canal' (probable Romano-British age) running SW–NE on the right of the Plate; and various extinct, meandering tidal creeks.

New Developments in Geophysical Prospection

facing p. 233

4. Ground-probing radar sondages and resistivity pseudosection over a shallow tumulus. (a) radar E–W section. (b) radar N–S section. (c) twin-probe pseudosection, N–S. Subsequent excavation features are superimposed.

Preface

This volume contains the proceedings of a Discussion Meeting jointly organised by the British Academy and the Royal Society, held at the Royal Society, London, on the 13th and 14th of February 1991. The meeting organisers were Professor M.J. Aitken (Oxford), Professor F.R. Hodson (London), Professor M.K. Jones (Cambridge), Professor A.M. Pollard (Bradford), Professor A.C. Renfrew (Cambridge) and Professor M.S. Tite (Oxford). The meeting was attended by over 300 people. On behalf of the organisers, I would like to thank the British Academy and the Royal Society for their support, and Professor Harris (London), Professor Hall (Oxford), Professor Cramp (Durham) and Dr. Moorey (Oxford) for chairing the various sessions.

A. M. POLLARD

Department of Archaeological Sciences,
University of Bradford,
Bradford BD7 1DP, UK.

Proceedings of the British Academy, **77**, 1–2

Introduction

M. J. AITKEN

*Research Laboratory for Archaeology and the History of Art, Oxford University,
6, Keble Road, Oxford OX1 3QJ, UK.*

The meeting at which the papers of this volume were presented was one of several jointly organised by the Royal Society and the British Academy, the first being '*The Impact of the Natural Sciences on Archaeology*' in 1969. The emphasis at that meeting was on the unique way in which dating techniques based in the natural sciences was providing the chronological framework for prehistoric archaeology—the trains were being provided with timetables, using the allegory of Sir Mortimer Wheeler. With that process now well established, but nonetheless still of vital importance and with dating techniques ever more refined and ingenious, the organisers of this 1991 meeting felt it appropriate to give priority to the views through the semi-opaque train windows which the natural sciences were revealing, as it were. So it was decided that dating techniques should be represented by posters—of which a list is given in the Appendix to this volume—and these did indeed stimulate substantial interest and discussion. Even so there was an *embarras du choix* and the programme represented only a selection of what might have been included; also, the focus was primarily on developments that had already borne archaeological fruit rather than those no further advanced than holding potential for the future.

The wealth of possible material for the meeting is in large part due to a revolution in the funding of archaeological science that began in the seventies. Following the 1969 meeting a report was prepared by Derek Allen and Martyn Jope, both of the British Academy, making the case for the infusion of science money into this hybrid field. In due course this was accepted by the Science Research Council, then under the chairmanship of Sir Sam Edwards, and research council funding, large to us in this field but small by comparison with the needs of big science, continues to the present despite economic vicissitudes. We should be grateful to those named above, and others, for their initial efforts as well as to successive research council chairmen who have looked upon us with a kindly eye. I say 'we' meaning those of other countries too because I believe that the funding initiatives in the United Kingdom were a trigger for similar action in many of the major countries of the world.

Finally I would like to recall an earlier volume on archaeological science that was placed on my desk by Christopher Hawkes when I took up my post at the Oxford University Research Laboratory for Archaeology some 34 years ago. *La Découverte du Passé*, published in 1952 by Picard (Paris) under the editorship of A. Laming, gave a remarkable foretaste of the richness and diversity of the archaeological science field as it now is. When the history of our subject comes to be written it will surely be recognised as an early, if not the earliest, milestone.

Past Human Environments

Proceedings of the British Academy, **77**, 5–23

Dendrochronology and Past Environmental Change

M. G. L. BAILLIE

Palaeoecology Centre, The Queen's University, Belfast BT7 1NN, UK.

Summary. The long oak tree-ring chronologies constructed in Ireland, England and Germany provide the background chronological framework for the archaeology of the past seven millennia in northern Europe. The chronologies also provide year-by-year records of the response of a biological system to climatic and environmental factors. Although each chronology and its consistent ring patterns can be investigated as a source of information on local change, the areal dimension provided by the geographical spread of chronologies means that comparisons can be made between responses through time.

Numerous parameters can be investigated spatially, from periods of growth initiation to periods of sample depletion, from ring-damage events to isotopic ratios within growth rings. Hopefully we can look forward to accumulating environmental information to add to the chronological backdrop. I shall consider several lines of research that have already produced indications of future possibilities.

1. Dendrochronology and environmental change

In northern European terms it is fair to say that dendrochronology has now supplied archaeology with precise time control. It is also fair to say that archaeology, which had barely come to terms with the interpretation of either raw radiocarbon or calibrated radiocarbon chronologies has been largely unprepared for the quantum leap in precision provided by dendrochronology. No methodology exists to deal with the integration of the new tree-ring dates with the pre-existing radiocarbon, typological and ancient historical

Read 13 February 1991. © The British Academy 1992.

chronologies (Baillie 1991a). What is certain is that the number of precise dates for sites in early historic, proto-historic and prehistoric times are destined to increase; these well-dated sites will serve to mark out the course of the archaeological record and will require the rest of the archaeological record to fit itself around them. Archaeologists will have to come to terms with what could be called 'marker' dates (Baillie 1988; 1991b).

Rather similar things could be said about any environmental information which may derive from the tree-ring records. We have precise calendrical records which will supply some dated environmental information. Unfortunately this tree-ring/environmental 'kit' has come without a set of instructions and as a result techniques and approaches are having to be developed to allow attempts at reconstruction. There are basically four approaches:

i) To read off some specific tree-ring parameter as a direct indicator of some past phenomenon e.g., fire scars, moon rings, small early vessels etc.

ii) To measure some physical property of individual growth rings in the same way that measurement of carbon-14 concentrations allowed reconstruction of past variations in radiocarbon concentrations in the atmosphere.

iii) To perform regressions between tree-ring data and climate variables in the hope of forming predictive relationships.

iv) To use a proxy or indirect approach wherein parameters such as periods of tree abundance, episodes of growth initiation or synchronous tree death are used to infer environmental change.

In this article approaches i), ii) and iii) will be touched on only briefly, as their contribution to any archaeological understanding is mostly represented by hopes for the future. The main aim is to demonstrate how dendrochronology allows us to begin to document several episodes in the archaeological past where environmental change can be inferred and where, already, some pictures are beginning to emerge. One such episode, around 4000 BC, will be used to demonstrate how we may be able to integrate proxy environmental evidence from dendrochronology with pre-existing radiocarbon evidence in order to specify some events at the beginning of the Neolithic in the British Isles.

2. The background

Dendrochronology effectively began with attempts to reconstruct long-term cycles of tree-growth in semi-arid America. A.E. Douglass, an astronomer, was interested in relationships between earth climate and solar activity and reasoned that in the arid southwest, with almost constant sunshine, the year-to-year variations in ring width would mostly be driven by variations in annual moisture availability. Any medium to long-term underlying trends might then be related to variations in solar output. As a result, in the early decades of this century, he produced long tree-ring chronologies and effectively reconstructed southwestern rainfall for the last 1500 years. Interestingly his basic thesis on solar variations also appeared to work and he noted that the apparently clear sunspot cycles, recorded in his chronologies, broke down in the 17th century—the Maunder minimum in solar activity (Zeuner 1958, 17). Of course the choice of location, with growth largely responding to one climatic variable, had made the task relatively straightforward.

One unfortunate side effect of Douglass's work was to fix in the minds of people that simplistic climate/tree growth relationships were to be expected. For example, in the 1960's, some workers were happily assuming that narrow rings in English oak trees were associated with drought. Indeed, on occasion, unsuccessful attempts were made to *date* ancient tree-ring records by coincidences between narrow rings and historically recorded droughts (Schove and Lowther 1957). Such attempts ignored the complex relationship between tree-growth and a range of climatic and other variables which pertain in temperate regimes (Pilcher and Hughes 1982). However one can see the attraction in attempting to identify phenomena in ring records which can be 'read off' as specific climate information and we will see an example below.

It needs to be understood that there are clear divisions between attempts to reconstruct 'climate'—which tends towards specific information—and attempts to reconstruct 'environment' where information can be much more general and much less quantified—at least in the first instance. Most recent research on climate reconstruction has moved away from the study of single trees or single chronologies to the analysis of widespread grids of chronologies. Virtually all such areal studies have as their primary aim the reconstruction of 'instrumental' style records—how wet, how dry, how cold, how hot? Working with large grids of chronologies is in part the result of the recognition of the limitations of single chronologies, however, it is also adopted as a preliminary step towards by-passing one of the most intractable problems in dendroclimatology; the problem of the use of trees from different sources in any long chronology.

With recent work in northern Europe we know now at annual resolution how some oaks and pines responded to short term alterations in climate/environment. One inevitable consequence, and we will see an example of this below, will be to move away from previous blanket assertions like 'this was a cold century' and to get closer to the reality of the very considerable variations in the seasons, years and decades which go to make up centuries. In addition, the spreading network of tree-ring chronologies should allow us to get away from the old, and previously inevitable, assumptions of the type which held that 'if it was cold in Britain it was cold everywhere'. Hopefully we will begin to see the regional variability which may be the key to reconstructing changes in the past circulation patterns of the globe.

2.1 Direct indicator approach

One of the most straightforward applications of dendrochronology to an environmental problem is the dating of fire-scars. In north America, where fire history has been studied extensively, records can be carried back for hundreds even thousands of years. Plots of fire frequency against time show periods when fires were rare or common. This proxy information can then be compared with environmental and archaeological information in order to separate out natural from human-induced change.

As was noted with Douglass's work, trees growing in limiting conditions can be extremely good indicators. In a more recent example, it has been observed that the narrowest 10% of growth rings in Sequoia dendron from Nevada show very good agreement with the Palmer Drought Index. This should allow reconstruction of frequencies over the last two millennia (Hughes 1989).

However, there can be difficulties associated with the interpretation of specific phenomena in tree-ring records. This is well exemplified in the case of an anomaly in European oak rings known as 'small early vessels' (SEV's). These anomalous rings make themselves obvious in that the hollow vessels formed at the beginning of an oak ring, usually in April to May, are abnormally small—diameters perhaps 0.06 mm or less compared to the normal 0.12 mm. These vessels fall below the resolving power of the human eye and the ring therefore appears as blurred or indistinct. The phenomenon tends to be rare, certainly in oaks in the British Isles, with only a few trees exhibiting such rings; indeed even those trees which exhibit SEV's may only exhibit one in a lifetime of several hundred years. So SEV's can be spotted fairly easily and it would be attractive if they could be related directly to some climatic variable. Existing literature from the Soviet Union (Bolychevtsev 1970) suggests that such rings are associated with severe frost causing damage to the growing tissue. However, an unpublished preliminary British study on long-lived oaks from Sherwood Forest, which attempted to relate SEV's to cold winters, could only be described as inconclusive. Interestingly, Fletcher (1975) did observe very clear and consistent SEV's seventeen years apart in the years AD 1437 and 1454 in many of the oak panels which he used in the construction of the 'English' type A art-historical chronologies. These observations were out of line with most other work in the British Isles, where no obvious SEV consistency has so far been observed. Indeed, this unusual feature served as a clue that the oaks concerned were probably not of English

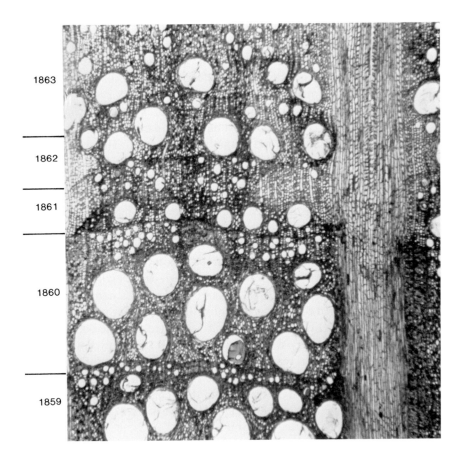

1863

1862

1861

1860

1859

Figure 1. Small Early Vessels in the growth ring for AD 1861 in an oak from Cadzow, Scotland. This could be a direct result of the severe cold conditions recorded for Christmas 1860.

origin. The situation was resolved and the SEV's better explained when it was proven that the oaks in question had come from the Eastern Baltic (Baillie *et al.* 1985; Eckstein *et al.* 1986). So perhaps we can still assume that there may be some relationships between SEV's and extreme cold conditions. We could therefore look to see if there are periods or areas in the British Isles in which they are more common. Figure 1 shows an extreme SEV in an oak from Cadzow in central Scotland in the growth ring for 1861. It can be seen that the spring vessels in this case are only 25% of normal size. The effect is so severe that ray tissue is also disrupted. This example highlights the problem with interpreting such phenomena. Jones (1959) cites a reference to oak being "the only indigenous deciduous tree to suffer notably from the severe weather of Christmas 1860". This seems to be evidence for a clear link between some SEV's and cold winters. Unfortunately, few trees show the effect and it seems possible that the presence of an SEV may register no more than a single night of extreme cold or wind chill. The SEV anomaly, one of the few known to occur in oaks, may therefore form a poor basis for defining cold winters but does require proper analysis.

A related phenomenon, certainly observed in French and German oaks, is included sapwood. Here severe frost damage can cause an oak to leave a ring of unconsolidated sapwood within its main stem. The date of such obvious rings can immediately be attributed to very extreme frost conditions. Again, as might be expected with hindsight, such effects were observed by Fletcher in his Baltic timbers (Tapper *et al.* 1978). The phenomenon is so far not recorded by British dendrochronologists and this may reflect our less continental climate. However it does raise the possibility that identification of such effects in ancient trees might allow the identification of episodes of anomalous cold. The observation of curious concentric weathering patterns on some bog oaks may be the results of just such cases.

Having raised the issue of 'frost' rings we must note Lamarche's observations of frost damaged rings in his upper tree-line bristlecone pines in California (Lamarche and Hirschboeck 1984). It was noted that the occurrence of these frost effects, again possibly produced in only one or two nights, were strongly correlated with years of climatic upset following large volcanic eruptions—well exemplified by a notable frost ring in 1884 following the Krakatau eruption of 1883 and leading to their courageous suggestion of a 17th century BC date for the Thera eruption on the basis of a severe frost ring event in 1627 BC.

Overall, outside areas of limiting conditions, observation of specific effects in tree-rings which are attributable to specific causes will always tend to be rare and fortuitous.

2.2 Physical measurement approach

The concentration of radiocarbon in tree-rings was mentioned above as an example of a global variable which could be reconstructed by analysis of a single sample effectively anywhere on Earth. Pearson measured the $^{14}C:^{12}C$ ratio in consecutive samples of Irish Oak from all periods of the last 7 millennia (Pearson *et al.* 1986) while Stuiver did the same, for the last 4500 years, using German wood (Stuiver and Becker 1986). So there is now a continuous record of past variation in radiocarbon concentration in the atmosphere, initially produced for correction of archaeological radiocarbon dates but now regarded as a proxy record of past solar variation. Although not overtly climatic, the radiocarbon to solar activity to Earth climate relationship has led to attempts to compare the past radiocarbon variations with proxy climatic records deduced from glacial activity (Wigley and Kelly 1990).

The only climatic variable likely to have a global component is temperature. Although temperature is strongly regional it is clearly dependant on the overall temperature of the globe; underlying trends should be detectable at a regional level. Rainfall and pressure on the other hand tend to be inherently regional in character, so attempts to infer these variables from tree-rings will normally be at a regional level. Isotopes used for climatic study include ^{13}C, deuterium (^{2}H) and ^{18}O. Unfortunately isotopic studies have a somewhat checkered history. The ratio of ^{16}O to ^{18}O in wood cellulose in theory holds the best hope for temperature reconstruction. One study on German oak produced a reconstructed temperature curve so similar to the Central England Temperature curve as to be almost unbelievable (Libby *et al.* 1976). Unfortunately other workers were less than convinced and no attempt appears to have been made to extend the record into the distant past (Wigley *et al.* 1978). The controversy remains and oxygen isotopes in tree-rings remain one of the great unexplored areas of climatic research.

Libby *et al.* also measured hydrogen/deuterium ratios and discerned a warming trend during the 19th century. Those results are borne out by Epstein and Krishnamurthy (1990) who measured the same ratios in trees from 23 different locations and found very consistent agreement on warming over the same period. Epstein and Krishnamurthy also reported carbon-13/12 ratios in growth rings and suggested quite strong and consistent climate signals with suggestions of consistent underlying warming over the last 1000 years. So the potential for detailed, widespread, measurements of oxygen, carbon and hydrogen stable isotopes seems enormous especially when coupled with the existence of precisely dated, seven millennia long, tree-ring chronologies from a number of areas.

One other physical parameter, which has been widely favoured in studies on conifers in Europe, is maximum late-wood density; which is taken to represent a relatively clear temperature record (Schweingruber *et al.* 1979; Hughes *et al.* 1984). The potential of the method is well exemplified in a recent reconstruction of summer temperatures in Fennoscandia (Briffa *et al.* 1990). In this work a linear regression equation relates summer temperature to both ring width and maximum latewood density in current and succeeding years. The resulting reconstruction is the longest so far reported at annual resolution. Their main conclusion is that for Fennoscandia at least the prevailing views on a centuries long medieval Warm Epoch followed by the centuries long Little Ice Age do not seem to hold. Most variability in their record is on a scale from years to decades. The potential in both isotope and density studies has to be considerable. Unfortunately their impact on archaeological understanding has so far been minimal.

2.3 The grid approach

Ideal situations for climate reconstruction are clearly those areas where growth is limited by one principle climate variable. Unfortunately in temperate areas such as Europe, such simple regressions are unlikely to be successful. The preferred approach in Europe, following the lead of Fritts in America (1976; Fritts *et al.* 1979), has been the establishment of large spatial grids of tree-ring chronologies and their regression onto climate variables such as temperature, rainfall and atmospheric pressure. The obvious complexity of regressing large grids of tree-ring data with large grids of climatic variables has led inevitably to some simplification of approach, admirably stated by Briffa *et al.* (1983) in their explanation of Fritts' procedures:

"They have used a transfer function approach where a set of dependant variables or *predictands* (such as atmospheric pressure at each of several locations, or the loadings on principal components of pressure patterns) is related, using canonical regression techniques, to a multivariate set of regressors or *predictors* (ring width series from a network of sites)".

This type of highly mathematical approach, applied to large grids of data, has so far been restricted to study of modern chronologies: in part this is because of the need for large numbers of chronologies, something not yet available for the distant past. It is also because most of the existing studies have involved attempts to verify reconstructions against existing instrumental records. Most of these exercises have been successful in showing that regression equations can produce reconstructions which account for significant proportions of the variance in the climatic data. Examples include reconstructions of English temperature and rainfall from a grid of 14 mostly British Isles chronologies (Briffa *et al.* 1983), atmospheric pressure from a similar grid (Briffa *et al.* 1986) and southern English riverflow from some seven chronologies in Britain and northern France (Jones *et al.* 1984). With more chronologies it becomes possible to undertake major experimental exercises. Briffa *et al.* (1987) used a grid of 75 modern chronologies to attempt "a series of exploratory reconstructions of European mean-sea-level pressure variations (over Europe) encompassing a number of...seasons...back to 1750". Their results were markedly good at reconstructing the known pressure patterns for the most extreme years but much less good for the remainder. It seems reasonable to assume that the current mathematical approaches will be refined and new approaches will be developed given the availability of the chronologies and the instrumental records. However, there seems little urgency to attempt long-term reconstructions until dendroclimatologists can maximise their success in explaining climatic variance from the tree-ring grids.

As noted above one of the major problems with attempting to extend such areal reconstructions back in time, beyond recent chronologies, relates to the fact that most long chronologies are inevitably composed of ring patterns from unknown sources. The dendrochronologist, usually building long chronologies for dating purposes, links from modern trees with known site provenance to historic timbers which can only be attributed to a region. So built into any long chronology will be potential changes in tree response to climate.

The extreme case would be a chronology which extends back to trees which grew on the surfaces of bogs. It seems unlikely that such trees would have the same response to climate as modern parkland oaks. Such considerations, in conjunction with the relatively small number of long chronologies and the limited success in reconstructing climate variables has so far inhibited attempts at long reconstructions.

2.4 The proxy approach

We now want to look at the potential for identification and interpretation of phenomena in the tree-ring record which allow 'archaeological' style inferences to be made about environmental change. Although in the study of such phenomena the climate variables can seldom be specifically identified and quantified, they do frequently provide markers in the record of the ancient past which at least point to periods where detailed analysis might be worthwhile. After all, so poor is our knowledge of past environments that any information is potentially valuable at least as a starting point.

The types of information which we can glean immediately from the precisely dated tree-ring records relate to phenomena such as episodes of widespread depletion in the sub-fossil record and episodes of extreme growth reduction (presumably episodes of extreme growth enhancement would also be of interest). To give an example, if oak trees have been growing continuously on the surface of a bog for 1500 years and suddenly that bog no longer supports trees then something has changed.

We can hazard a guess that the change is environmental and that it was detrimental for tree-growth; a useful working hypothesis might be that conditions became wetter. A qualification would have to be put in to separate local effects from widespread effects. For example, oaks dying out on a single bog could be explained by some local change in drainage pattern; if oaks die out synchronously on bogs hundreds of kilometres apart then we are probably seeing the effects of environmental change (Leuschner and Delorme 1988).

Once we have specified any environmental event, we can look for other precisely-dated information with which to test our hypothesis. We can also pose the question of the likely effects of any significant increase in wetness on early agricultural societies; if things are bad enough to wipe out oaks on bogs how were things on dry land? We can then look to the archaeological record for signs of associated change. Unfortunately, most of the time, the archaeological record lacks the time control necessary to make direct comparisons with suggested environmental effects derived from tree-rings.

Exactly such thinking has been occasioned by the discovery that some Irish oaks tended to put on their *narrowest* growth rings at the times of large volcanic dust-veil events, as marked in the Greenland ice-cores (Baillie and Munro 1988). We also know that when the Irish oaks suffered at 207 BC and AD 540 there are historical records of atmospheric effects and famines affecting human populations from Europe to China (Baillie 1991b). There are quite plausible suggestions of similar juxtapositions of environmental effects and human stress in both the 1620's BC and in the mid-12th century BC (Baillie 1989a; 1989b; 1990a). Interestingly if we hypothesise increased wetness in the 17th century BC we already know that bog oak systems which had been continuously regenerating on *both* East Anglian and Lancashire peatlands since 3200 BC, are interrupted some time after 1680 BC (Baillie and Brown 1988). However for the purposes of this paper we will concentrate on two events which allow us to draw in both environmental deductions from dendrochronology and dated archaeological evidence to demonstrate the power of this proxy approach.

2.4.1 Case 1: the 208 BC event

During the construction of the Belfast 7000 year oak chronology some thousands of sub-fossil oaks were collected from northern Irish bogs. It proved possible to construct a continuous year-by-year chronology from 5289 BC to 949 BC and from 947 BC to 229 BC (Pilcher *et al.* 1984). At 229 BC (197 $\pm$ 9 BC estimated death date allowing for missing sapwood) bog oaks cease to be represented in the random collections; what happened? Subsequently it transpired that there was a large volcanic dust-veil event registered in Greenland at 210 $\pm$ 30 BC (Hammer *et al.* 1980). Irish archaeological oaks show a 'narrowest' ring event at 207 BC (Baillie and Munro 1988); Lamarche observes a frost ring at 206 BC in American bristlecone pines (pers. comm. but see also Lamarche and Hirschboeck 1984). Pang and Chou (in Wiesburd 1985) point out records of atmospheric effects, summer cold and severe famines in China at the same time; Forsyth (1990) is able to accumulate similar records from early Roman sources relating to the middle of the same decade; Hollstein's German oaks show a severe reduction in ring width (Hollstein 1980); Becker and Schirmer (1977) indicate the initiation of a major phase of river gravel deposition. The Becker and Schirmer case is particularly interesting. They made a point of stressing a depositional phase of river gravel oaks beginning in 226 BC—'About 220 BC a renewed phase of flooding began to destroy the riverine forest...(shown by) 46 cross-dated trunks from eight exposures...(this was) obviously the most important horizon of (the) Holocene Main Valley...simultaneously evident in the Main and Danube area..." (Becker and Schirmer 1977, 307). When this horizon was being referred to in the early 1980's (Baillie 1982, 236) no specific environmental event was known about, so the specific 226 BC date for the initiation of a flooding phase was not regarded as significant. However now that we know of the 208–204 BC dust-veil event, with its implications for the demise of the Irish bog oaks around 200 BC, the date 226 BC from Germany takes on an added importance. Does it, as appears at face value, represent some sort of environmental downturn starting *before* the 208 BC event?—if so the 208 BC event may simply be superimposed on some pre-existing change.

The reason for raising this issue is because of the very high chronological resolution provided by dendrochronology and historical information; a few years become important in interpretation of events. It becomes important to know if Becker and Schirmer's depositional phase really started pre-208 BC.

One key element in their 1977 paper related specifically to the dating— "...the Iron-Roman Age tree-ring patterns have been dated absolutely, following their successful correlation with the ring sequences of Roman oak bridges ...(Hollstein 1967...)" (Becker and Schirmer 1977, 307). So their ring patterns were actually dated against Hollstein's chronology. However, we know that until the late 1970's Hollstein had a 26 year error in his Roman-period chronology—he had mistakenly allowed the dating of his chronology, for the period before the 4th century AD, to be based on an historical reference to the bridge at Köln having been built in AD 310 (Hollstein 1980). Various workers both archaeological (Baatz 1977) and dendrochronological (Schmidt and Schwabedissen 1978) pointed out that there had to be an error in the placement of the chronology. By 1980 this error had been corrected by 26 years (a tree-ring date of AD 310 after correction became AD 336 (Hollstein 1980)). So it seems that Becker and Schirmer's 226 BC initiation of a German flooding event, dated against Hollstein's uncorrected chronology, should be moved forward by 26 years and actually refers to an initiation in 200 BC! If correct, and the deduction appears to be borne out by contemporary comments by Becker and Delorme (1978, 59), we can add to the list of environmental factors associated with the 208 BC event. The initiation of a 350 year depositional phase, in some German river valleys, immediately after the event suggests some significant environmental trigger mechanism. So is the observed demise of bog oaks in the north of Ireland and the deposition of river gravel oaks in Germany direct evidence for a climatic downturn which registered around (though not necessarily everywhere around) the

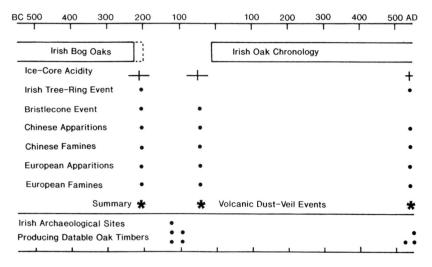

Figure 2. Accumulating evidence for three historically recorded, dust-veil related, environmental events in 208 BC, 44 BC and AD 536. The strange distribution of tree-ring dated archaeological sites in Ireland is included for comparison.

northern hemisphere? Is the combined evidence sufficient to confirm that after the 208 BC dust-veil conditions in northern Europe became a lot wetter?

Interestingly the 208 BC event is not the only one in the first few centuries BC. Although nothing shows up in Irish oaks, there is an exactly similar package of ice-core, bristlecone, Chinese and European information related to the important dust-veil event of 44–42 BC. The possible archaeological significance of these events becomes apparent when reference is made to Figure 2. When the Irish tree-ring chronologies are plotted for the period 500 BC to AD 500 the 197 ± 9 BC to 13 BC gap is apparent. The indicated dust-veil events could be classed as independent information. However, it is the five tree-ring dated archaeological sites which are the most remarkable. In twenty years of sample accumulation only five Irish archaeological sites have produced timbers datable by dendrochronology in the thousand years from 500 BC to AD 500. All five lie between 208 BC and 44 BC; they are two major sections of bog trackway, two major sections of linear earthwork and the timbers from the ritual temple built at Navan Fort, the ancient capital of Ulster, in 95/94 BC. Something archaeological must have changed; perhaps new people or new social organisation or even something as mundane as changed conditions which favoured the survival of timbers.

2.4.2 Case 2: The early Neolithic event

If we trace back slightly further in the history of the development of the

Belfast oak chronology, there was a time, before its extension to 5289 BC, when the long chronology started at 3938 BC (Pilcher *et al.* 1977; Baillie 1982). Indeed, quite a lot of difficulty was encountered in splicing the extension onto the long chronology. Such chronology building problems are normally due to depletions in the number of available oaks (Baillie 1979). However, once the chronology had been successfully extended little further thought was given to the period of difficulty.

The date 3938 BC does however begin to take on some potential significance when, in the course of outlining an English prehistoric chronology, it is discovered that in Lancashire it is possible to build a bog oak chronology from 1680 BC to 3916 BC and another from 4023 BC to 4989 BC. Extensive random sampling fails to turn up any bog oaks crossing the period 4023 BC to 3916 BC. So in two areas, at around the same time, difficulties are associated with chronology construction using oaks which had grown on the surface of peat bogs! More interesting still, the very period at which there is a depletion in bog oaks is a period when English tree-ring workers are able to find oaks from an archaeological site, from river gravels and from submerged coastal sources (Morgan *et al.* 1987; Hillam *et al.* 1990). Indeed the last ring of the archaeological timbers—from the Sweet track in the Somerset levels—is now known to have grown in 3807 BC. Now in every case—a track across wet bogland—oaks deposited in river gravels and submerged coastal oaks—there is some suggestion of potential increased wetness or increased runoff. (The term 'submerged coastal oaks' is used quite deliberately in preference to 'submerged forest' for the simple reason that these submerged oak trees may not have grown where they are now lying but may have been deposited in these coastal estuarine sites by water action—this is currently an open question). When this is added to the bog oak depletions which again give rise to questions of increased wetness it becomes apparent that, again, something is going on; we can suggest an episode during which there was environmental change.

What may be more surprising is that in this case we may be able to bring in more archaeology than simply the Sweet Track. For the purposes of this paper all the British and Irish Neolithic and Mesolithic radiocarbon dates accumulated by the CBA up to 1980 were tabulated. These form a quite reasonable sample and they are plotted in Figure 3. Now the problem for anyone trying to work with Neolithic radiocarbon dates *and tree-ring dates* is that the two are incompatible. It is extremely difficult to convert radiocarbon dates into any sort of useful real-age ranges without extending their ranges to the point of absurdity. However, with the availability of the high-precision radiocarbon calibration curve (Pearson *et al.* 1986) it is possible to convert tree-ring dates to tight ranges of radiocarbon years. So we

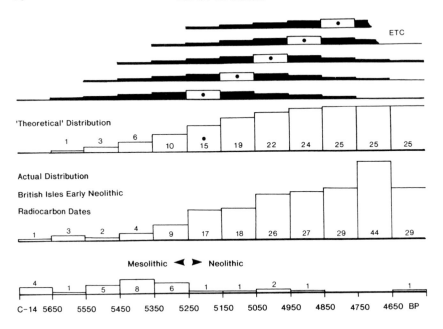

Figure 3. Suggested explanation for the observed distribution of Neolithic radiocarbon dates. Accumulated 'smeared' distributions for each century of the early-Neolithic (marked with dots) would account for the observed distribution. This approach suggests a sudden start to the Neolithic and demise of the Mesolithic.

can look at the environmental information in terms of radiocarbon years and compare this with the archaeological radiocarbon dates.

One obvious question in this context is "when does the Neolithic in the British Isles start?" Other workers have been seduced into belief in an 'earliest' Neolithic by the handful of very early radiocarbon dates for the Neolithic site at Ballynagilly in northern Ireland (Williams 1989) and by the occasional occurrence of cereal sized grass pollen in pre-elm decline deposits (Edwards and Hirons 1984). None of this evidence is very convincing and if Ballynagilly were taken out of the equation there would be essentially no archaeological evidence for an earliest Neolithic in the British Isles at all. The Ballynagilly dates are highly likely to have been affected by 'old wood' considerations, especially as the house was constructed using riven oak planks. Williams highlights this point but then makes the bizarre decision to *exclude* dates on the planks themselves while *including* dates on undifferentiated charcoal, and excludes the perfectly acceptable dates for the house fabric itself (*op. cit.* 512). As a non-believer in the early Ballynagilly dates, a different approach is advocated here.

Although the 'tail' of Neolithic radiocarbon dates extends back to 5800 BP (39th century bc), common sense and a realistic approach to the smearing

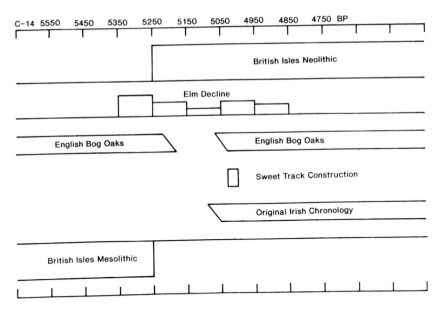

Figure 4. Simplified diagram, on a radiocarbon timescale, showing the end of the Mesolithic, the start of the Neolithic, the elm decline, a presumed environmental dislocation in bog oak survival and the construction of the Sweet Track. The close proximity of all these parameters raises the question of the role of environmental change in the Neolithic colonization of the British Isles.

of radiocarbon dates would suggest that the first serious Neolithic activity is around 5300 BP (33rd century bc). This can be justified by crudely modelling the likely spread of radiocarbon dates from the first century of Neolithic activity and accumulating similar spreads from each successive century. This approach can be justified on the strength of the eight century spread of 90% of the 62 routine radiocarbon dates associated with the English Neolithic tree-ring complex (Baillie 1990b). The effect of such modelling is shown in Figure 3 and the fit to the observed distribution suggests that this approach is on the correct lines. It is interesting to note that the main cluster of Mesolithic radiocarbon dates ends around 5400 BP (34th century bc).

In Figure 4 this simplified Mesolithic transition is indicated along with the spread of radiocarbon dates for the (almost certainly synchronous) elm decline (Edwards 1985), the accurate 'radiocarbon' dates for the English bog oak 'gap', the Sweet Track and the original end of the Belfast long chronology. It may be an illusion but it is possible that in this Figure we may be able to 'see' the Neolithic colonisation of the British Isles in an environmental context. Given the close proximity of something environmental happening at around the time of the colonisation, the question then becomes whether the Neolithic colonisation was prompted by some environmental pressure?

It should be noticed in this context that *two* German tree-ring laboratories also experienced difficulties in their chronology construction around 4000 BC (Leuschner and Delorme 1984, 1988; Becker pers. comm.); so the environmental event, if there was an event, may have been widespread and extended in character. It would be a pity to leave this discussion without making one minor point. It is worth pointing out that the placement of the Sweet Track does, as would always have seemed sensible, fall *after* the suggested start of the Neolithic. This is important because the two dates are, to a large extent, arrived at independently.

What does this all mean? We have looked at two episodes where dendrochronology supplies not only time control but hints of environmental change. Irrespective of the fact that we cannot quantify those changes in degrees centigrade or in millimetres of rainfall, we can assert with some conviction that there is more than a suggestion of both environmental and social change at these times. We can also reasonably ask what else was going on at the same times which might be traced in the archaeological record. Dendrochronology is opening up a new kind of window into the past and suggesting significant events which until now have been virtually invisible. We have looked at two examples but there are others with every bit as much substance, for example at AD 536 (Baillie 1991b), 1159 BC (Baillie 1989b), 1628 BC (Baillie 1990a) and 3195 BC (Baillie 1989a). Obviously there must be others. At least some of these are periods of abrupt change and suggest that the concept of punctuated equilibrium requires further consideration in the archaeological record.

3. Conclusion

There appears to be unlimited potential for the reconstruction of various aspects of past environmental change from tree-ring records.

References

Baatz, D. 1977: Bemerkungen zur Jahrringchronologie der römischen Zeit. *Germania* 55, 173–179.

Baillie, M.G.L. 1979: Some observations on gaps in tree-ring chronologies. In Aspinall, A. and Warren, S.E. (editors) *Symposium on Archaeological Sciences* (Bradford, University of Bradford) 19–32.

Baillie, M.G.L. 1982: *Tree-Ring Dating and Archaeology* (London, Croom-Helm).

Baillie, M.G.L. 1988: Marker dates—turning prehistory into history. *Archaeology Ireland* 2(4), 154–155.

Baillie, M.G.L. 1989a: Do Irish bog oaks date the Shang Dynasty? *Current Archaeology* 117, 310–313.

Baillie, M.G.L. 1989b: Hekla 3—just how big was it? *Endeavour* 13(2), 78–81.

Baillie, M.G.L. 1990a: Irish tree-rings and an event in 1628BC. In Hardy, D.A. (editor), *Thera and the Aegean World III Vol. 3* (London, Thera Foundation) 160–166.

Baillie, M.G.L. 1990b: Checking back on an assemblage of published radiocarbon dates. *Radiocarbon* 32, 361–366.

Baillie, M.G.L. 1991a: Suck-in and smear: two related chronological problems for the 1990's. *Journal of Theoretical Archaeology* 2, 12–16.

Baillie, M.G.L. 1991b: Marking in marker dates: towards an archaeology with historical precision. *World Archaeology* 23, 233–243.

Baillie, M.G.L. and Brown, D.M. 1988: An overview of oak chronologies. In Slater, E.A. and Tate, J.O. (editors), *Science and Archaeology, Glasgow 1987* (Oxford, British Archaeological Reports British Series 196) 543–548.

Baillie, M.G.L. and Munro, M.A.R. 1988: Irish tree-rings, Santorini and volcanic dust veils. *Nature* 332, 344–346.

Baillie, M.G.L., Hillam, J., Briffa, K. and Brown, D.M. 1985: Re-dating the English art-historical tree-ring chronologies. *Nature* 315, 317–319.

Becker, B. and Delorme, A. 1978: Oak chronologies for Central Europe: their extension from Medieval to Prehistoric times. In Fletcher, J. (editor), *Dendrochronology in Europe* (Oxford, British Archaeological Reports International Series 51) 59–64.

Becker, B. and Schirmer, W. 1977: Palaeoecological study on the Holocene valley development of the River Main, Southern Germany. *Boreas* 6, 303–321.

Bolychevstev, V.G. 1970: Annual rings in oak as an index of secular cycles of climatic fluctuation. *Lesoved*, Moskva, 15–23. (English translation in Fletcher, J.M. and Linnard, W. (editors), *Russian Papers on Dendrochronology and Dendroclimatology 1962–1972* (Oxford, Research Laboratory for Archaeology, Oxford University) 1977).

Briffa, K.R., Jones, P.D., Wigley, T.M.L., Pilcher, J.R. and Baillie, M.G.L. 1983: Climate reconstruction from tree-rings: Part 1 Basic methodology and preliminary results for England. *Journal of Climatology* 3, 233–242.

Briffa, K.R., Jones, P.D., Wigley, T.M.L., Pilcher, J.R. and Baillie, M.G.L. 1986: Climate reconstruction from tree-rings: Part 2 Spatial reconstruction of summer mean sea level pressure patterns over Great Britain. *Journal of Climatology* 6, 1–15.

Briffa, K.R., Wigley, T.M.L., Jones, P.D., Pilcher, J.R. and Hughes, M.K. 1987: Patterns of tree-growth and related pressure variability in europe. *Dendrochronologia* 5, 35–57.

Briffa, K.R., Bartholin, T.S., Eckstein, D., Jones, P.D., Karlen, W., Schweingruber, F.H. and Zetterberg, P. 1990: A 1400-year tree-ring record of summer temperatures in Fennoscandia. *Nature* 346, 434–439.

Eckstein, D., Wazny, T., Bauch, J. and Klein, P. 1986: New evidence for the dendrochronological dating of Netherlandish paintings. *Nature* 320, 465–466.

Edwards, K.J. 1985: The elm decline. In Edwards, K.J. and Warren, W.P. (editors), *The Quaternary History of Ireland* (London, Academic Press) 288–289.

Edwards, K.J. and Hirons, K.R. 1984: Cereal pollen grains in pre-elm decline deposits: Implications for the earliest agriculture in Britain and Ireland. *Journal of Archaeological Science* 11, 71–80.

Epstein, S. and Krishnamurthy, R.V. 1990: Environmental information in the isotopic record in trees. *Philosophical Transactions of the Royal Society of London* A330, 427–439.

Fletcher, J.M. 1975: Relation of abnormal earlywood in oaks to dendrochronology and climatology. *Nature* 254, 506–507.

Forsyth, P.Y. 1990: Call for Cybele. *The Ancient History Bulletin* 4.4, 75–78

Fritts, H.C. 1976: *Tree-Rings and Climate* (London, Academic Press).

Fritts, H.C., Lofgren, G.R. and Gordon, G.A. 1979: Variations in climate since 1602 as reconstructed from tree-rings. *Quaternary Research* 12, 18–46.

Hammer, C.U., Clausen, H.B. and Dansgaard, W. 1980: Greenland ice sheet evidence of post-glacial volcanism and its climatic impact. *Nature* 288, 230–235.

Hillam, J., Groves, C.M., Brown, D.M., Baillie, M.G.L., Coles, J.M. and Coles, B.J. 1990: Dendrochronology of the English Neolithic. *Antiquity* 64, 210–220.

Hollstein, E. 1967: Jahrringchronologien aus vor-römischer und römischer zeit. *Germania* 45, 60–84.

Hollstein, E. 1980: *Mitteleuropäische Eichenchronologie* (Mainz am Rhein, Phillip von Zabern).

Hughes, M.K. 1989: The tree-ring record. In Bradley, R.S. (editor), *Global Changes of the Past* (Boulder, Colorado, UCAR/Office for Interdisciplinary Earth Studies) 117–137.

Hughes, M.K., Schweingruber, F.H., Cartwright, D. and Kelly, P.M. 1984: July-August temperature at Edinburgh between 1721 and 1975 from tree-ring density and width data. *Nature* 308, 341–344.

Jones, E.W. 1959: *Quercus L.* in biological flora of the British Isles. *Journal of Ecology* 47, 169–222.

Jones, P.D., Briffa, K.R. and Pilcher, J.R. 1984: Riverflow reconstruction from tree-rings in southern Britain. *Journal of Climatology* 4, 461–472.

LaMarche, V.C. Jr. and Hirschboeck, K.K. 1984: Frost rings in trees as records of major volcanic eruptions. *Nature* 307, 121–126.

Leuschner, von H.H. and Delorme, A. 1984: Verlängerung der Gottingen Eichen-jahrringchronologien für Nord- und Süddeutschland bis zum Jahr 4008 v. Chr. *Forstarchiv* 55. 1–4.

Leuschner, von H.H. and Delorme, A. 1988: Tree-ring work in Göttingen—absolute oak chronologies back to 6255 BC *Pact* II.5 Wood and Archaeology, 123–132.

Libby, L.M., Pandolfi, L.J., Payton, P.H., Marshall, J. III., Becker, B. and Giertz-Sienbenlist, V. 1976: Isotopic tree thermometers. *Nature* 261, 284–288.

Morgan, R.A., Litton, C.D. and Salisbury, C.R. 1987: Trackways and tree trunks—dating Neolithic oaks in the British Isles. *Tree-Ring Bulletin* 47, 61–69.

Pearson, G.W., Pilcher, J.R., Baillie, M.G.L., Corbett, D.M. and Qua, F. 1986: High-precision ^{14}C measurement of Irish oaks to show the natural ^{14}C variations from AD 1840 to 1520 BC. *Radiocarbon* 28, 911–934.

Pilcher, J.R. and Hughes, M. 1982: The potential of dendrochronology for the study of climate change. In Harding, A.F. (editor) *Climate Change in Later Prehistory* (Edinburgh, Edinburgh University Press) 75–84.

Pilcher, J.R., Baillie, M.G.L., Schmidt, B. and Becker, B. 1984: A 7272-year tree-ring chronology for Western Europe. *Nature* 312, 150–152.

Pilcher, J.R., Hillam, J., Baillie, M.G.L. and Pearson, G.W. 1977: A long sub-fossil tree-ring chronology from the north of Ireland. *New Phytologist* 79, 713–729.

Schmidt, B. and Schwabedissen, H. 1978: Jahrringanalytisches untersuchungen an Eichen der römischen zeit. *Archäologisches Korrespondenzblatt* 8, 331–337.

Schove, D.J. and Lowther, A.W.G. 1957: Tree-rings and Medieval archaeology. *Medieval Archaeology* 1, 78–95.

Schweingruber, F.H., Braker, O.U. and Schar, E. 1979: Dendroclimatic studies on conifers from Central Europe and Great Britain. *Boreas* 8, 427–452.

Stuiver, M. and Becker, B. 1986: High-precision decadal calibration of the radiocarbon time scale, AD 1950–2500 BC. *Radiocarbon* 28, 863–910.

Tapper, M., Fletcher, J. and Walker, F. 1978: Abnormal small earlywood vessels in oak. In Fletcher, J. (editor), *Dendrochronology in Europe* (Oxford, British Archaeological Reports International Series 51) 339–342.

Weisburd, S. 1985: Excavating words: a geological tool. *Science News* 127, 91–96.

Wigley, T.M.L. and Kelly, P.M. 1990: Holocene climatic change, 14-C wiggles and variations in solar irradiance. *Philosophical Transactions of the Royal Society of London* A330, 547–560.

Wigley, T.M.L., Gray, B.M. and Kelly, P.M. 1978: Climatic interpretation of δ^{18}O and δD in tree-rings. *Nature* 271, 92–94.

Williams, E. 1989: Dating the introduction of food production into Britain and Ireland. *Antiquity* 63, 510–521.

Zeuner, F.E. 1958: *Dating the Past* (London, Methuen).

PLATE 1

THE YSTAD AREA
LATE MESOLITHIC LANDSCAPE, CA. 3500 BC*

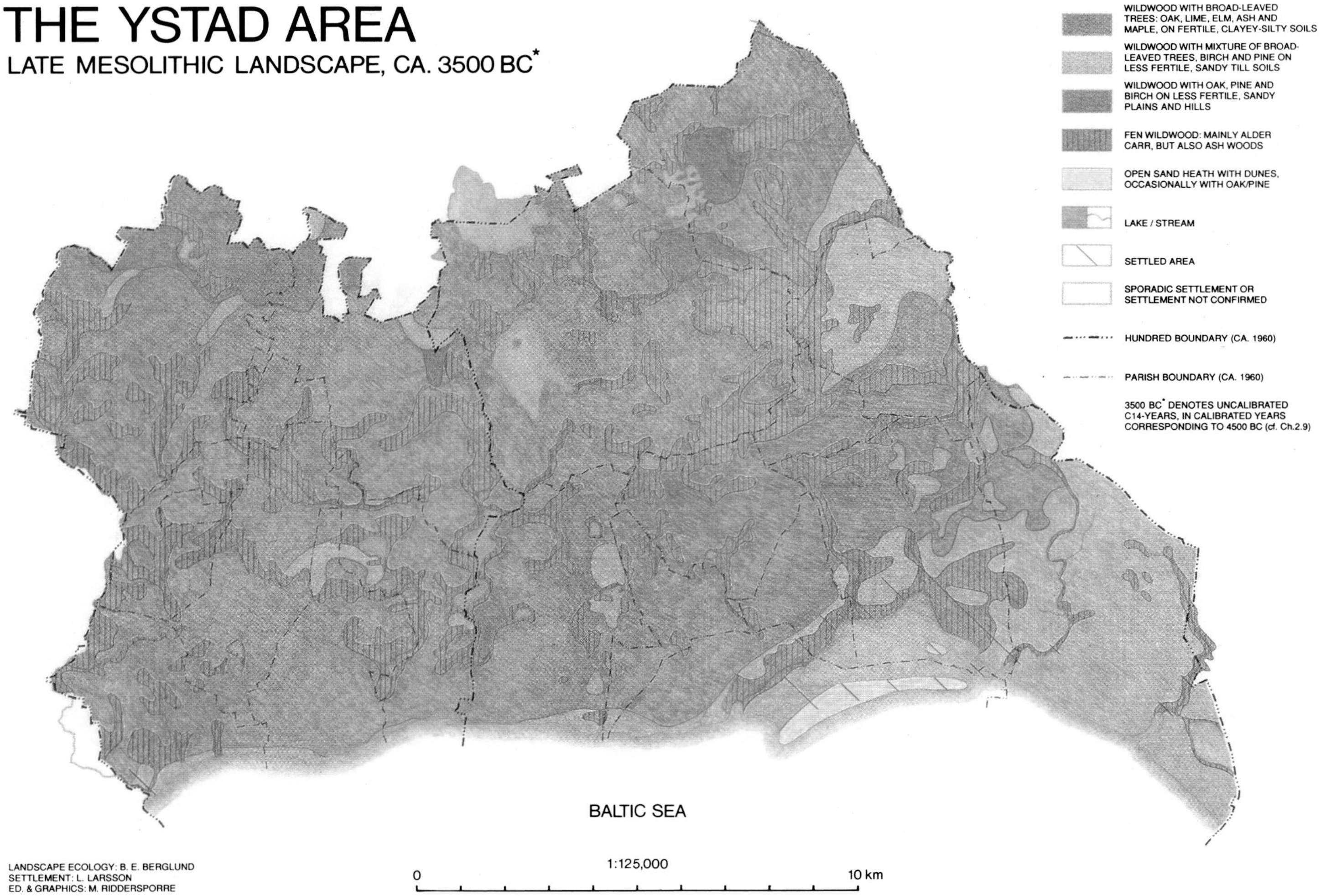

WILDWOOD WITH BROAD-LEAVED
TREES: OAK, LIME, ELM, ASH AND
MAPLE, ON FERTILE, CLAYEY-SILTY SOILS

WILDWOOD WITH MIXTURE OF BROAD-
LEAVED TREES, BIRCH AND PINE ON
LESS FERTILE, SANDY TILL SOILS

WILDWOOD WITH OAK, PINE AND
BIRCH ON LESS FERTILE, SANDY
PLAINS AND HILLS

FEN WILDWOOD: MAINLY ALDER
CARR, BUT ALSO ASH WOODS

OPEN SAND HEATH WITH DUNES,
OCCASIONALLY WITH OAK/PINE

LAKE / STREAM

SETTLED AREA

SPORADIC SETTLEMENT OR
SETTLEMENT NOT CONFIRMED

HUNDRED BOUNDARY (CA. 1960)

PARISH BOUNDARY (CA. 1960)

3500 BC* DENOTES UNCALIBRATED
C14-YEARS. IN CALIBRATED YEARS
CORRESPONDING TO 4500 BC (cf. Ch.2.9)

BALTIC SEA

1:125,000

0   10 km

LANDSCAPE ECOLOGY: B. E. BERGLUND
SETTLEMENT: L. LARSSON
ED. & GRAPHICS: M. RIDDERSPORRE

PLATE 2

THE YSTAD AREA
LATE VIKING AGE LANDSCAPE, CA. AD 1000

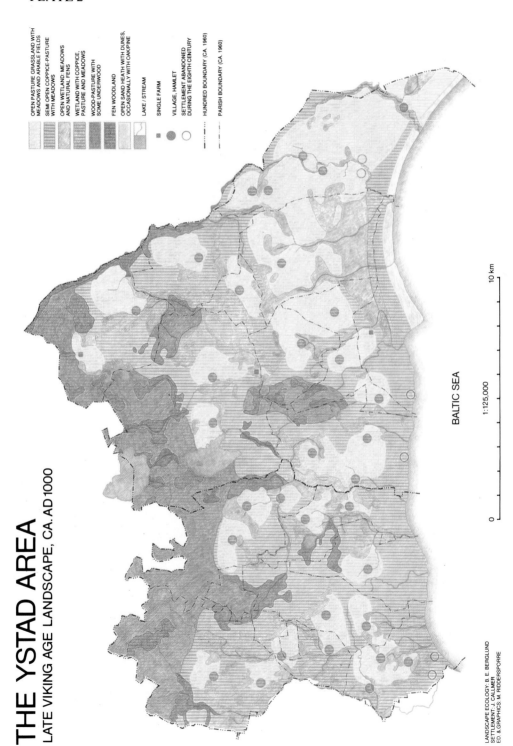

OPEN PASTURE GRASSLAND WITH MEADOWS AND ARABLE FIELDS WITH MEADOWS

SEMI OPEN COPPICE-PASTURE WITH MEADOWS

OPEN WETLAND: MEADOWS AND NATURAL FENS

WETLAND WITH COPPICE, PASTURE AND MEADOWS

WOOD-PASTURE WITH SOME UNDERWOOD

FEN WOODLAND

OPEN SAND HEATH WITH DUNES, OCCASIONALLY WITH OAK/PINE

LAKE / STREAM

SINGLE FARM

VILLAGE, HAMLET

SETTLEMENT ABANDONED DURING THE EIGHTH CENTURY

HUNDRED BOUNDARY (CA. 1960)

PARISH BOUNDARY (CA. 1960)

BALTIC SEA

1:125,000

0   10 km

LANDSCAPE ECOLOGY: B. E. BERGLUND
SETTLEMENT: J. CALLMER
ED. & GRAPHICS: M. RIDDERSPORRE

Proceedings of the British Academy, **77**, 25–37

Landscape Reconstructions in South Sweden for the Past 6000 Years

B. E. BERGLUND

Department of Quaternary Geology, Lunds Universitet, Tornavägen 13,
S-223 63 Lund, Sweden.

Summary. Interdisciplinary research on the cultural landscape history since the introduction of agriculture has been performed within a coast-inland area of South Sweden—the so-called Ystad project. Palaeoecological and ecological research has been combined with archaeological, historical and geographical research. Landscape ecological maps have been reconstructed for ten time-slices on the basis of the following source material: present environment— subsoils, hydrology, modern as well as historical vegetation (AD 1700, 1815, 1915, 1985); past environment—lake/mire stratigraphy, shoreline changes, pollen and charcoal analyses; settlement history —archaeology, place names, written sources (from AD 1200), land survey acts, etc. Certain assumptions have been made on past land use and vegetation dynamics. The results are compiled in a map sequence (in conventional radiocarbon years) for 3500, 2700, 800 BC, AD 200, 1000, 1300, 1700, 1815, 1915 and 1985. Conclusions can therefore be drawn on landscape ecological patterns and processes through time.

1. Background to an interdisciplinary project

The present cultural landscape is the result of the interaction between man and environment. This means that it can be explained only after inter-disciplinary studies focused on changes in time and space. A team of scientists from Lund University have been collaborating within the framework of the project "The Cultural Landscape during 6000 Years", colloquially known as "The Ystad Project", since 1982. About 25 scholars from six departments/

Read 13 February 1991. © The British Academy 1992.

disciplines have been involved in this project, all with a holistic view of the landscape and its long-term changes—historical landscape ecology.

The general aims of the project have been as follows:

i) To describe changes in society and the landscape in a representative area of southern Sweden;

ii) To analyse the causes behind these changes and especially to emphasise the relation between land use, vegetation and fauna, primary production and consumption on one hand, and population pressure, social structure, economy, and technology on the other hand;

iii) To correlate and compare the investigation area with other areas in Sweden as well as other areas in Europe;

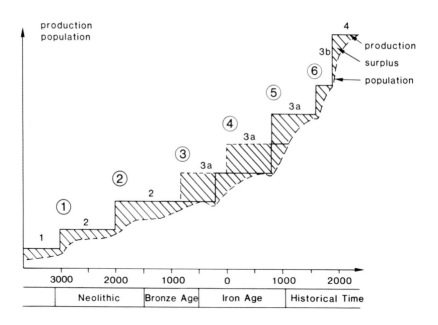

CAUSES FOR CHANGES OF SOCIETY AND ENVIRONMENT:

Population pressure	⎫		Climate	⎫	
Social organization		Social	Hydrology		Environmental
Economy		factors	Biota		factors
Technology	⎭		Soils	⎭	

Figure 1. Multi-causal model for long-term changes of the cultural landscape used as a general hypothesis for the Ystad Project. Encircled figures 1–6 refer to expansion phases sometimes indicated in pollen diagrams (e.g., Berglund 1988). Time-scale in radiocarbon years.

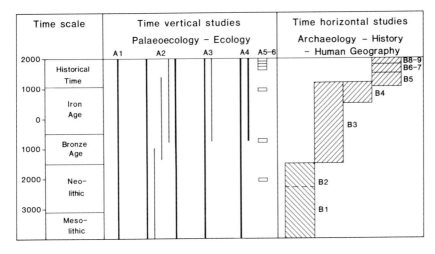

Figure 2. Project organisation with participating university disciplines and sub-projects plotted against time.

iv) To contribute to a scientific exchange between participating disciplines, particularly concerning research approach, methods, terminology, etc.;

v) To contribute to the management of the natural environment and ancient monuments.

When initiating the project, we agreed on a general hypothesis about the development of the agrarian landscape, characterised by phases of expansion, consolidation, and regression. This pattern was first identified and described by palaeoecologists (e.g., Berglund 1969), and later discussed by archaeologists (Welinder 1975, and others). In our project we have proposed a dynamic multi-causal theory for the observed changes during prehistoric and historical times. We have illustrated this as a staircase for cultural landscape development (Figure 1).

The organisation of the project has been based on the hypothesis of the assumed expansion phases in the cultural landscape. The research projects have been of two kinds: (i) time-vertical studies, dealing with landscape changes in a long-term perspective, and (ii) time-horizontal studies, which are multidisciplinary studies dealing with selected periods of special importance for changes in society and landscape.

The time-vertical studies have been mainly palaeoecological and ecological in character, and have provided the framework for the time-horizontal studies. The arrangement of the sub-projects in time is shown in Figure 2. The details of the sub-projects have been presented by Berglund (1988). It ought to be mentioned that the natural science projects dealt with vegetation history, palaeohydrology, soil erosion, vegetation reconstructions, and bio-production during selected time slices. Although one discipline has been mainly responsible for each sub-project, scientists from different disciplines collaborated within each. This means that there was close cooperation between researchers from six departments at the University of Lund during the period 1982–88, in some cases also including specialists from other universities or institutes. In addition, scientists from outside Sweden have been invited to cooperate.

The main publications of the project are three monographs, one about prehistoric society (Callmer *et al.* 1992), one about medieval society (Anders-son and Anglert 1989), and one interdisciplinary synthesis (Berglund 1991).

2. The study area

After careful consideration, the area adjacent to the town of Ystad on the south coast of Scania—the southernmost province of Sweden—was chosen as a suitable study area. Physiogeographically it is divisible into three land-scape zones from the coast towards the inland (Figure 3):

i) a coastal landscape with sandy soils (below 25 m elevation), today fully exploited for agriculture and settlement,

ii) an outer hummocky landscape with clayey silty soils (mainly 25–75 m), today fully exploited for agriculture,

iii) an inner hummocky landscape with clayey or stony soils (mainly 75–100 m), today partly forested and less suitable for agriculture.

This zonation implies a gradient from central to marginal settlement, which would also apply to prehistoric and historical times. It is representative of the present-day cultivated plain extending through southern and western Scania. With archaeological-historical and palaeoecological studies in each zone, it will be possible to make correlations and comparisons in time and space. We assumed that agrarian expansion reached the marginal area from the settlement at the coast. During historical time, big estates dominated the study area, and since medieval times, the town of Ystad has been the com-mercial centre. It is therefore possible to study the relationship between this centre and the surrounding countryside during most of historical time.

The studies have been concentrated in four focal areas also shown in Figure 3. They are assumed to be representative of each landscape zone. The source material was considered to be of high quality, including palaeoecolo-gical and archaeological evidence, as well as written documents and maps. The distribution of sites with pollen diagrams and other palaeoecological

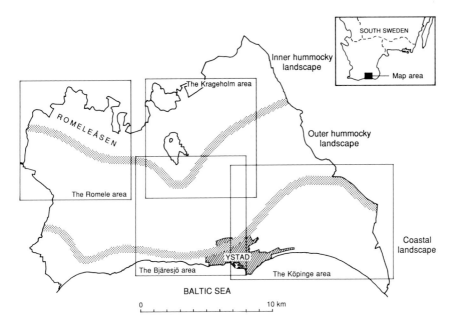

Figure 3. Study area around the town of Ystad with the three landscape zones and four main focal areas indicated.

studies is shown in Figure 4. Good sites with continuous records of lake sediments or peat deposits are rare and not evenly distributed. Today only three lakes exist, and most peat deposits have been exploited for fuel.

We regard this study area as representative of southernmost Scandinavia, physiogeographically a lowland area with nutrient-rich, clayey soils situated in a nemoral forest region. From a settlement-historical point of view it is also related to other areas in South Scandinavia and areas around the South Baltic. The situation with a fertile coastal area contrasting to a less fertile inland area is typical of many landscapes in South and South-Central Sweden.

3. Source material for landscape-ecological mapping

One main task in this project was to compile evidence of past environment and settlement into maps illustrating the past landscape, in a way similar to that of modern maps. For the entire area, survey maps were constructed at a scale of 1:50,000 (published at 1:125,000). Ten time slices were selected (see Figure 6). For some small key areas and for a few periods, more detailed reconstructions were made at a scale of 1:10,000 (published at 1:25,000). Environment (vegetation, hydrology, etc.) has been combined with settle-

B. E. Berglund

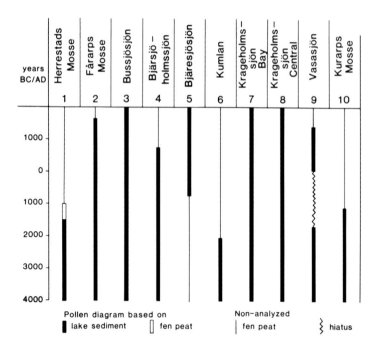

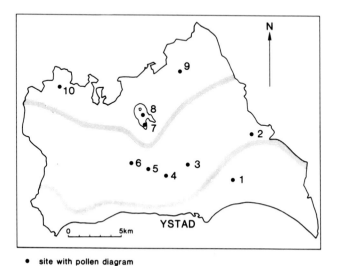

• site with pollen diagram

Figure 4. Survey scheme illustrating the time-span for each palaeoecological site with a pollen diagram. Site location is indicated on the survey map.

Table 1. Source material for landscape reconstruction

Present environment:
  Subsoil maps
  Hydrology maps (1812)
  Vegetation maps
  Economic maps
  Agricultural statistics
Past environment:
  Lake and mire stratigraphy
  Shoreline changes
  Pollen analyses
  Charcoal analyses
  Land survey maps (1690-)
  Economic maps (1920-)
  Taxation records (1300-)
Settlement history:
  Archaeology
  Place-names
  Taxation records (1300-)
  Land survey acts (1690-)
  Population statistics (1700-)
  Economic maps (1920-)
  Travel reports (1750-)

ment and land use. Table 1 gives a survey of available source material for present and past environment as well as settlement history.

The vegetation reconstructions presented in the survey maps are based on various sources. For historical time, environmental information has been available in written records including maps. This applies to the time periods 1985, 1915, 1815, and the 18th century, which makes this series of maps quite accurate. The 14th-century map is based on some written documents beside knowledge of ancient settlement and results of archaeological excavations and palaeoecological studies. The vegetation is also interpreted from retrogressive analysis of the 18th-century map. In a similar way the Viking Age landscape is reconstructed on the basis of a combination of archaeological/palaeoecological information and a retrogressive analysis of the 14th-century map. However, the vegetation of the five prehistoric periods is mainly based on palaeoecological and archaeological results from the project. This means that the human impact is traced by means of pollen-analytical correlations as well as archaeological inventories. These reconstructions are tentative mappings which rely on a few investigated sites regarded as representative of areas with similar ecological conditions (soils, hydrology, etc.).

The settlement distribution in prehistoric as well as historical time has been compiled and outlined in survey maps (Figure 5). This information is fundamental for indications of settled places, particularly the density and, as

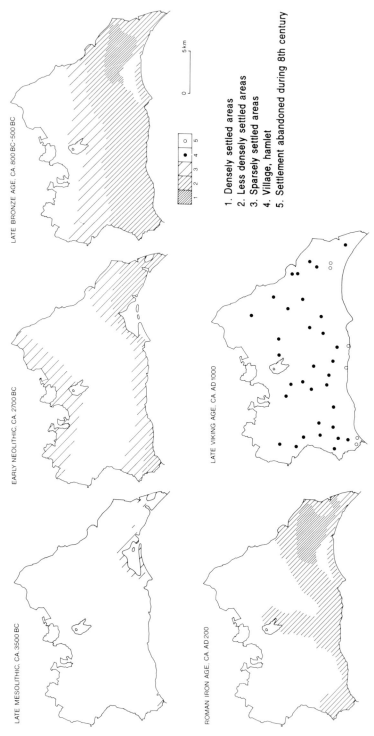

Figure 5. Settlement changes from the Mesolithic to the Early Middle Ages. These maps are intended to give a picture of the most important changes in settlement.

a consequence, the land use and vegetation differentiation in the landscape. This is a complement to the palaeoecological information which is better suited for general landscape changes through time than for precise spatial changes.

For the more detailed reconstructions of landscape and vegetation, slightly different methods have been used (Olsson in Berglund 1991). Beside relevant palaeoecological information from nearby sites, a protein-based model for human nutrition has been applied. Information on human dietary consumption was obtained from archaeological and palaeoecological evidence.

4. Assumptions about vegetation dynamics with increasing human impact

The interpretations concerning the spatial distribution of vegetation types are based on several assumptions, particularly the fact that all natural, or less disturbed, vegetation is to some extent a reflection of soil fertility, topography, and hydrology. This can be applied also to conditions in the past. Another assumption is that human impact on the natural ecosystems in an agrarian economy leads to deforestation and the creation of secondary woodlands and grasslands (cf. Rackham 1986, Pott 1988). When subdividing the ground into two categories according to soil moisture, we recognise two main developmental trends along with increasing human impact (Table 2).

All vegetation/land-use categories mentioned here have been given certain symbols on the coloured landscape historical maps. The terminology of woodlands mainly follows Rackham (1986).

5. Regional landscape reconstructions

The periods with survey landscape reconstructions can be characterised in the following way, here selectively illustrated (Figure 5; Plates 1 and 2):

3500 BC, Late Mesolithic. Hunting camps at the coast in the southeast, otherwise sporadic. Possibly small clearings. More or less closed wildwoods, mosaic because of wetlands and soil differentiation.

2700 BC, Early Neolithic. Agrarian economy introduced. Settlement mainly along the coast and sporadically in the inland area. In the settled area half-open landscape with wood pastures, coppiced woods, meadows, and arable. In the intermediate hummocky landscape more or less untouched woodlands. Later during the Neolithic and Early Bronze Age settlement concentrated on the coast.

Table 2. Vegetation development through time in an agrarian
economy

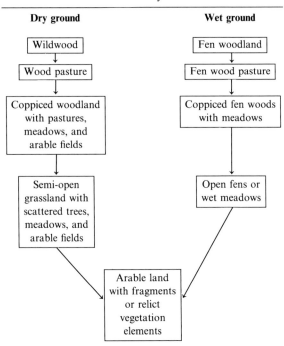

800 BC, Late Bronze Age. Settlement concentrated in the coastal area,
particularly in the southeast, and the outer hummocky landscape. Coastal
area semi-open grassland with scattered trees, pastures, meadows, and arable
fields. Outer hummocky landscape with coppiced woodland, and meadows
and arable fields around settled places. Fen woodlands opened for coppicing
and pastures close to settled places. Inland area with wood pastures used
extensively, possibly in a transhumance system.

AD 200, Roman Iron Age. Settlement concentrated in the coastal area, the
outermost hummocky landscape, and in a lobe towards the inland along a
river-lake valley. Coastal area semi-open grassland as before. The zone with
coppiced woodland in the outer hummocky landscape reduced because of
settlement concentration. Vast wood pastures in the outer and inner
hummocky landscape.

AD 1000, Viking Age. Settlement in villages at the coast as well as in the
outer hummocky landscape. In the inland possibly sporadic single farms.
Villages surrounded by semi-open grassland—infield/outfield pattern. Also
fen woodlands exploited for coppicing, grazing, and mowing.

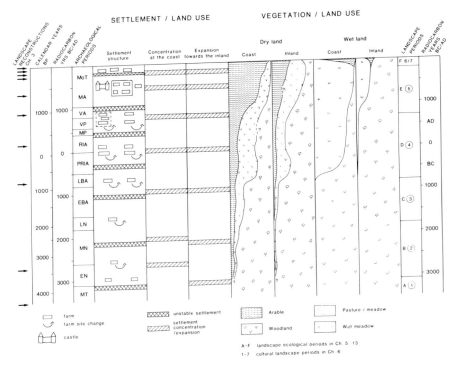

Figure 6. Synthesis of long-term landscape changes in the Ystad area during 6000 years. Settlement/land use is illustrated by symbols according to a simplified model. Changes in vegetation/land use are illustrated by approximate proportions of four main land-use categories based on pollen diagrams. Archaeological periods have been given the following abbreviations: MT = Mesolithic Time, EN = Early Neolithic, MN = Middle Neolithic, LN = Late Neolithic, EBA = Early Bronze Age, LBA = Late Bronze Age, PRIA = Pre-Roman Iron Age, RIA = Roman Iron Age, MP = Migration Period, VP = Vendel Period, VA = Viking Ages, MA = Middle Ages, MoT = Modern Times.

14th century. Settlement in villages as before. Now also church villages and the first estate fortresses. The town of Ystad on the coast. The inland colonised by the first single farms in the Late Middle Ages. Landscape semi-open, mosaic character with grasslands for grazing and mowing, coppiced wood stands, on dry land as well as on wet lands.

18th century. Settlement and landscape more or less as before, but inland woodlands also more exploited. Landscape extremely mosaic and diverse, with dry and wet pastures/meadows occupying large areas.

1815. Settlement and landscape as before, but woodlands and grasslands decreasing because of expanding arable land. Some villages are broken up and settlement starts to be scattered.

1915. Increased scattered settlement caused by changed village organisation. Expanding arable fields at the expense of grasslands, woods, wetlands. Former wetlands drained. Untouched woodlands (hunting woods) only at the estates.

1985. Expanding scattered settlement, and expansion of the area of the town of Ystad. Expansion of arable land at the expense of grassland, woods, wetlands. Agrarian monocultures. Plantations of coniferous trees. Still preserved "old" landscape: woods on the estates, grasslands in the inland area and in military areas.

6. Synthesis of the cultural landscape development

Our view of the long-term landscape changes is illustrated in the sequence of ten landscape-historical maps, and also in a time-vertical diagram (Figure 6) where settlement and vegetation changes are juxtaposed against land use. This results in the definition of seven landscape-ecological periods which are comparable for southern Scandinavia. This means that we regard the interaction between society and environment to be more dynamic and complex than assumed by the expansion/regression hypothesis. However, most of our landscape periods end with a settlement concentration leading to woodland regeneration, later followed by a new settlement expansion. We believe that, in general, landscape changes are caused by changes in society. Environmental factors such as climate and hydrology mainly have a long-term effect on the landscape. At least in prehistoric times society was flexible and adapted easily to ecological changes. For an agrarian society there seems to have been a surplus in this region of natural resources throughout the past.

References

Andersson, H. and Anglert, M. (editors) 1989: By, huvudgård och kyrka: Studier i Ystadområdets medeltid. *Lund Studies in Medieval Archaeology* 5. (Stockholm, Almqvist and Wiksell).

Berglund, B.E., 1969: Vegetation and Human Influence in South Scandinavia during Prehistoric time. In Berglund, B.E. (editor), Impact of Man on the Scandinavian Landscape during the Late Post-Glacial. *Oikos Supplement* 12, 9–28.

Berglund, B.E., 1988: The cultural landscape during 6000 years in South Sweden—an interdisciplinary project. In Birks, H.H., Birks, H.J.B., Kaland, P.E. and Moe, D. (editors), *The Cultural Landscape—Past, Present and Future.* (Cambridge, Cambridge University Press), 241–254.

Berglund, B.E. (editor), 1991: The Cultural Landscape during 6000 Years in Southern Sweden. *Ecological Bulletin* 41.

Callmer, J., Larsson, L., and Stjernquist, B. (editors), 1992: The Archaeology of the Cultural Landscape: Fieldwork and Research in a South Swedish Rural Region. *Acta Archaeologica Lundensia* (Stockholm, Almqvist and Wiksell).

Pott, R., 1988: Entstehung von Vegetationstypen und Pflanzengesellschaften unter dem Einfluss des Menschen. *Düsseldorfer Geobotanisches Kolloquium* 5, 27–54.

Rackham, O., 1986: *The History of the Countryside.* (London, Dent).

Welinder, S., 1975: Prehistoric agriculture in Eastern Middle Sweden. *Acta Archaeologica Lundensia* (Stockholm, Almqvist and Wiksell).

Proceedings of the British Academy, **77**, 39–59

Soil Micromorphology in Archaeology

M.-A. COURTY

*C.N.R.S., UA 723, Laboratoire d'Hydrologie et de Géochimie Isotopique,
Université de Paris Sud, 91045 Orsay Cedex, France.*

Summary. Soil micromorphology consists of the integrated use of various microscopic techniques for studying the arrangement and the nature of components that form sediments and soils. The power of this analysis in archaeology is to provide key information which can discriminate the sedimentary signatures diagnostic of human-related activities from those resulting from natural phenomena.

Soil micromorphology has became popular in the last decade in archaeology, although the potential of the microscopic approach has been well known for more than fifty years, due to the recent increase in interest in site formation processes. This type of analysis can be used to achieve a detailed environmental reconstruction of human palaeolandscapes or to identify the various kinds of domestic and specialised activities which are involved in the formation of living floors and of anthropogenic structures.

The future progress of soil micromorphology in archaeology requires us to enrich our knowledge of the sedimentary dynamics of cultural processes and to increase the number of well-trained scientists in this new field of investigation. A better integration of the analysis at the microscopic scale with the field perception should help to improve the characterisation of site formation processes whilst the excavation is taking place.

1. Introduction

In archaeology, the study of sediments and soils has been shown to be an essential component of environmental reconstruction which may concern either palaeolandscapes and human impact at a regional scale, or site formation processes ruled by both natural factors and human activities (Butzer

Read 13 February 1991. © The British Academy 1992.

1982; Hassan 1978; Gladfelter 1981; Stein and Farrand 1985). To achieve one or both of these objectives, specialists in sedimentary archaeology have developed various approaches in relation to their academic origin and depending on their laboratory facilities. Scientists with rather different competencies are now facing a particular challenge: to demonstrate the sagacity of their methodological choice and the efficiency of their approach.

In the recent years, soil micromorphologists have striven to meet the challenge by demonstrating that the microscope was an essential tool to analyse ancient soils and site formation processes (Courty et al. 1989). The objective of this paper is to analyse the present situation of soil micromorphology in archaeology by considering: (i) how this approach was developed, (ii) how it has enriched our knowledge of archaeological sediments, and (iii) what is the present situation. Although the future of soil micromorphology in archaeology is apparently promising, it may be worthwhile to discuss, in conclusion, how this relatively young method of investigation should progress in order to rapidly achieve its full maturity.

Before entering the debate, it may be useful to outline the method. Soil micromorphology is the study under the optical microscope of thin sections prepared from undisturbed and oriented samples after they have been impregnated by synthetic resin. For an efficient coordination between field observations and microscopic investigations, soil thin sections have to be larger (ca. 12 × 7 cm or more) than the standard petrographic ones, but have the same thickness (25 μm). A continuous observation from the field scale down to high magnification, permitted by scanning electron microscopes, allows an exhaustive characterisation (nature, shape, size, frequency, etc.) of elementary components and the study of their arrangement. A high level of significance is given to specific attributes, which are subdivided according to their origin into three well-defined groups:

i) Sedimentary features which are diagnostic of the source of the sediments, the mode of transport and depositional conditions (Figure 1).

ii) Pedological features that give information about the dynamics of each soil-forming process and about the interaction of these processes through time (Figure 2).

iii) Anthropogenic features related to human activities, which can be identified at various scales, such as mineral or organic components of human origin or which may correspond to specific fabrics induced by human transformations (Figure 3). Both human-induced fabrics and anthropogenic components can have been produced intentionally or accidentally.

The high efficiency of this approach is due to the use of standardised optical and crystallographic procedures to observe transparent thin sections

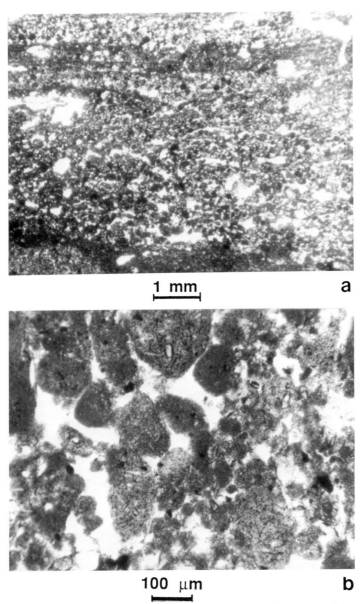

1 mm   a

100 μm   b

Figure 1. Compound sedimentary features diagnostic of the source of sediments, of the mode of transport and of depositional conditions: (a) the clear micro-layering observed at low magnification indicates repeated episodes of low energy water reworking (run-off) interrupted by phases of desiccation; (b) the well rounded aggregates observed at high magnification relate to air transportation by saltation ("pseudo-sands"); most aggregates consist of dense calcitic fine silt which have been eroded by wind from superficial crusts formed on bare soil surface. Buried soil formed during the late third millennium B.C. in Upper Mesopotamia, Abu Hjeira 2, northeastern Syria (director M. Lutz).

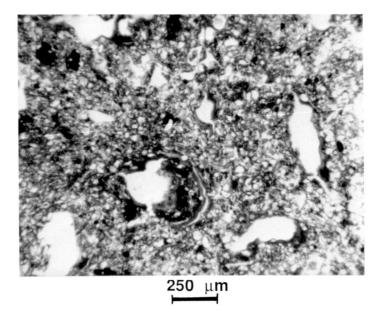

250 μm

Figure 2. B horizon of an argillic brown earth formed under a forest cover: the diagnostic fabric consists of abundant clay coatings in the channels. The dark colour of the coatings is due to the fine addition to the clay of micro-contrasted particles which indicates that the soil surface was not densely covered by the vegetation. Late Holocene argillic brown earth on loess deposits, Paris Basin.

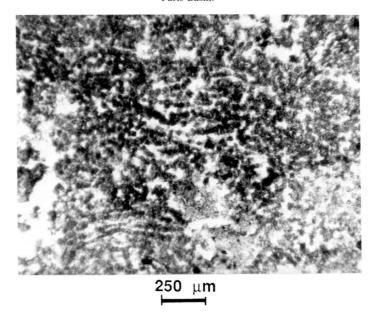

250 μm

Figure 3. Typical open fabric of a wood ash layer which has not suffered subsequent trampling or alteration by post-depositional processes. The good preservation of the plant pseudomorphs indicates firing around 500°C. Mesolithic ash layer, cave of Abeurador, south-eastern France (director J. Vaquer).

of standard thickness. Moreover, this representation makes easier the perception of spatial relationships between components, fabrics and features which
is essential to enable the reconstruction of the sequential evolution of soils
and sediments through time.

2. The advancement of soil micromorphology in archaeology

2.1 The academic context

Two decisive periods have marked more than half a century of continuing
research in archaeological sedimentology. The first was in the late 1950's
when interest in prehistoric sediments increased considerably, especially in
Europe (Campy 1982; Farrand 1975; Laville 1976; Miskovsky 1974). Quaternary geologists and prehistorians essentially worked together on the chrono-
stratigraphy of prehistoric sequences, emphasising the palaeoclimatic
implications. They gave little consideration to the regional significance of the
sedimentary signal recorded at the micro-regional scale of archaeological
sites. Field stratigraphical interpretations were supported by analytical data,
the validity of which had never been evaluated. Particle size analysis
was routinely performed because it is easy to handle both technically and
scientifically.

For academic reasons, individuals sharing a common interest in
archaeological sediments have rapidly formed a scientific community that
has been rather independent of related disciplines in earth sciences (classical
sedimentology, geochemistry, pedology, etc.). Consequently, archaeological
sedimentology has not fully profited from the technical and scientific pro-
gresses accomplished in these various fields. Furthermore, the results
achieved in archaeological sedimentology have not been critically evaluated
by the larger community of earth science specialists. This situation may
explain why soil micromorphology was not introduced at this stage in
archaeological sedimentology, although the microscopic approach was
entering its golden age in soil science, and was already familiar to soil
scientists dealing with archaeological soils (Romans and Robertson 1983).

An important change marked archaeological sedimentology in the late
1970's when Karl Butzer, followed by others, clearly stated that archaeological sediments are singular because they relate to interactive processes ruled
by human beings and natural factors (Butzer 1982). Geoarchaeologists
suddenly realised that past humans had contributed to the sedimentation
process of archaeological sites not only with lithics, bones or plants but with
mineral components which may have substantially affected the original
sedimentary signal (Stein 1985). This new generation of archaeological
sedimentologists has much debated the necessity of a careful examination of

sediments to identify the cultural components of the site matrix (Stein 1985). They have, however, never considered the necessity of adapting methods and related techniques to achieve the new goals. Using methods similar to those of their predecessors, they have been mostly able to detect anthropogenic influence on sediments but have not been able to recognise the human activities involved.

At the same time, soil micromorphology was introduced into archaeology by earth scientists who were external to this new trend of archaeological sedimentology. Familiar with the microscopic scale from their basic training at university, they naturally thought the use of thin sections was necessary when facing archaeological sediments and soils. They spontaneously joined the group of soil micromorphologists and have remained highly pragmatic when characterising sedimentary signatures of cultural activities. Evolving rather far from the theoretical debate of archaeology, they however realised that the introduction of the soil micromorphological approach was throwing a new light on contextual archaeology (Fisher and Macphail 1985; Goldberg 1979, 1981; Courty and Fedoroff 1982, 1985).

At the same time, following the lead of André Leroi-Gourhan, French archaeologists have been discussing the dynamics of formation of living floors. They have essentially taken into consideration the spatial distribution of artefacts and their typological and technological characteristics, whereas they have made little use of the sedimentary attributes because the close relationship between the sedimentary matrix and cultural processes was still poorly documented (Audouze 1985; David *et al.* 1973; Rigaud 1979).

2.2 The present situation of soil micromorphology in archaeology

2.2.1 The scientific position

Since its modest beginning in the late 1970's, soil micromorphology has been continually progressing in archaeology, especially in Western Europe where there has been an increasing demand for micromorphological investigations from archaeologists of various origins. Two orientations are now appearing although they share some common interest:

i) An environmental approach in which the micromorphological study of soils and sediments leads to the environmental reconstruction of human palaeolandscapes at a regional or micro-regional scale (site level). Beyond the characterisation of naturally-induced phenomena, the recognition of human influence (through devegetation, cultivation, etc.) on palaeolandscapes is an essential objective of the micromorphological analysis (Courty 1990; Macphail *et al.* 1987, 1990; Romans and Robertson 1983).

ii) A cultural approach which is oriented towards the recognition of human activities analysed in a spatio-temporal perspective. The essential objective is to integrate an accurate knowledge of the sedimentary matrix into the traditional archaeological approach of studying artefacts for a comprehensive functional analysis of a site (Courty *et al.* 1989).

These two approaches are widely accepted although they both face some difficulties.

Many colleagues, either in Quaternary geology or soil science, still deny that the microscopic scale should be an imperative level of perception in landscape analysis. They essentially achieve landscape reconstruction by analysing at the field level, spatial relationships between stratigraphical units of both pedogenic and sedimentary origin. Analytical data and micromorphological observations are used to complete the diagnosis of morphological properties recognised at high levels of organisation (horizon, profile, site regional scale). Their attitude is surprising considering that the efficiency of the microscopic approach for palaeogeographic reconstruction has been largely demonstrated by sedimentologists working with consolidated rocks.

The difficulties in contextual archaeology are different. We face three kinds of reaction:

i) A positive attitude, where results are well accepted but have limited impact because they are not properly integrated into the archaeological construction. This is essentially a problem of dialogue due to important differences in the interpretative systems used in the naturalistic approach and those of social sciences.

ii) Suspicion: total refutation is probably less common now than in the beginning when the identification of anthropogenic deposits based on the use of thin sections was not always accepted by archaeologists. It is however common to meet a certain scepticism and surprise regarding the accuracy of information that can be obtained by soil micromorphology. In this case, archaeologists often require a preliminary study performed without providing the basic contextual data which are essential for a comprehensive interpretation of the thin sections. The real soil micromorphological study will only start if the test was able to give convincing results.

iii) A constructive attitude has recently appeared from archaeologists who have fully evaluated the potential of soil micromorphology. They regard the microscopic study of thin sections as the logical continuation of the excavation because it not only reveals the constitution of the sedimentary matrix but also questions the validity of the field criteria used for the supposedly objective description of facts and for the collection of data during the excavation. They have realised that the micromorphological characteristics of archaeological sediments have to be taken into account when discussing field evidence and that an efficient field strategy requires the understanding of dynamics at different spatial scales from the macro-regional scale down to the microscopic level. Undoubtedly, in this perspective, soil micromorphology has reached a new plateau that we had not even suspected when we started to work for archaeologists. This situation implies that when dealing with cultural processes the micromorphological approach should be handled by archaeologists themselves because the concepts debated are the ones of archaeology and the objectives are those of contextual archaeology.

2.2.2 Achievements

i) Palaeoenvironmental changes and archaeological implications.

The recognition in thin sections of the successive pedological phases recorded during the historical development of a soil is probably the most diagnostic result that can be used to document past-environmental change (Fedoroff and Goldberg 1982; Kemp 1985; Macphail 1986). Each phase is defined by a group of pedological features which relate to elementary soil-forming processes (e.g., biological activity, translocation of clay, accumulation of secondary carbonates, etc.). Their intrinsic properties and their spatial distribution provide information about the hydric regime of the soil during each phase of development and about the vegetation cover (Fedoroff *et al.* 1990), (Figure 2). The characteristics of the transition between two pedological phases aid in elucidating the dynamics of the transformation and the factors which induced the change (climate, self-degradation of the soil-system, human impact). A sequential chronology can thus be established not only in polycyclic palaeosols formed during a few thousand years, but also in any kind of stratigraphical unit which may be less than a few hundred years old (Figure 4). The results achieved shed new light on stratigraphical sequences which can only be simply interpreted as the succession of accumulation phases, interrupted by periods of soil development. Each unit appears, in most cases, to be the result of a complex imbrication of sedimentary and pedological events which have been more or less simultaneous.

Micromorphological investigations have shown to be highly helpful in discriminating *in situ* soils or palaeosols from pedosediments which are no longer in their primary situation because they have been reworked by sedimentary processes (Goldberg 1987), (Figure 5). The distinction is often difficult in the field because *in situ* palaeosols and sediment derived from palaeosols may present similar morphological properties. Particle size distribution and routine soil analyses can rarely resolve this question. This explains the common errors of chronostratigraphical interpretation which do not use soil micromorphological data (Goldberg 1979).

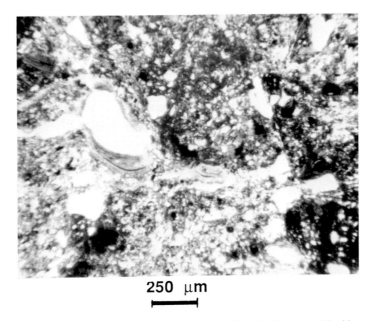

250 μm
|———————|

Figure 4. Polycyclic palaeosol developed during the last Interglacial period. The hierarchy of pedological fabrics and features allows recognition of the succession of several phases of soil development under a forest cover interrupted by degration phases of the soil cover (minor colluviation and cryoturbation). Iville palaeosol, Paris Basin.

250 μm
|————————|

Figure 5. Massive sandy clay unit which results from the colluvial reworking of a palaeosol developed during the last Interglacial period. Pre-existing pedological features have been strongly altered and are not recognisable in the homogeneous dusty clay fine mass. Archaeological unit with Middle Palaeolithic industry, site of Villejuif, Paris Basin (director Ph. Andrieux).

ii) Distinction between natural factors and human influence.

The study in thin section of archaeological sediments from various cultural periods, and collected in diverse geological and climatic locations, has permitted the differentiation of anthropogenic sediments from natural ones (Courty *et al.* 1989). This term implies that human agencies directly influenced the formation of the deposits, either by controlling their accumulation or by inducing transformations of natural sediments. Sediments which are totally related to cultural processes, both in the mode of deposition and in the nature of constituents, are termed anthropogenic. An ash unit is, for example, a typical anthropogenic sediment. The similarities observed in a large variety of cultural settings reveal the nature of the combustible used and the history of the combustion (Wattez 1988), (Figure 2). Living floors are another common type of anthropogenic sediments which are characterised by a specific fabric produced by trampling (Figure 6).

In other cases, human activities are only partly responsible for the formation of the sediments, which may be of natural origin. For example, human influence in most of ancient cultivated soils consists of structural modifications to natural soils, in addition to a minor input of anthropogenic constituents (manure, liming, etc.), except in the case of plaggen soils and garden soils in urban environments which may be totally anthropogenic (Courty *et al.* 1989).

Not all archaeological sediments are anthropogenic in origin. Evidence of human influence, recognised at the microscopic level in the nature of basic components or in their arrangement, is often rare (Figure 7) or even absent (Figure 8). In theses cases, post-depositional processes may have strongly obliterated cultural features (Courty and Fedoroff 1982; Courty *et al.* 1989). It may also suggest that human activities have not affected the sedimentary matrix, which should be confirmed by the study of artefacts. The absence of anthropogenic features may even indicate that artefacts are not in their primary position because the anthropogenic signal has been erased by subsequent reworking.

For example, the study of thin sections has been shown to provide essential information in discriminating human-related units from biogenic accumulations in some cave deposits because the two types of sediments may show similar characteristics in the field (Wattez *et al.* 1990), (Figure 9).

iii) Dynamics of cultural processes.

Thin section study of anthropogenic sediments can aid in the accurate recognition of the different groups of cultural deposits which have been theoretically distinguished by Karl Butzer (1982).

Primary cultural deposits relate to accumulation on the soil surface during the utilisation of an activity area; they may have been altered by

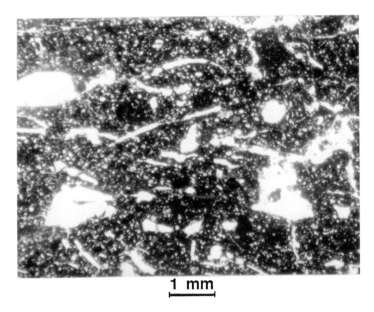

Figure 6. Typical fabric of a living floor induced by repeated trampling and by addition of very fine anthropogenic debris and soil fragments (dark spots). Neolithic Pre-ceramic site of Netiv Hagdud, Jordan Valley (director O. Bar Yosef).

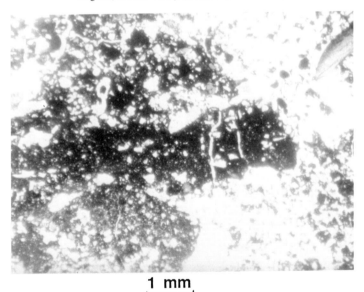

Figure 7. Relict living floor consisting of a trampled sub-surface at the bottom (dense fine layer) and an active layer on the top rich in anthropogenic constituents (ash, bones). The surrounding open sandy matrix has been intensively reworked by biological activity. Late Magdalenian archaeological layer, site of Verberie, Oise valley, Paris Basin (director F. Audouze).

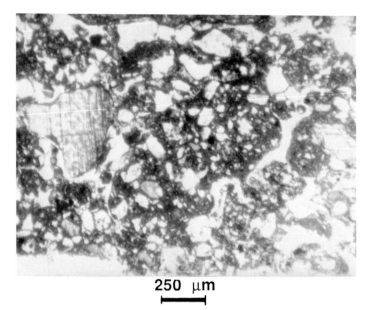

250 μm

Figure 8. Archaeological unit strongly reworked by post-depositional processes which consist of detrital sedimentation, dissolution of carbonates, cryoturbation and biological activity. Anthropogenic constituents are only observed at high magnification in the fine mass (bone fragments); evidence for human-related fabric is not recognisable. Mousterian layer VIII, cave of Vaufrey, south-western France (director J. Ph. Rigaud).

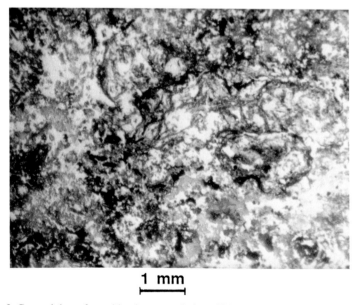

1 mm

Figure 9. Grey ash layer formed by the accumulation of bird excrement which has been burnt, possibly by humans. Mesolithic layer, cave of Fontbreguoua, south France (director J. Courtin).

post-depositional processes. A large number of ash layers are primary cultural deposits (Figure 3), as well as living floors (Figure 6).

Secondary cultural deposits are primary deposits which have suffered important modifications in their original settings, either because they have been displaced (e.g., dumped ashes cleaned from a fire place, Figure 10) or because there was a significant change in the utilisation of the activity area. In the latter case, secondary cultural deposits appear finely mixed with primary cultural ones which relate to the latest phase of human activity.

Tertiary cultural deposits correspond to the cultural disturbances defined by Butzer (1982). They have been totally removed from their original settings because of spatial rearrangement or cleaning (e.g., digging of ditch, dumping; Figure 11) and may have been reutilised for a specific purpose (e.g., terracing).

The distinction among these three groups is essentially based on the study of the spatial relationships of the elementary constituents, rather than their intrinsic characteristics which may not always have been strongly modified through reutilisation and displacement.

At the present stage, we are able to decipher the effects of successive reworking and of subsequent alteration by natural processes. We are certainly limited to the specific identification of a few cultural signals because our reference system is still incomplete. Comparison with features obtained in controlled conditions, from experiment or from ethnoarchaeological studies, has appeared to be essential in evaluating the respective role of all the cultural processes which interact to result in specific sedimentary signals.

2.2.3 The academic situation

Soil micromorphology in archaeology is rapidly gaining maturity although its real progress is modest. Most senior scientists in archaeological sedimentology are not using soil micromorphology and its possibilities are essentially being exploited by young scientists. In addition to technical or financial problems, beginners have to face several difficulties:

i) There are practical problems in the preparation of thin sections because only a few departments of archaeology or environmental archaeology have the basic equipment. In many cases, thin sections have to be made in departments of soil science which cannot always respond rapidly to the increasing demand.

ii) Absence or scarcity of reference materials ("benchmark" thin sections, published catalogues, etc.). Each researcher is more or less trying to build his or her own reference collection which is not only time-consuming but also casts doubt upon the validity of the interpretation achieved. The recently

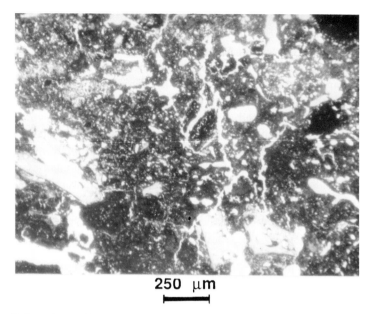

250 μm

Figure 10. Secondary anthropogenic deposits: dumped ash cleaned from a fire place, finely mixed with domestic refuse (bones) and soil fragments which have been intensively trampled while the soil was water saturated (well-expressed dusty clay coatings in cavities). Mesolithic layer of the shelter of Bavans, eastern France (director G. Aimé).

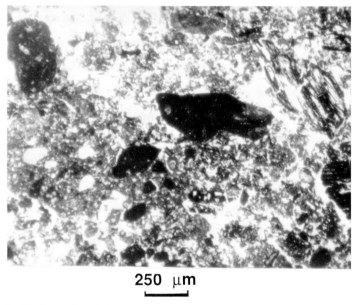

250 μm

Figure 11. Tertiary cultural deposits: domestic refuse (ash, animal dung) and debris from construction materials (living floors, bricks) dumped in a pit. Neolithic Pre-ceramic site of Netiv Hagdud, Jordan Valley (director O. Bar Yosef). The main difference from Figure 10 is the very open fabric which indicates that the dumped deposits have not suffered any trampling.

published handbook "Soils and Micromorphology in Archaeology" (Courty *et al.* 1989) should partly fill the gap although it cannot be not exhaustive.

iii) Lack of training fully oriented towards the objectives of soil micromorphology in archaeology. This problem is probably more crucial for the few young and audacious archaeologists that are now following this approach.

iv) An important time investment before being able to make comprehensive descriptions of thin sections and to achieve coherent interpretation.

v) Difficulty of corroborative scientific evaluation because of insufficient communication between practitioners, despite a number of international fora.

vi) Necessity to produce results rapidly to answer the demand of archaeologists (e.g., in rescue projects). In these cases, the contribution of soil micromorphology consists mostly of fastidious description, the conclusions being often superficial or obscure to the archaeologist.

These different limitations explain why many young scientists involved in this field make little profit from the information recorded in thin sections and are not using the optimal potential of soil micromorphology in archaeology. This situation may become detrimental to the future of the discipline.

3. Perspectives

Discussing the future of soil micromorphology in archaeology implies that we can effectively solve our present difficulties and that we should decide what are our long term scientific objectives. Predictions are always delicate and may benefit from the lessons of the past. Soil micromorphology has now been used in soil science for nearly half a century and it may be worthwhile to comment upon a few points of its history.

3.1 Lessons from soil micromorphology in soil science

Technical difficulties in the preparation of high quality and large sized thin sections have limited for a long while the development of soil micromorphology in many soil departments, although others had considerably improved the technique more than fifteen years ago. Technical problems cannot thus explain why soil micromorphology is used in soil science in a non-systematic manner when utilisation of routine soil analyses has been standardised for more than 50 years.

Scientific difficulties have been, and still are, probably more limiting because soil scientists often have a basic training in agronomical sciences (especially in France and the USA) which includes only a limited background in geology and generally no knowledge of petrography. Soil micromorphology in soil science is taught in a large number of soil science and earth science departments, but this basic knowledge is apparently insufficient and intensive courses in soil micromorphology have recently been created.

Soil scientists have commonly escaped their knowledge deficiencies in two ways :

i) Those with a sufficient background in petrography have focused on the weathering of mineral constituents and have paid little attention to the overall organisation of soil constituents.

ii) Others have been using only scanning electron microscopes, and related microprobe techniques, without investigating the intermediate levels of organisation between the field and the ultramicroscopic level.

A large number of soil micromorphologists have, however, overcome the inherent difficulties of thin sections and have been able to handle properly a multi-scale approach, both through time and through spatial scales.

For many years, soil micromorphology has been essentially promoted in studies dealing with soil genesis. In this field a few experts have achieved world-wide experience and are considered to possess the key to interpretation. Unfortunately, most of the available textbooks are essentially devoted to the description of thin sections (Bullock *et al.* 1985; Brewer and Sleeman 1988; Fitzpatrick 1984) whereas there is a lack of a general textbook dealing with the interpretation of pedological features recognised at the microscopic scales in modern and ancient soils. Moreover, soil micromorphologists have performed few experiments which could help to corroborate their conclusions (see, for example, Mücher and de Ploey 1990). This explains why they are often accused of working from intuition. On the other hand, in the numerous regional studies of soil-landscapes, soil micromorphology has been commonly used, but only as one of many techniques.

Soil micromorphology has suffered a clear decline in this field since the 1970's because the understanding of soil genesis is not at present a predominant objective of soil science.

In the recent years, soil micromorphology has however largely expanded its field of application to biological, physical and chemical aspects of soils (e.g., structural modification under farming practises, deterioration of the soil ecosystem by man, behaviour of heavy metals in soils, etc.), (see, for example, Bresson and Boiffin 1990; Thompson *et al.* 1990). Because in these cases soil micromorphology is combined with other methods to answer specific questions, the logic of the micromorphological investigation can be more efficiently evidenced. It seems that through this direction, soil micromorphology is progressing successfully in soil science.

3.2 The future of soil micromorphology in archaeology

3.2.1 Scientific objectives

The lessons from soil science suggest that we should not be too ambitious in hoping to obtain the maximum benefit from soil micromorphology in the next few years. Our progress is not only dependent upon technical or financial factors. The most important and the most delicate question is whether we have the conceptual capacities to process the impressive quantity of data already collected and continually increasing. Our immediate objectives should then be:

i) to normalise the collection of data not only at the microscopic level but also in the field which may have important implications on field strategies adopted by archaeologists;

ii) to build reference systems by using standardised, or at least well-defined procedures (especially for experiments) and to publish them rapidly; great care has to be taken in their elaboration in order to avoid invalidating former results although some may have to be revised.

We should be modest in our aims and restrict our interpretation to data that we can identify by using our reference systems. Hypotheses can however be formulated on features of unknown origin by taking other criteria into account, for example the artefactual context.

We should rapidly develop the utilisation of more powerful techniques (SEM, STEM, microprobes, etc.) for the characterisation of constituents which are poorly determined in thin sections: impregnation by fat, blood or urine and other kinds of organic matter, phosphatic residues, etc. We should however be aware that sophisticated techniques are always fascinating and that they can easily divert the research from its primary goals. The petrographic microscope is certainly not self-sufficient but is absolutely necessary to make the link between field observations and any other kind of investigation on specific components of the sedimentary matrix (from grain size to molecular content).

We are also expecting from the progress achieved in image analysis an increase in systematic interpretation. The first attempt to understand structural modifications of soils by human trampling is already promising (Whitbread and Goldberg 1991). Image analysis should provide an efficient way to standardise our observations and to achieve a satisfactory level of quantification.

We are aware that the development of soil micromorphology in archaeology requires a close collaboration with archaeologists. This implies that we first have to facilitate the dialogue by making achievements in soil micromorphology accessible to all archaeologists. An effort has to be made in this direction by using a simple but strictly codified terminology. It is also highly important that all archaeologists accept that we are not providing them with data but that we are combining complementary approaches to meet common objectives.

The objectives of soil micromorphology in archaeology are those of contextual archaeology: to consider human activities through time and through space by analysing spatio-temporal relationships between the sedimentary matrix and its artefactual content. Our short experience has already shown that a large range of human activities has been recorded at the sedimentary level and that the signals of those activities can be deciphered. In the near future, for example when working on hunting sites which have been well preserved, we should be able to identify by their sedimentary signatures : outside fireplaces, cooking zones, eating zones, inner-hut fire places, rest zones, storage zones, passage zones. This ambitious objective faces more practical limitations than scientific problems. We are not going to impregnate the entire site and conduct the excavation under the microscope. Important choices have to be made right in the field which means that the micromorphological study begins with, and is part, of the excavation.

3.2.2 Academic organisation

The entrance of soil micromorphology into archaeology raises the important problem of academic institutions. The practical aspects of the preparation of thin sections can be easily solved until departments in archaeology or environmental archaeology can get their own equipment. The more delicate question is whether there is a scientific environment favourable to micromorphological investigations in archaeology. The full development of soil micromorphology in archaeology, especially when dealing with cultural aspects, requires the complete integration of the method with the archaeological methodology, started in the field, continued in the laboratory and achieved in publications. The inherent difficulties in soil micromorphological research can however handicap beginners, who may not find advisers in this field within departments of archaeology. From our own experience, one cannot hope to gain a solid level of expertise by spending hours with the microscope, even with a good knowledge of the related literature. A constant discussion with colleagues of what is seen under the microscope is absolutely essential to test the objectivity of observations and the logic of interpretation.

4. Conclusions

We can expect environmental change, induced by natural factors or by humans, to have been recorded in sedimentary materials only when the perturbation has been strong enough to modify their singular properties. The recognition in the field of these modifications is essentially limited by the fact that observable properties at this level of organisation are the resultant of complex interactions between elementary components of various sizes (atomic, molecular, nanometre, microscopic, etc.). Observations of thin sections prepared from undisturbed samples provide substantial information about most reactions which have affected the basic constituents of sediments (sand-, silt- and clay-sized mineral particles and organic components). These reactions are characterised by their specific signals which may relate to sedimentary changes, pedological modifications or man-induced transformations. The interpretation of each signal and the recognition of its succession can aid in the elucidation of the historical development of a given pedogenised sediment which may have been influenced by man. The microscopic scale thus allows an accurate perception of the dominant processes which are broadly identified at the field level. This approach is also essential to decipher minor events which have been offset by dominant processes.

For these two reasons, soil micromorphology offers environmental archaeology the opportunity to accurately identify man-induced transformations on ancient landscapes and to reconstruct landscape evolution with a very fine time resolution.

In contextual archaeology, soil micromorphology appears as an innovative approach which has already shed a new light in the recognition of cultural influences on the sediments. The most promising achievements expected concern the functional analysis of archaeological sites which implies that we should rapidly be able to decipher sedimentary signals related to the everyday life of our ancestors.

The singularity of the micromorphological approach requires a well defined system of concepts and methods and specific training. Soil micromorphology should consequently be a full branch of instruction in archaeology with a large diversity of objectives. We have to be cautious that the promotion of this new sub-discipline does not however create a community of scientists who are so specialised that their results will remain inaccessible to others. This pitfall can be avoided by demonstrating how investigations at microscopic scales performed by specialists can change the field perception of any archaeologist.

In conclusion, the successful future of soil micromorphology in archaeology implies not only that the number of practitioners should increase, but also that dialogue with archaeologists should be considerably improved.

References

Audouze, F. 1985: L'apport des sols d'habitat à l'étude de l'outillage lithique. In Otte, M. (editor), *La Signification Culturelle des Industries Lithiques (Actes du Colloque de Liège)* (Oxford, British Archaeological Reports International Series 239) 58–68.

Bresson, L.-M. and Boiffin, J. 1990: Morphological characterisation of soil crust development stages on an experimental field. *Geoderma* 47, 310–25.

Brewer, R. and Sleeman, J.R. 1988: *Soil Structure and Fabric* (Adelaide, CSIRO Division of Soils).

Bullock, P., Fedoroff, N., Jongerius, A., Stoops, G. and Tursina, T. 1985: *Handbook for Soil Thin Section Description* (Wolverhampton, Waine Research Publishers).

Butzer, K. 1982: *Archaeology as Human Ecology* (Cambridge, Cambridge University Press).

Campy, M. 1982: *Le Quaternaire Franc-comtois: Essai Chronologique et Paléoclimatique* (Besançon, Thèse de Doctorat ès Sciences naturelles, n°159, Faculté des Sciences et Techniques de l'Université de Franche-Comté).

Courty, M.-A. 1990: *Environements Géologiques dans le Nord-ouest de l'Inde. Contraintes Géodynamiques au Peuplement Protohistorique (Bassins de la Ghaggar-Saraswati-Chautang)* (Université de Bordeaux I, Thèse de Doctorat ès Sciences Naturelles).

Courty, M.-A. and Fedoroff, N. 1982: Micromorphology of a Holocene dwelling. *PACT* 7, 257–55.

Courty, M.-A. and Fedoroff, N. 1985: Micromorphology of recent and buried soils in a semi-arid region of north-west India. *Geoderma* 35, 285–332.

Courty, M.-A., Goldberg, P. and Macphail, R.I. 1989: *Soils and Micromorphology in Archaeology* (Cambridge, Cambridge University Press).

David, F., Julien, M. et Karlin, C. 1973: Approche d'un niveau archéologique en sédiment homogène. In *L'homme Hier et Aujourd'hui, Recueil d'étude en hommage à André Leroi-Gourhan* (Paris, Cujas) 65–72.

Farrand, W.R. 1975: Sediment analysis of a prehistoric rockshelter: the Abri Pataud. *Quaternary Research* 5, 1–26.

Fedoroff, N. and Goldberg, P. 1982: Comparative micromorphology of two late Pleistocene palaeosols (in the Paris Basin). *Catena* 9, 227–51.

Fedoroff, N., Courty, M.-A. and Thompson, M.L. 1990: Micromorphological evidence of palaeoenvironmental change in Pleistocene and Holocene palaeosols. In Douglas, L.A. (editor), *Soil Micromorphology: A Basic and Applied Science* (Amsterdam, Elsevier) 653–665.

Fisher, P.F. and Macphail, R.I. 1985: Studies of archaeological soils and deposits by micromorphological techniques. In Feiller, N., Gilbertson, D.D. and Ralph, N.G.A. (editors), *Palaeoenvironmental Investigations: Research Design, Method and Data Analysis* (Oxford, British Archaeological Reports International Series 258) 93–112.

Fitzpatrick, E.A. 1984: *Micromorphology of Soils* (London, Chapman and Hall).

Gladfelter, B.G. 1981: Developments and directions in geoarchaeology. In Schiffer, M.B. (editor), *Advances in Archaeological Method and Theory 4* (New York, Academic Press) 343–363.

Goldberg, P. 1979: Micromorphology of Pech de l'Azé II sediments. *Journal of Archaeological Science* 6, 17–47.

Goldberg, P. 1981: Applications of micromorphology in archaeology. In Bullock, P. and Murphy, C.P. (editors), *Soil Micromorphology. Vol. 1: Techniques and Applications* (Berkhamstead, A.B. Academic Publishers) 139–150.

Goldberg, P. 1987: Soils, sediments and Acheulean artefacts at Berekhat Ram, Golan Heights.

In Fedoroff, N., Bresson, L.-M. et Courty, M.-A. (editors), *Micromorphologie des Sols/Soil Micromorphology* (Plaisir, Association Française pour l'Etude du Sol) 583–589.

Hassan, F.A. 1978: Sediments in archaeology: methods and implications for palaeoenvironmental and cultural analysis. *Journal of Field Archaeology* 5, 197–213.

Kemp, R.A. 1985: The Valley Farm soil in southern East Anglia. In Boardman, J. (editor), *Soils and Quaternary Landscape Evolution* (London, John Wiley and Sons) 179–96.

Laville, H. 1976: Deposits in calcareous rockshelters: analytical methods and climatic interpretation. In Davidson, D.A. and Shackley, M.L. (editors), *Geoarchaeology* (London, Duckworth) 137–155.

Macphail, R.I. 1986: Palaeosols in archaeology: their role in understanding Flandrian pedogenesis. In Wright, V.P. (editor), *Palaeosols* (Oxford, Blackwell) 263–290.

Macphail, R.I., Courty, M.-A. and Gebhardt, A. 1990: Soil micromorphological evidence of early cultivation in north-west Europe. *World Archaeology* 22, 53–69.

Macphail, R.I., Romans, J.C.C. and Robertson, L. 1987: The application of micromorphology to the understanding of Holocene soil development in the British Isles, with special reference to early cultivation. In Fedoroff, N., Bresson, L.-M. and Courty, M.-A. (editors), *Micromorphologie des sols/Soil Micromorphology* (Plaisir, Association Française pour l'Etude du Sol) 647–657.

Miskovsky, J.-Cl. 1974: *Le Quaternaire du Midi Méditerranéen: Stratigraphie et Paléoclimatologie d'après l'étude Sédimentologique du Remplissage des Grottes et Abris-sous-Roches (Ligurie, Provence, Bas-Languedoc, Roussillon, Catalogne).* (Université de Provence, Etudes Quaternaires 3).

Mücher, H.J. and de Ploey, J. 1990: Sedimentary structures formed in aeolian-deposited silt-loams under simulated conditions on dry, moist and wet surfaces. In Douglas, L.A. (editor), *Soil Micromorphology: A Basic and Applied Science* (Amsterdam, Elsevier) 155–160.

Rigaud, J.-Ph. 1979: Contribution méthodologique à l'étude d'un sol d'occupation. *Revista do Museu Paulista, Sao Paulo* XXVI, 189–199.

Romans, J.C.C. and Robertson, L. 1983: The general effect of early agriculture on the soil. In Maxwell, G.S. (editor), *The Impact of Aerial Reconnaissance on Archaeology* (London, Council for British Archaeology Research Report 49) 136–141.

Stein, J.K. 1985: Interpreting sediments in cultural settings. In Stein, J.K. and Farrand W.R. (editors), *Archaeological Sediments in Context* (Orono, Center for the Study of Early Man) 5–19.

Stein, J.K. and Farrand, W.R. (editors) 1985: *Archaeological Sediments in Context* (Orono, Center for the Study of Early Man).

Thompson, M.L., Fedoroff, N. and Fournier, B. 1990: Morphological features related to agriculture and faunal activity in three loess-derived soils in France. *Geoderma* 46, 329–49.

Wattez, J. 1988: Contribution à la connaissance des foyers préhistoriques par l'étude des cendres. *Bulletin de la Société Préhistorique Française* 85, 353–366.

Wattez, J., Courty, M.-A. and Macphail, R.I. 1990: Burnt organo-mineral deposits related to animal and human activities. In Douglas, L.A. (editor), *Soil Micromorphology: A Basic and Applied Science* (Amsterdam, Elsevier) 431–440.

Whitbread, I. and Goldberg, P. 1991: Micromorphological aspects of Bedouin tent deposits and their implications in archaeology. *Society for American Archaeology, New Orleans, April 24–28, 1991,* in press.

Artefact Studies

Proceedings of the British Academy, **77**, 63–108

Lead Isotope Studies in the Aegean (The British Academy Project)

N. H. GALE & Z. A. STOS-GALE

Isotrace Laboratory, Department of Nuclear Physics, Keble Road,
Oxford OX1 3RH, UK.

Summary. In 1988 the British Academy awarded one of three special grants for collaborative research in the humanities for a project, initiated from Oxford, entitled "Science and archaeology: Bronze Age trade in the Mediterranean". Within this project stress is laid on the collaboration of archaeologists with archaeological scientists in an attempt to study ancient 'trade' by welding together more traditional approaches (textual evidence, typology, distribution of artefacts, tomb paintings, underwater archaeology, etc.) with scientific studies of the provenance of ceramics and metals and of the organic contents of vessels. The work involves colleagues in Cambridge, Athens, London, Manchester and Oxford. A major aspect of Bronze Age trade was probably that in metals such as copper, silver, lead and gold. Though it has long been a goal for archaeological science to find a way to establish the ore sources that supplied the metal for particular archaeological objects, it has been only in the past ten years that success has come through the application of comparative lead isotope analyses of ores and artefacts. The contribution of these and other archaeometallurgical methods to the aims of the British Academy project are outlined in this paper.

1. The British Academy Project

In the context of new developments in archaeological science our topic has double relevance. It was our intention that both the organisation of the British Academy Group Research Project and the subject of provenancing metals using lead isotopes should engender new developments in archaeologi-

Read 13 February 1991. © The British Academy 1992.

cal science. The British Academy Project has the title "Science and Archaeology: Bronze Age Trade in the Aegean and Adjacent Areas". It was conceived by the present authors, who formed a team involving archaeologists at Oxford, Cambridge, and the British School of Archaeology at Athens together with archaeological scientists at Oxford, Manchester, London and the Fitch Laboratory, Athens (see, for the personnel and a discussion of the aims of the project, Knapp 1989; Knapp and Cherry 1990). Exciting developments in new fields of archaeological research have often not been fully exploited because of the diversity of disciplines involved. We hope to make a major advance by integrating a variety of research strengths in a comprehensive study of an archaeological problem.

There have of course been a number of occasions before this when archaeologists and scientists have planned together collaborative work on a single archaeological site. In such ventures archaeological science (for instance, geophysical prospection, dating, environmental studies, etc.) often plays a rather subservient role, as a handmaiden to archaeology, producing data for interpretation by others or, worse, relegation to appendices of little apparent relevance in a site report. We hope to go beyond this, in demonstrating the validity of archaeological science as an academic discipline in its own right, just as within the Earth Sciences isotope geochemistry or geophysics have advanced the overall subject in ways not available to more traditional geological approaches. We selected a broad archaeological theme, depending on material from a host of sites, which we hope to advance by fusing together the methods of archaeology and archaeological science to achieve a result impossible for either alone. That theme is Trade in the Bronze Age Aegean. Both disciplines need to be brought together to establish the character and the details of such trade or exchange. The archaeological approach from excavation, field survey, typology, the decipherment of ancient texts and the study of Egyptian tomb paintings is no less necessary than the techniques of the natural sciences. Archaeological science can perhaps contribute most directly in the attempt to identify non-local materials, and to isolate or eliminate likely sources for these materials, be they ceramics, metals or organic residues. If we can make any progress with that, we can then try to build models of ancient trade and try to discover its importance to Bronze Age societies and its possible impact on their development. To give proper consideration to historical reconstruction and cultural issues, scientific analyses and statistical techniques must be incorporated in a research design that fosters basic quantitative research and builds interlocking arguments amongst data, analysis and interpretation.

One aspect of Bronze Age trade is that in metals, perhaps especially in the copper and tin which comprise the metallic alloy which names this period, but also in gold, silver and lead. There can be no doubt that metals were of considerable importance in the Bronze Age of the Eastern Mediterranean, on the one hand as prestige objects which took part in the move to increasing social stratification such as the gold hilts of swords and the bronze daggers elaborately inlaid with gold, silver and niello, and the elaborate gold jewellery, all from the Mycenaean Shaft Graves (Iakovides 1974, 274–280; Hood 1978, 176–186, 190–207). No less important was the use of bronze for domestic utensils (Hood 1978, 170–172), in the provision of tools (Renfrew 1972, Plate 17) which transformed carpentry and ship-building and in weapons (Renfrew 1972, Plate 22; Iakovides 1982) and armour (Iakovides 1974, 282–283; Warren 1975, 128) which revolutionised war. Most of this paper discusses new developments in using comparative lead isotopic analyses of artefacts and metal ores to trace the ore sources which supplied the metals for this trade.

2. Lead isotopes

Let us now turn to the main focus of this paper: advances in the use of variations in the isotopic composition of lead for the provenancing of metals. It was just over 21 years ago that Brill (1970) reviewed progress in the beginnings of the archaeological use of lead isotopes in a lecture delivered in London in another symposium organised jointly by the Royal Society and the British Academy and published in the Philosophical Transactions of the Royal Society. We hope to show that we have progressed a little since then. My own (N.H.G.) introduction to the subject sprang out of collaborative work in cosmochemistry with the Max-Planck-Institut für Kernphysik in Heidelberg, when the then Director, Wolfgang Gentner, suggested joint work on the sources of silver for the Archaic and Classical Greek coinage (Gale *et al.* 1980). Subsequently the enthusiasm of Colin Renfrew steered us towards research in the Bronze Age Aegean.

3. Provenancing metals

The attempt to trace ancient metal objects back to the ore deposits/mines which supplied the metal from which they were made has a long history (e.g., Desch 1928, Marechal 1966, Junghans *et al.* 1968). Most of that history is of a succession of ill-fated efforts to establish trace and minor element patterns of the chemical composition of metal objects which might group sets of artefacts, and might be related to similar patterns of chemical compositions in ore deposits. Coles (1982, 287–291) has expressed the deep disappointment of archaeologists with the confusion introduced into Bronze Age studies by the misleading and false interpretation of trace element analyses of metals.

The failure of such an approach is well documented and was to be expected from the beginning (Catling 1964, 12; Gale and Stos-Gale 1982). First, ore deposits are not homogeneous in chemical composition, even on the small scale (e.g., Thompson 1958; Chernykh 1966; Griffitts et al. 1972; Bowman et al. 1975; Constantinou 1982). Second, the process of smelting metal from an ore involves the addition of fluxing minerals to separate, as slag, the unwanted gangue minerals in the ore from the desired metal. The fluxes introduce a chemical pattern different from that in the ore, the partitioning of elements between slag and metal varies from element to element and depends also on furnace temperatures and atmospheres (e.g., Tylecote et al. 1977), whilst some elements are relatively volatile and may in part be lost in furnace fumes. Subsequent processes like fire refining or cupellation can cause further changes in chemical composition. Third, chemically representative samples are not simple to obtain from relatively impure ancient metals which are themselves inhomogeneous in chemical composition (e.g., Slater and Charles 1970), whilst corrosion can alter their original composition.

These disadvantages are not shared by comparisons of the isotopic composition of lead in an ore deposit with that of lead in an artefact made of metal from that ore. This is true whether we are talking of objects made of lead itself, or of silver, copper, bronze, iron or zinc containing traces of lead deriving from that in the original ore deposit. On the one hand the isotopic composition of lead in an ore deposit varies (with rare exceptions) by quite a small amount, less than about $\pm$ 0.3%. On another, the isotopic composition of lead in metal obtained from ore by extractive metallurgy is identical with that in the ore, and is constant throughout a metal artefact. The isotopic composition remains unaltered by subsequent purification of the metal, by the processes of making objects from the metal, or by subsequent corrosion of the objects (Barnes et al. 1978).

All this would be of no avail unless the isotopic composition of Pb were different in different ore deposits. Fortunately this is so. This is because three of the terrestrial isotopes of lead are partly radiogenic in origin, being derived from the radioactive decay of $^{238}U\{^{206}Pb\}$, $^{235}U\{^{207}Pb\}$ and $^{232}Th\{^{208}Pb\}$. Since mass spectrometers measure isotope ratios, we usually report analyses in terms of such ratios. These lead isotopic ratios record the time integrated record of the U/Pb and Th/Pb ratios of the sources in which the lead developed. In most cases ore deposits of lead/silver, of copper, of gold, of tin, of iron, of zinc, etc., contain vanishingly small amounts of uranium or thorium, so that after ore formation the isotopic composition of the lead which they contain will not change. (For more detailed discussions of the basic aspects of lead isotope geochemistry and systematics see Gale and Mussett 1973; Köppel and Grünenfelder 1979; Faure 1986; Gulson 1986).

The lead isotopic composition frozen into such an ore deposit which also

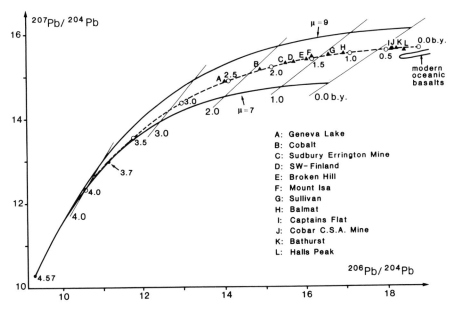

Figure 1. Lead isotope ratios for conformable ore deposits which appear approximately to fit a single-stage growth curve having μ ($= ^{238}U/^{204}Pb$ at the present day) of about 8. The data come from a compilation by Kanasewich (1968). The numerals on the curve are dates B.P. in billions (10^9) of years.

had a relatively straightforward geological history will, to first order, reflect the geological age of that ore deposit. Such well behaved ore deposits are typified by the large, strata bound, conformable (stratiform, see Stanton and Russell 1959) ore deposits for which the Holmes-Houtermans single-stage evolutionary model was originally formulated (Holmes 1946). Figure 1 shows how the isotopic compositions of such ores lie on a curve according to the age of the deposit; nowadays the evolution of the isotopic composition of such ores is described by slightly more complicated models due to Stacey and Kramers (1975) and Cumming and Richards (1975). Fine structure deviations from such simple models will result for most ore bodies, since in practice the lead which they contain has had a complicated history. This may have involved residence in the Earth's mantle, a period of crustal residence accompanied possibly by metamorphism, erosion and sedimentation, until the lead and other metals were finally extracted during a volcanic cycle, or by the action of hot brines, and concentrated into an ore deposit. (See, for example, Barnes (1989) for an elementary account of modern ideas about ore deposition). Relatively rare deposits may reflect extreme isotopic anomalies not related to their apparent age. Figure 2 shows how such extremely anomalous, rare, ore deposits, as Ivigtut, Joplin or Idaho, plot completely away from the

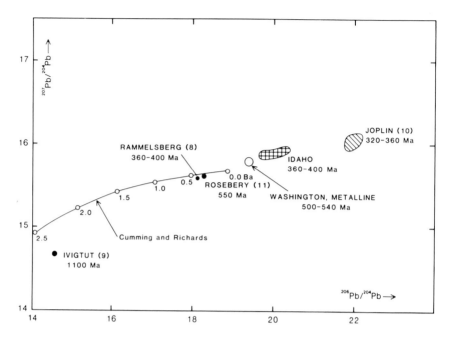

Figure 2. Lead isotope ratios for some ore deposits which are grossly anomalous (Ivigtut, Metalline, Idaho, Joplin) and for others (e.g., Rammelsberg) which lie (more typically) only a little away from the curve predicted by the model of terrestrial lead evolution devised by Cumming and Richards (1975) to describe the conformable ore deposits.

curve describing the conformable deposits; the more usual situation is exemplified by the Rammelsberg ore deposit, which plots just a little off the Cumming/Richards model curve. The usual situation, where the isotopic composition of lead in an artefact is related to first order to the age of emplacement of the ore deposit from which its metal came, is a useful advantage of lead isotope provenancing, since it can guide one in seeking possible ore deposits for which detailed lead isotope measurements should be made. There is of course no similar feature or advantage for chemical analyses.

One possible problem which would affect any technique for the provenancing of metals is that of possible melting down for re-use of diverse artefacts made from metal derived from a variety of ore sources. This has been considered in detail (Gale and Stos-Gale 1982, 1985; Gale *et al.* 1985; Stos-Gale *et al.* 1986; Pernicka 1989) and Pernicka *et al.* (1984) have devised a technique which combines lead isotope and trace element analyses in such a way as to prove whether mixtures exist or not. Use of this, together with archaeological arguments and the fact that we do not observe the smeared out lead isotope compositions for artefacts which would characterise mixing, shows that it is not a problem for the Bronze Age Mediterranean. Possible problems with the addition of tin or the practice of liquation in the Bronze Age have also been discounted (Gale and Stos-Gale 1982, 1985; Stos-Gale *et al.* 1984; Pernicka *et al.* 1990).

4. Methodology and techniques of measurement

One of the most important developments of this provenancing method has been its use for a wide ranging, but well defined, archaeological research programme in the Mediterranean world. This has necessarily meant that the lead isotope compositions have had to be determined for the many copper and lead-silver deposits in this region. In assigning the provenance of, say, a copper object to a copper ore deposit on the basis of a match between their lead isotope compositions it is vital to discover whether the lead isotopic compositions of the relevant ore deposits can be distinguished, the one from the other. One important factor which is decisive for this is the accuracy with which lead isotope ratios can be determined. Since the whole range of lead isotope compositions yet found in ore deposits is only about 8%, and most fall in a region covering a range of only about 1.7%, it is clearly necessary to be able to determine lead isotope ratios with an accuracy of less than or equal to about $\pm$ 0.1%.

This was not possible until 1969. Before that the methods used for isotopic analysis of lead by thermal ionisation mass spectrometry (TIMS) involved the use of 1 microgram or more of lead in the nitrate or sulphide form, and reproducibility was no better than $\pm$ 1%. In 1968 Catanzaro *et al.* published a triple Pt filament TIMS technique which allowed lead isotope ratios to be measured to about $\pm$ 0.05% at the 95% confidence level, but the technique required 1000 microgram samples, too high for most archaeological applications. This did however allow the United States National Bureau of Standards (NBS, now NIST) to prepare three international lead isotope reference standards, so that henceforward all laboratories could place their lead isotope analyses on an absolute basis. In 1969 Cameron *et al.* published a technique using a silica gel emitter which allowed of the order of 300 nanograms of lead to be isotopically analysed. [In fact Akishin *et al.* (1957) in Russia had published a similar technique a decade earlier, and Amov (1968) in Bulgaria also anticipated the American work, but these developments took a long time to be widely known in the west]. It was however not until 1973 that Barnes *et al.* at NBS in the USA, and independently Arden and Gale (1974) in Oxford, published low blank (blanks of about 1 nanogram) chemical separative techniques for lead and a silica gel emitter technique which allowed 100 nanogram samples of lead to be measured to $\pm$ 0.1% (at 95% confidence level). Since almost all the work in this field published by Brill involved analyses made at NBS, all of Brill's analyses published prior to 1974 are of an accuracy too low to be of any use. All Oxford work in lead isotope analysis applied to archaeology postdates 1976 and has the requisite modern precision and is moreover on an absolute basis by reference to the NBS lead isotope standards. An exciting new development has been the use of an internal standard ^{202}Pb—^{205}Pb tracer against which to correct fractionation in the mass spectrometer, which for all lead isotope ratios reduces the absolute 2 sigma error to $\pm$ 0.01% (Todt *et al.* 1984) but, the tracer being very expensive, this has not yet been used in archaeological applications.

5. Interpretation

Provenancing using lead isotope analyses is simple in principle, involving just comparative measurements of lead isotopic compositions of artefacts and ore deposits and the search for matches of composition, but there are many traps for the unwary. (For an extended review of the use of lead isotopes in provenance studies see Gale 1991).

The method of comparison and interpretation introduced and used by Brill is illustrated in Figure 3, adapted from one of his papers (Brill *et al.* 1974). The diagram is constructed from data obtained for some 400 specimens of various archaeological materials and ores from all over the ancient world. For analyses of new artefacts matches were sought with the regions of isotopic composition shown on the diagram, labelled L, X, E, S, etc. This approach, perhaps understandable in the early days when few isotopic analyses were available, in fact displays almost all the faults of interpretation which spring first to mind. First, the so-called lead isotope fields depend on both ores and artefacts from all over the ancient world and are labelled merely according to the geographical origin of most of the ores or artefacts within a given field; these are clearly not coherent groups and their use also involves some circularity of argument. Secondly there is mostly only an analysis of one ore from each ore deposit, so the extent of the field of isotopic composition for a given ore deposit remains unknown. Thirdly the ore analyses are almost solely of lead ores from deposits which do not contain copper, tin, etc, yet the artefacts include, for instance, bronzes which cannot possibly have been derived from such ore deposits. Fourthly the artefacts include glasses, glazes, pigments, bronzes, lead metal, debased silver from the Bronze Age to Roman times from all over the ancient world, amongst all of which one should hardly be seeking groupings with such gay abandon. Fifthly the fields are too catholic in their embrace; for instance that labelled

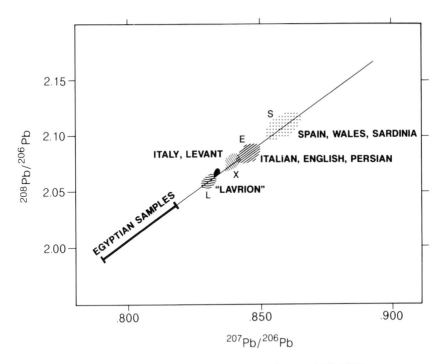

Figure 3. The lead isotope "fields" used by Brill and his colleagues (1974; 1988) to attempt to interpret lead isotope analyses in an archaeological context.

E includes ores and/or artefacts from Italy, England and Persia. Even the field labelled L for Lavrion includes ores and objects having nothing to do with that famous ore deposit in Attica upon which the wealth of ancient Athens depended. Gale (1980, 175, Figure 8) has shown by comparison how restricted is the true Lavrion field, constructed from our analyses of Lavrion ores only. And so on.

Though this approach was perhaps natural in the early days it seems unfortunate for it still to be in use (Brill 1988); progress cannot be achieved in this way. Progress can come only from the laborious construction of lead isotope fields for ore deposits in the region of interest and by the comparison of like with like: copper artefacts with copper deposits, lead/silver artefacts with lead/silver ore deposits, etc. Fieldwork is therefore essential, not only to collect ores from known geological horizons for isotopic analysis but also to establish the exact character of the mineral assemblages in particular ore deposits, and to differentiate between ore deposits and mere mineral occurrences which can never have been used at any period.

Fieldwork is also necessary to look for any traces of associated mining activities and to explore mines and slag heaps for ceramics or charcoal to date

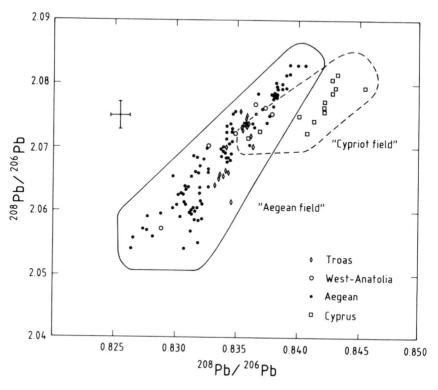

Figure 4. The so-called portmanteau "Aegean field" for lead isotope analyses of Aegean ores posited by Pernicka *et al.* (1984).

the activities. One will be immeasurably more confident about lead isotope evidence that a third millennium copper alloy dagger from Crete was made from copper from the Cycladic island of Kythnos against the background of the dating to that period of the copper slag heap on that island, by ceramic and accelerator C-14 dating (Gale and Stos-Gale 1989b; Stos-Gale 1989).

The vital importance of fieldwork in providing a proper basis for lead isotope studies is recognised by the Turkish/American team led by Aslihan Yener and by the German team also engaged in metal provenancing, and one cannot praise too highly the excellent fieldwork in Anatolia led by Gunther Wagner. Nevertheless we would not go along with the pessimism expressed by his colleagues (Pernicka *et al.* 1990, 282–283) that the lead isotope composition of lead in ore deposits is usually not unique, so that an assignment is not possible of an artefact to a single ore deposit. Their pessimism springs from constructing diagrams of what they call an Aegean lead isotope field (see Figure 4, adapted from Abbildung 28 of Pernicka *et al.* 1984), with which they try to compare analyses of artefacts made of lead, silver, and copper alloys. At first sight it does seem that ore deposit is overlapping with ore deposit and that not much discrimination between them is possible.

This is a key point for provenancing using lead isotopic analyses; one must be able to discriminate between ore sources if one is to be able to trace a metal artefact to its ore source. We believe that diagrams like that reproduced in Figure 4 have some problems. First, it plots together on one diagram data from lead/silver deposits *and* copper deposits. Second, it depends in fact predominantly on isotopic analyses of Pyrite-Blende-Galena (PBG) ore deposits which contain no copper recoverable in ancient times, so that it is incorrect to compare copper alloy objects with most of it except for those parts representative of Cyprus or Lavrion. Third, we know that lead was not exploited in the Bronze Age Aegean except where it contained silver above a certain lower limit (Gale and Stos-Gale 1981a; Gale *et al.* 1984; Pernicka 1989); this diagram does not distinguish between the ore deposits which have silver above or below that limit. Fourth, the individual ore deposits are not distinguished so that possible structure in this diagram is ignored. Fifth, it displays only two out of the three Pb isotope ratios (a usual feature of papers from Heidelberg/Mainz), so that possible extra discrimination available by using all the data is missed. We have emphasised in many papers (e.g., Stos-Gale *et al.* 1984; Gale and Stos-Gale 1985; Gale and Stos-Gale 1989b) the necessity of using all three lead isotope ratios in order to obtain both maximum discrimination between ore sources and maximum confidence in assigning a metal artefact to an ore source, but it is only recently that others have begun to take up this point (Reedy and Reedy 1988; Sayre *et al.* 1990; Yener *et al.* 1991).

A first look at the isotopic evidence for some of the copper ore deposits in the Aegean (see Figure 5) brings out some of these points. First, the structure is evident, which is obscured if all the lead deposits are plotted also on the same diagram. Second, the extra discrimination afforded by use of all the data is illustrated, for example, by the overlap between the Kythnos and Cypriot fields in the upper diagram and the complete separation of these ore deposits in the lower diagram. Separation of two ore deposits in *one* lead isotopic diagram is clearly sufficient proof that their isotopic 'fingerprints' can be distinguished. Each of the two lead isotopic diagrams used in this paper is of course a particular section through the three-dimensional cloud of data points with coordinates $^{208}Pb/^{206}Pb$, $^{207}Pb/^{206}Pb$, $^{206}Pb/^{204}Pb$.

6. Separation of lead isotope fields for ore deposits

Discrimination between two ore deposits having similar lead isotope compositions is vital to metal provenancing; it depends not only on the precision

COPPER ORES IN THE AEGEAN ANATOLIA AND SINAI

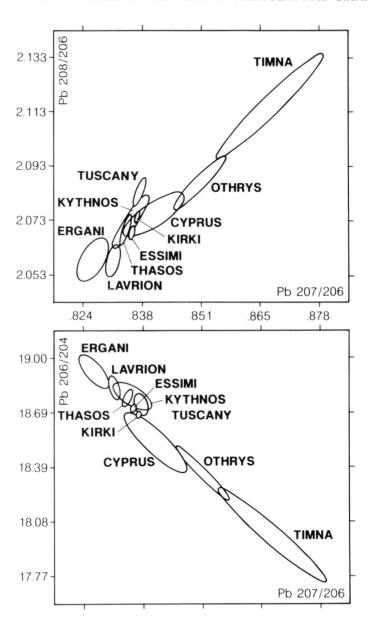

Figure 5. The two available ordinary bivariate lead isotope fields for some Mediterranean copper ore deposits.

and accuracy of the isotopic analyses, but also on the proper definition of the range of isotopic compositions found in each ore deposit. Some ore deposits seem to have, for samples collected from various positions within the deposit, lead isotopic compositions which are constant within the experimental uncertainty of $\pm$ 0.1% [such as Balya in Turkey (Begemann *et al.* 1989) and Bleiberg in Austria (Köppel and Köstelka 1976)]. These are the exception rather than the rule, and it is always necessary to make a number of different analyses for different samples through the deposit in order to establish its isotopic field. Until we began work in this field in Oxford it had been very rare for more than one or two lead isotope measurements to be made for a single ore deposit. Without at least ten to twenty analyses for a deposit the range of compositions characteristic of that deposit (its lead isotope field) remains poorly known, and the degree of its possible overlap with nearby fields cannot be assessed with any confidence. This point was emphasised by Gale and Stos-Gale (1982), Stos-Gale *et al.* (1986), Gale (1986), Gale and Stos-Gale (1989a) and was re-emphasised by Reedy and Reedy (1988).

It is in this vital question of possible overlap of ore deposit lead isotope fields and of data analysis that important recent advances have been made. We illustrate this in terms of the available copper deposits in the Aegean, the locations of which are shown in Figure 6, and some in the Central and Eastern Mediterranean, such as those in Tuscany (Figure 7) for some of which there is disputed evidence that they may have been exploited at least by Etruscan times (see, for instance, Camporeale 1989). We shall also consider important copper deposits (see Figure 8) in Timna (Rothenberg 1988), in Cyprus (Muhly *et al.* 1982), in Ergani Maden (Griffitts *et al.* 1972), in the Taurus Mountains (Yener *et al.* 1989, 1991) and in the Troas and its hinterland (Pernicka *et al.* 1984; Sayre *et al.* 1990).

First a digression about how we construct, from lead isotope measurements of a number of different ore samples from a particular ore deposit, the lead isotope field of that deposit. Our initial approach (e.g., Stos-Gale *et al.* 1986) was to plot the data for the three isotope ratios involved on two diagrams and to draw an envelope around the error bars of the outlying data, as shown in Figure 9 (for one of the two possible diagrams) for ores and litharge from the Cycladic island of Siphnos, which has direct and indirect evidence for Bronze Age lead-silver mining (Gale and Stos-Gale 1981a, 195–203).

This was not very sophisticated, and we have now written a computer graphics programme (PICTURE) which, for the data points for each ore deposit, plots these diagrams together with ellipses drawn around the data for each ore deposit and calculated at a chosen statistical confidence level. This method depends on the assumption that the lead isotope ratio data for a given ore deposit are distributed according to a tri-variate normal distribu-

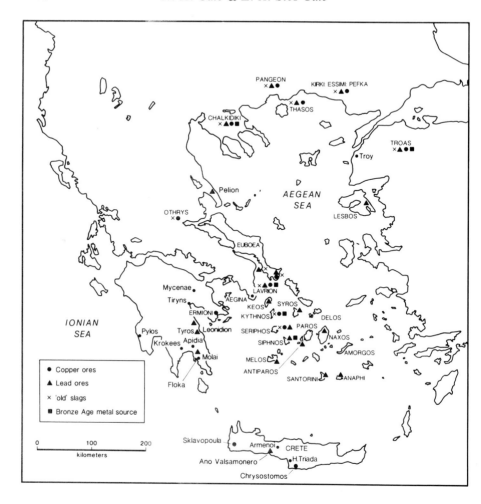

Figure 6. Locations of the principal copper and lead deposits around the Aegean.

tion function. We stress again that to define properly the field of each ore deposit at least 20 *geologically well-selected* ore samples are needed from each deposit, which again emphasises the need for fieldwork. For fewer samples something can be done with the use of F-tests and Hotelling's T^2 tests, but the true extent of the fields and proper assessment of overlapping will remain uncertain. Another approach to plotting bivariate lead isotope ratio diagrams, with ellipses drawn at preselected confidence levels (with or without the use of Hotelling's T^2 distribution for small samples), is to use the programme RAPLOT within the Brookhaven multivariate statistical software (Sayre 1975), now available for IBM PC compatible desktop computers.

Figure 7. Locations of the important copper and lead deposits in Tuscany.

We digress a little to consider briefly why we use lead isotope ratios rather than, as advocated by Reedy and Reedy (1988), the fractional atomic abundances (fractional compositions) of the four isotopes of lead [^{204}Pb, ^{206}Pb, ^{207}Pb, ^{208}Pb], which they claim to be less correlated than the ratios (one must in fact choose only three of these fractional abundances; they are not completely independent, their sum being unity). In fact their analysis shows rather marginal differences between the correlations for atomic abundances *versus* ratios, but there is a more fundamental reason for choosing ratios. All mass spectrometers used for accurate isotopic work in geochemistry or archaeology produce their primary data as ratios, for technical reasons partly connected with the techniques used for correcting for fractionation during an analysis (e.g., Dodson 1963); *all lead isotope data in the literature has been produced as ratios.* So far the vast majority of lead isotope data produced for

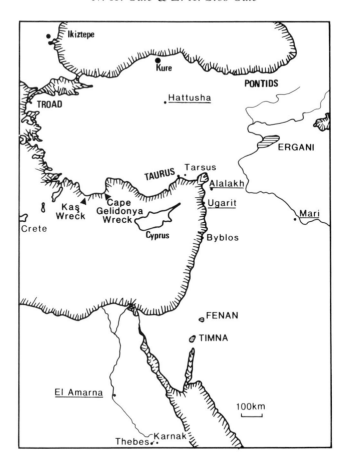

Figure 8. Approximate locations of important copper deposits in Timna, Fenan, Cyprus, Ergani Maden, the Taurus Mountains and the Troas. The locations are also shown of the Bronze Age shipwrecks of Cape Gelidonya and Ulu Burun (Kas) excavated by Bass (1967, 1986).

archaeology has been obtained using single collector mass spectrometers where the ion beams for the different isotopes were switched rapidly and sequentially into the collector; unavoidable instability in the thermal ionisation process forced the data to be obtained as ratios of ion beam currents, with interpolation procedures to take account as far as possible of the time varying ion currents (Webster 1960; Dodson 1963; Wasserburg *et al.* 1969; Wasserburg 1987, 134–138). Modern mass spectrometers often have software which allows the data to be printed out as fractional atomic abundances, but this data is secondary, having been computed from the directly measured ratio data. The atomic abundance data is therefore, due to propagation of errors, always less accurate than the primary ratio data; the primary ratio data is therefore the first choice for multivariate statistical analysis, other

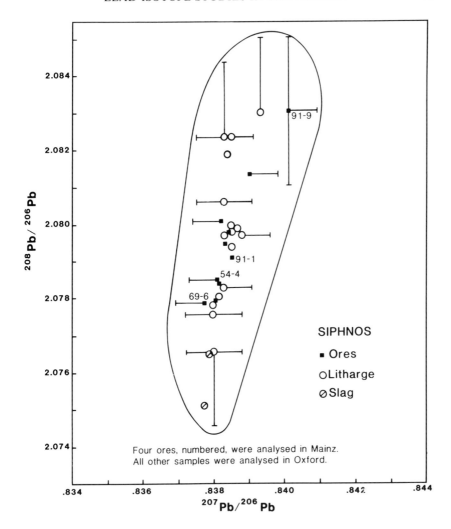

Figure 9. One of the two ordinary bivariate lead isotope fields for the lead-silver ores from the Cycladic island of Siphnos.

things being equal. In practice it seems to make little difference whether one uses the ratios we select, another choice of ratios, or the atomic abundances. We have empirically investigated the effect of such alternative choices of input data for the BMDP programme 7M (discriminant analysis) and the Brookhaven programmes RAPLOT, CONDIST, ADCORR and ADSEARCH; we find no differences, within computational error, between the computed probabilities etc., which result from the different choices of input data type. Sayre (pers. comm.) reports the same conclusion.

Figure 5 shows 90% confidence level fields (a confidence level used also by Sayre and his colleagues in two-dimensional plots of lead isotope data, e.g., Yener *et al.* 1991), produced using the programme PICTURE, for some relevant copper ore deposits, including most of those in the Aegean and the Central and Eastern Mediterranean. It covers nearly the same range of isotopic compositions as the large Aegean "field" (see Figure 4) drawn by the Mainz/Heidelberg team, but it includes only copper deposits and reveals the structure within the larger "field" and the possibility of assigning individual artefacts to individual ore sources not shown by their approach. It also shows that the overlaps in the upper diagram (of Figure 5) between Kythnos and Cyprus, and Essimi with Cyprus, vanish in the lower diagram. The large extent of the isotopic field for Timna is due to the presence of uranium in some of the copper ores there, so that evolution away from the isotopic composition at deposition has continued until the present day.

The necessity of using all three isotope ratios is clear in attempts to unscramble the apparent overlapping of ore deposit lead isotope fields in the lower third of Figure 5. We also need to have a method of assigning statistical probabilities of the lead isotope data for one ore deposit falling into the isotopic field of another deposit, and for estimating the probability that the isotopic composition of an artefact assigns it to one ore deposit rather than another. We clearly need to combine all three isotopic ratios together in some form of multivariate statistical analysis. Since we know in advance that each geologically well defined ore deposit constitutes a group for statistical purposes, we can use the method of stepwise discriminant function analysis, for which the BMDP programme 7M is appropriate. (We used this approach first in Gale 1986). Figure 10 shows the result of using this approach to investigate the possible overlap between the lead isotope data for copper deposits on Kythnos and Cyprus, and the possible overlap of each with the fields for Essimi and Kirki in the Rhodope Mountains (Greece, see Figure 6); both the scatterplot illustrated and the numerical data generated by BMDP 7M give good separations of these copper ore deposits. [In subsequent discussion we shall present just the scatterplots of the first two Canonical variables, but in each case where we refer to good separation being obtained between two ore deposit lead isotope fields it should be understood that the numerical probabilities of all the samples from one field belonging to a nearby field are less than 5%. The enclosing lines drawn around samples from the same ore deposit are merely to guide the eye; they have no statistical significance.]

Figures 11 and 12 show how other apparent possible overlaps between copper ores in Tuscany, Kythnos and Cyprus, and between the very large

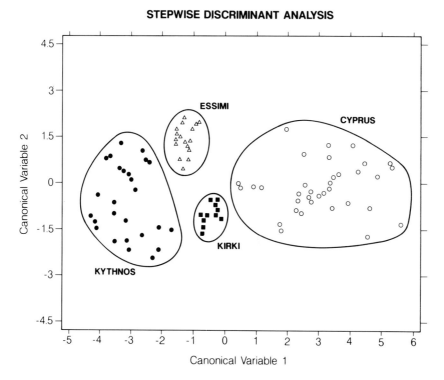

STEPWISE DISCRIMINANT ANALYSIS

Figure 10. Stepwise trivariate discriminant function analysis used to show that the lead isotope data for the copper ore deposits of Cyprus, Kythnos, Essimi and Kirki can be resolved from each other. For brevity only the scatterplot of the canonical discriminant functions are shown. The outlines have no statistical significance, and are drawn merely to guide the eye.

Anatolian copper mine of Ergani Maden in Turkey and Lavrion in Attica are easily resolved by discriminant analysis involving all three lead isotope ratios.

We cannot afford to leave out of account the copper deposits in Turkey in any investigation of copper sources which may have played a part in the Bronze Age metals trade, especially for sites in the North Eastern Aegean. Here however we meet a dilemma which has been pointed up also by the Smithsonian Laboratory (Sayre *et al.* 1990). Although rather thorough field-work has been carried out in Turkey by the team led by Gunther Wagner, in which over a five year period they have visited and briefly described in excess of 150 ore and slag deposits (Wagner *et al.* 1989 and references therein), there are currently only about 80 lead isotope analyses published for these deposits, many of which are lead rather than copper deposits. Four of the deposits account for 29 of the analyses, so that most deposits have one, or at the most two, analyses, and many remain completely unanalysed. In common with the Smithsonian Laboratory we find that there are too few analyses of the

STEPWISE DISCRIMINANT ANALYSIS

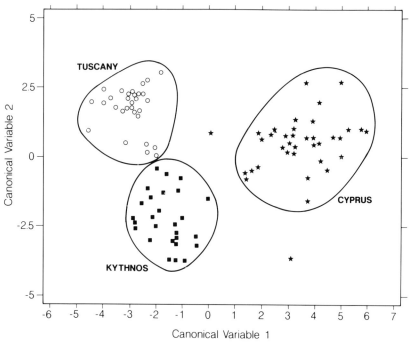

Figure 11. Discriminant function (trivariate) analysis used to resolve lead isotope data for the copper deposits of Tuscany, Kythnos and Cyprus.

Anatolian Black Sea sources, and from many other parts of Anatolia, for meaningful statistical characterisation. We have already dealt with the Ergani Maden mine; in addition one has from the German work enough data to characterise the Keban copper ore source at the headwaters of the Tigris and Euphrates rivers, the Kure mine on the Black Sea coast NNW of Ankara, and two groups of mines in the Troad region of Northwest Anatolia designated Troad 1 and Troad 2 in Figure 13, which shows the data in one of the two available ordinary lead isotope diagrams. We should mention here that Troad 1 embraces the deposits and slags designated by the German team as TG13A, TG14, TG15, TG16A, TG17A, TG142H, TG144C, TG144D, TG145A, TG146A, TG147A, TG150, TG152; Troad2 is made up of TG19, TG128B, TG130A, TG133B, TG133E, TG134A, TG137A, TG140A, TG143B. It should be emphasised that Troad1 and Troad2 are formed only by associating together two groups of ore and slag samples which have similar lead isotope ratios; there seems to be too little geological information to provide a sure geological basis to form these two "fields". Each group consists of over 8 different deposits, mostly with one analysis each, linearly

STEPWISE DISCRIMINANT ANALYSIS

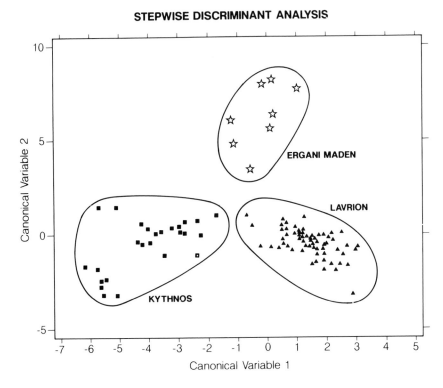

Figure 12. Discriminant function (trivariate) analysis used to resolve lead isotope data for the copper deposits of Ergani Maden in Anatolia, Lavrion in Attica and Kythnos.

distributed over a distance of about 100km. We shall accept these two Troad "fields" provisionally for the present, but only as a matter of convenience for the immediately succeeding discussion.

Figure 13 shows that we do not need to use statistics to see that there is no problem of overlap as far as the Keban and Kure mines are concerned, but at first sight there is an apparent problem with overlap between the Kythnos field and the Troad1 and Troad2 fields. Discriminant analysis (Figure 14) shows good separation of the Troad2 field, and rather good separation of the Troad1 field from the Kythnian field, with just a few Kythnos data points straying into the Troad1 field.

The Smithsonian Laboratory has analysed a number of possible copper ores from the Taurus Mountains (Yener *et al.* 1991). Figure 15 shows a partial overlap of the Taurus 2A field with Cyprus in one conventional bivariate diagram which is resolved in the other, whilst Figure 16 shows that complete separation is obtained by resorting to trivariate stepwise discriminant analysis.

SOME AEGEAN and ANATOLIAN ORES

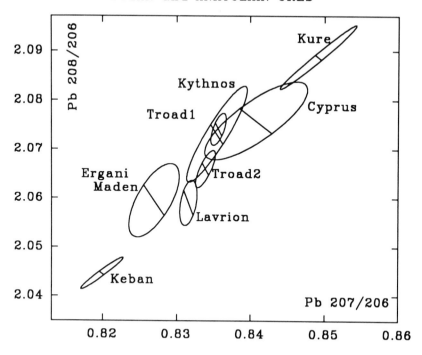

Figure 13. One of the two available ordinary bivariate lead isotope diagrams for copper ores, including the Anatolian deposits of Keban and Kure and two groupings of deposits in the Troad.

There is no space for overmuch repetition of such case studies here; suffice it to say that we have encountered only one serious overlap of lead isotope composition for copper ores in the Aegean, Central and Eastern Mediterranean. That is for the island of Thasos (locality given in Figure 17) which overlaps with Kythnos. Discriminant analysis does not completely resolve this overlap. This must be set in context, by noting that copper ores are insignificant in amount on Thasos and that the thermoluminescence date obtained for a copper slag heap there at Makrirarchi is 260 ± 160 BC (Pernicka and Wagner 1988, 229). Even more persuasive evidence that we do not have to worry about Thasos as a significant source of copper in the Bronze Age are our lead isotope analyses of a series of Late Bronze Age bronze objects, mainly knives, from Dr. Koukouli-Chrysanthaki's (1982 and references therein) excavations on Thasos, shown in Figure 18. Statistical analysis is not needed to see that not a single artefact is consistent with having been made from Thasian copper ores, whose lead isotopic fields are shown by the ellipses. Indeed the wide range of isotopic composition of the Thasian bronzes shows that the Thasians were, in the Late Bronze Age, using a wide

DISCRIMINANT ANALYSIS OF ORES FROM KYTHNOS, TROAD1, TROAD2.

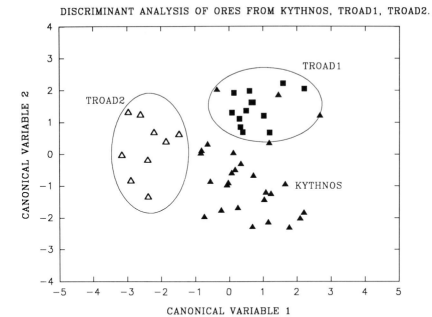

Figure 14. Discriminant function (trivariate) analysis showing good separation of the Troad1 and Troad2 "fields" from the Kythnian copper ores and slags.

variety of copper sources, which they would not be likely to have done if copper were easily available on their own island and they had the knowledge to exploit it. This sort of evidence, that in the period under review the local people did not exploit their own meagre resources and that therefore the resource in question cannot have been used abroad in that period, seems to us admissible extra evidence in the rare cases where partial overlap of ore source lead isotope compositions prevents more direct conclusions.

7. Oxhide ingots

We stress again that in the Bronze Age Mediterranean which forms the focus of our British Academy Project, overlapping ore fields are very rare. We now examine briefly the conclusions which lead isotope analyses allow us to draw about an important part of the copper trade in the Bronze Age Mediterranean. This took the form of the transport of copper ingots weighing on average about 29 kilograms and of a characteristic shape. They are called oxhide ingots by reason of a fancied resemblance of their shape to the flayed skin of an ox. The most comprehensive archaeological accounts of these

N. H. Gale & Z. A. Stos-Gale

AEGEAN, TUSCAN AND ANATOLIAN ORES

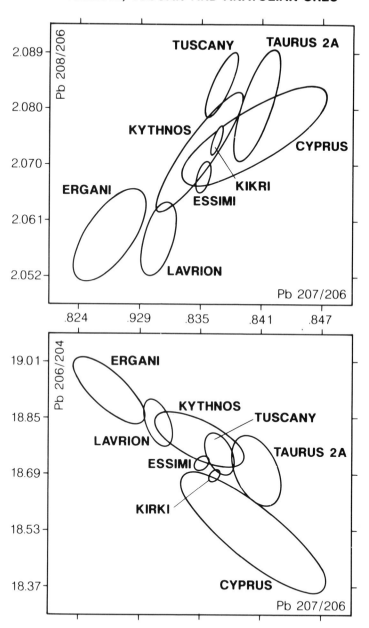

Figure 15. The two available ordinary bivariate lead isotope diagrams showing, amongst other things, a partial overlap between the Taurus2A field and the Cypriot field.

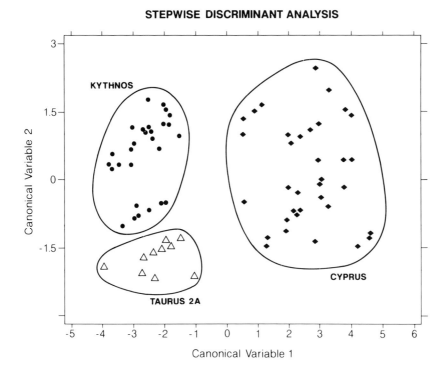

STEPWISE DISCRIMINANT ANALYSIS

Figure 16. Trivariate stepwise discriminant function analysis produces complete separation of the lead isotope data for Cypriot and Taurus2A copper ores.

ingots are given by Buchholz (1959) and Bass (1967), both of whom provide many illustrations of typical examples.

Figure 19 is a map of the distribution of find spots of oxhide ingots around the Mediterranean. For the finds on land, which often consist only of fragments, it is difficult to estimate the number of whole ingots represented, but it is about 130, with about 20 on Cyprus, 37 on Crete, roughly 50 on Sardinia, 22 in Greece (chiefly Mycenae and Kyme) and one each in Sicily and Lipari. Two Bronze Age shipwrecks have been excavated off the coast of Turkey by Bass at Cape Gelidonya (Bass 1967) and Ulu Burun (Kaş; Bass 1986); the localities are shown in Figure 8. There were 38 ingots on the Cape Gelidonya wreck and more than 200 on the Ulu Burun wreck, so that about 65 per cent of all known ingots have been found on only two shipwrecks.

That indicates the scale of the trade in copper in the oxhide ingot form alone (or at least that *intended*; how many ships foundered with their cargoes, how many voyages were successful?), with at least 6 metric tonnes of copper as oxhide ingots on the Ulu Burun ship alone. The distribution of find spots on land suggests that these ingots were almost exclusively transported by

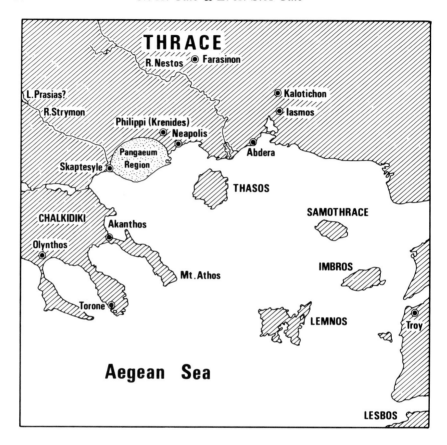

Figure 17. The locality of the island of Thasos in relation to its hinterland on the mainland.

ship. They have been found overwhelmingly either on islands or at mainland sites not far from the sea; sites which in the main have other evidence for international trade.

Before our work there was no evidence about the origin of these ingots, though the common view was that they represented trade in copper from Cyprus, based chiefly on the idea that Cyprus was a copper rich island with evidence for copper metallurgy and on which a few oxhide ingots had been found. Our first lead isotope analyses proved that the 13th century BC oxhide ingots found on Cyprus were indeed consistent with having been made from Cypriot copper ores (Gale and Stos-Gale 1986). Figure 20 gives the evidence for that as it appears in a discriminant analysis scatter plot, showing that lead isotopic analyses of Cypriot copper oxhide ingots fall inside the region defined by Cypriot copper ores. [We shall use such discriminant analysis scatter plots throughout the rest of this section; it is implicit that the BMDP

LBA THASOS BRONZES IN RELATION TO THASOS ORE FIELD

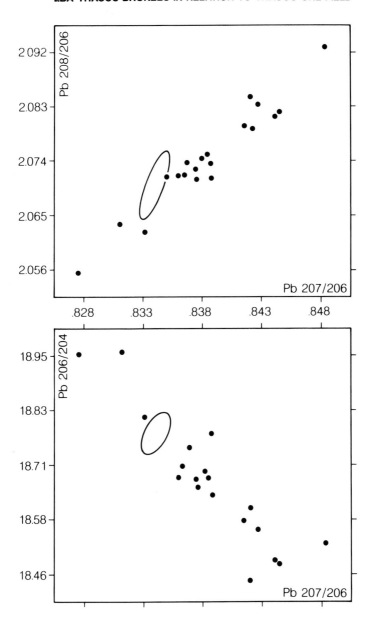

Figure 18. The two ordinary bivariate lead isotope diagrams for Late Bronze Age copper alloy artefacts excavated in Thasos by Dr Koukouli-Chrysanthaki, showing that none fall inside the lead isotope field (elliptical outline) for Thasian ores and copper slags.

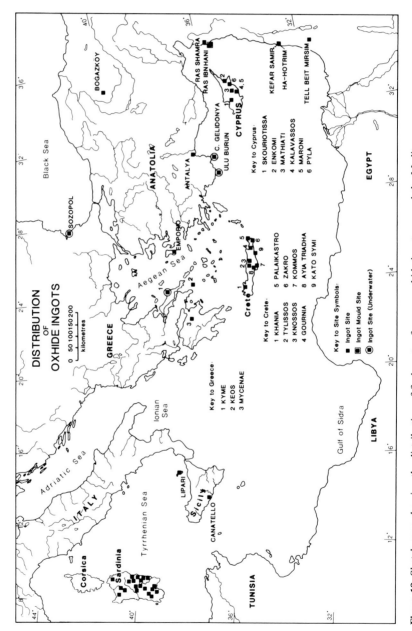

Figure 19. Sketch map showing the distribution of find spots of copper oxhide ingots around the Mediterranean.

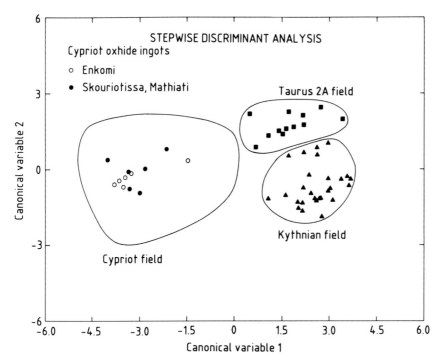

Figure 20. Trivariate discriminant function analysis showing that the lead isotope analyses for the copper oxhide ingots found on Cyprus group with the lead isotope analyses of Cypriot ores.

7M calculated probabilities of the ingots belonging to the field discussed are greater than 70% and mostly greater than 90%]. We also discovered another trace element characteristic of copper extracted from Cypriot copper ores in the Late Bronze Age; it has Au and Ag values falling in a restricted field (Stos-Gale *et al.* 1986, Figure 8; Gale 1989, Figure 29.11). Figure 21 shows that the Cypriot copper oxhide ingots also fall into this Au-Ag field. We have both a lead isotope and a Au/Ag fingerprint for copper produced from Cypriot copper ores in the Late Bronze Age; fingerprints which we can use to trace the movement overseas of Cypriot copper

A surprise was in store when we came to examine the 16th Century BC oxhide ingots found at Hagia Triadha and Tylissos on Crete. Figure 22 shows an ordinary lead isotope diagram for these ingots in relation to the Cypriot lead isotope field; we do not need statistics to see that these were not made of Cypriot copper. Provided that the two sources of copper clearly involved are not isotopically anomalous we can deduce from the Cumming and Richards (1975) model that these ingots were predominantly made of copper coming from a Precambrian ore source unknown in the Aegean but certainly known in Iran or Afghanistan. This may not be so far fetched if we recall that

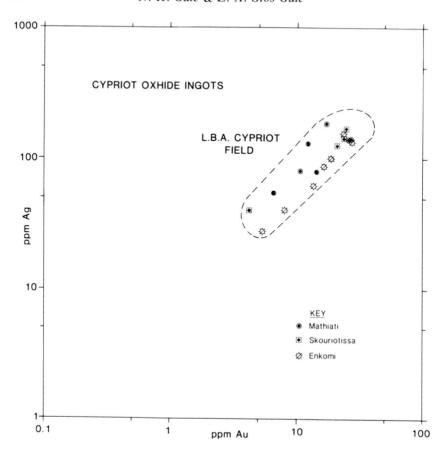

Figure 21. Gold and silver analyses of copper oxhide ingots found on Cyprus, showing that they fall within the field defined by analyses of copper alloys excavated from Late Cypriot archaeological sites.

the Minoan and Mycenaean source of lapis lazuli is thought to have been in Afghanistan (Hermann 1968) and that part of the tin trade to Crete came through Mari (Dossin 1970), possibly also from tin sources in Afghanistan (Shareq and Abdullah 1977; Cleuziou and Berthoud 1982). These are the earliest oxhide ingots known and, since they are not made of Cypriot copper, suggest strongly that the start of the Mediterranean copper trade in this form had nothing to do with Cyprus.

At Mycenae a complete copper oxhide ingot (illustrated by Iakovides 1974, 297) was excavated by Tsountas; twelve fragments of oxhide ingots (illustrated in Gale 1989, Figure 29.15) were excavated by Wace (1953) as part of the Poros Wall Hoard. Figure 23 shows that these 13th Century BC

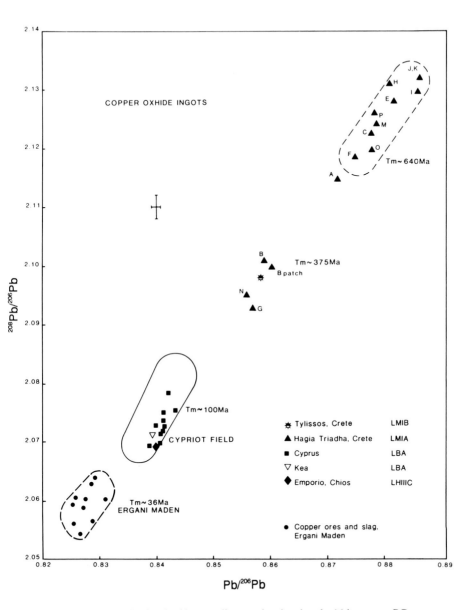

Figure 22. An ordinary bivariate lead isotope diagram showing that the 16th. century BC copper oxhide ingots excavated at Hagia Triadha and Tylissos on Crete fall far outside the Cypriot field.

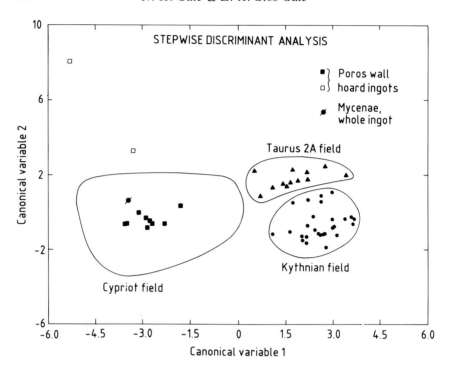

Figure 23. Trivariate discriminant function analysis of lead isotope analyses of the copper oxhide ingot and fragments excavated at Mycenae, showing that they group with copper ores from Cyprus.

oxhide ingot fragments are made of Cypriot copper, so that there was then at least some trade bringing Cypriot copper to Mycenae.

What of the copper oxhide ingots on the two Bronze Age shipwrecks off the coast of Turkey? Figure 24 shows that all 15 analysed ingots from the 13th century BC Cape Gelidonya ship were clearly made from Cypriot copper. Figure 25 shows that Cyprus also supplied the copper for the 4 analysed oxhide ingots from the Late 14th Century BC Ulu Burun ship, though this ship was carrying bun ingots which are not all of Cypriot copper. We can at least be sure that some Cypriot copper was being carried through the Mediterranean in the Late Bronze Age, though to establish quantitatively the overall picture many more ingots from these ships should be analysed.

Turning to Sardinia, there has been a modern tendency to ascribe the large numbers of oxhide copper ingot fragments found there to indigenous manufacture from Sardinian ore deposits, though the earliest discussion of these ingots saw them clearly as an import from the Eastern Mediterranean (Pigorini 1904). Modern scholars, thinking of the copper deposits on Sardinia, have tended to reject an Eastern origin for these oxhide ingots

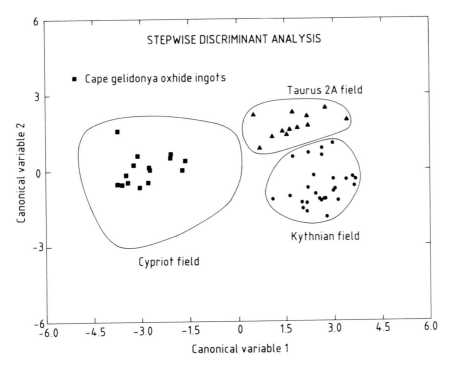

Figure 24. Trivariate discriminant function analysis of lead isotope analyses of copper oxhide ingots from the 13th century BC shipwreck excavated by Bass at Cape Gelidonya off the coast of Turkey.

found on Sardinia as an absurd example of "coals to Newcastle", though the modern example of cheap imports of coal from Poland to Britain should perhaps have given them pause in putting forward so simplistic an argument. Economic considerations aside, there is also the example from the ancient world that the Romans carefully distinguished copper from different ore deposits as of different quality (Pliny, NH.XXXIV.II).

In fact Sardinia is not noted for its reserves of copper, but rather for its deposits of lead. For example, the total production of copper minerals from Sardinia in the period 1851–1948 was 75,000 tonnes, compared with 3,147,000 tonnes of lead minerals in the same period (Sarda 1949, 59). That the reserves of copper in Cyprus are overwhelmingly larger is shown by the fact that in Cyprus one mine (Mavrovouni) exported 131,093 tons of copper concentrates in the year 1938 alone (Bear 1963, 58). Moreover there are only about six small copper mines of any account at all in Sardinia, whilst in Cyprus there are more than 30 cupriferous ore bodies, each vastly larger than any in Sardinia. The probability of ancient discovery of copper in Cyprus is vastly larger than in Sardinia.

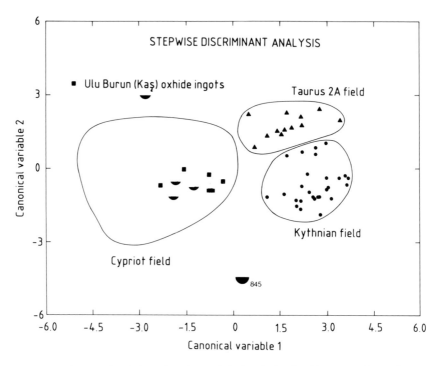

Figure 25. Trivariate discriminant function statistical analysis of lead isotope analyses of copper oxhide and bun ingots from the late 14th. century BC shipwreck excavated by Bass at Ulu Burun off the coast of Turkey.

Our comparative lead isotope analyses of Sardinian copper ore deposits and oxhide ingots found on Sardinia do not support the idea that the ingots were made of Sardinian copper; there is no match (Gale and Stos-Gale 1987). Figure 26 shows that there is a very clear match between the oxhide ingots found on Sardinia and Cypriot copper ores. Moreover Figure 27 shows that the oxhide ingots found on Sardinia display also the range of Au/Ag contents characteristic of Late Bronze Age Cypriot copper. Significantly, analyses depicted in the same figure of characteristic Sardinian Nuragic bronzes [from Santa Maria in Paulis, (Macnamara *et al.* 1984)] *both* have Au/Ag analyses lying outside the Cypriot field *and* have lead isotope characteristics consistent with their manufacture from Sardinian copper ores (Gale and Stos-Gale 1987, Figure 7.15). Present evidence suggests that we should see the Sardinian ingots as the successful Western extreme of the trade in Cypriot copper exemplified by the ill-fated Cape Gelidonya and Ulu Burun ships.

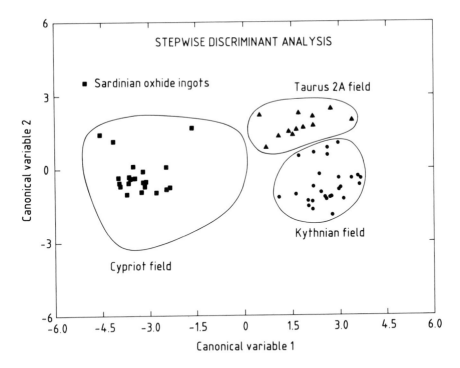

Figure 26. Trivariate discriminant function analysis of lead isotope analyses of copper oxhide ingots found on Sardinia, showing that they group with Cypriot copper ores.

8. The British Academy Project

We conclude by summarising very briefly something about what, within the purview of the British Academy Project, we have discovered about the metals trade in lead, silver, and copper in the Bronze Age Mediterranean by the application of the approaches sketched out in this paper. Figure 28 shows in histogram form the sources of lead and silver found to have been used at different periods of the Bronze Age in the Aegean. Very briefly, the chief sources of lead, silver and the cupellation by-product litharge in the Early Bronze Age were the Cycladic island of Siphnos (Gale 1980) and the mainland mines at Lavrion in Attica (Gale and Stos-Gale 1981a). In the Late Bronze Age Lavrion becomes the dominant source, with an indication that a very little lead and silver may have been coming from the deposits in the Halkidiki (Stos-Gale and MacDonald 1991). A major finding has been the Late Bronze Age trade in lead (and silver?) through the Cycladic islands from Lavrion to Thera and Crete (Gale and Stos-Gale 1981b; Stos-Gale and Gale 1982; Stos-Gale and Gale 1984; Gale *et al.* 1984; Stos-Gale 1985).

Figure 29 is a similar histogram for the sources of copper. It is based

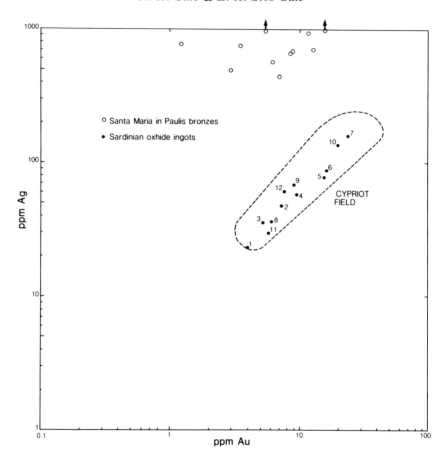

Figure 27. Gold and silver analyses of copper oxhide ingots found on Sardinia, showing that they fall within the field established by analyses of Late Bronze age copper alloy objects excavated in Cyprus.

chiefly on the analysis of copper and copper alloy artefacts, rather than the raw material represented by the copper oxhide ingots. It suggests that for copper in the Cyclades and Crete the dominant Early Bronze Age source seems to have been the Cycladic island of Kythnos (Stos-Gale 1988), with a little copper coming even then from Lavrion and other sources. By the Late Bronze Age the dominant source of copper for the Mycenaeans and the Minoans becomes Lavrion in Attica, with a little copper from Cyprus and other sources. When we examine the source of the copper most frequently used for making objects we find that Cyprus does not have the dominance in the Mycenaean and Minoan worlds which examination of the copper oxhide ingots might suggest, a fact in itself which raises interesting archaeological

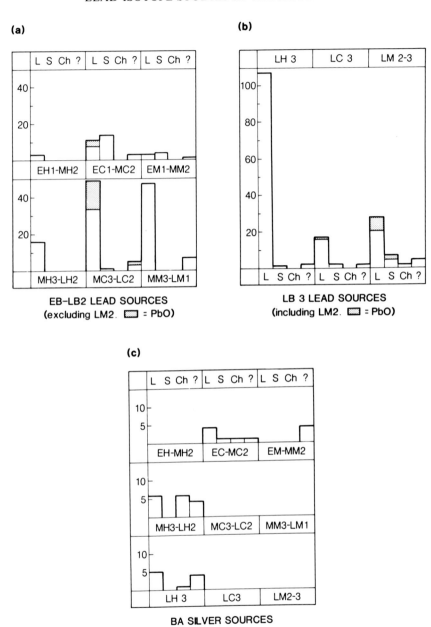

Figure 28. A histogram summarising present knowledge of the sources of lead and silver used at various periods in the Aegean.

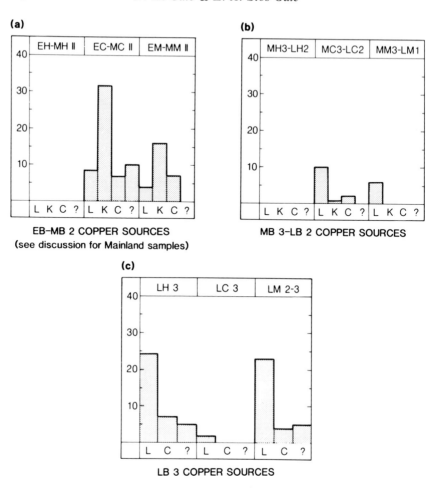

(L = Lavrion, K = Kythnos, C = Cyprus, ? = Unknown)

Figure 29. A histogram summarising present knowledge of the sources of copper used at various periods in the Bronze Age in the Aegean.

questions. We have of course to admit that many more artefacts need to be analysed to substantiate this view, and to trace through time the evolution of the metals trade in the Aegean. But, in conclusion, we think that it can be claimed that there have been advances in the use of lead isotopes in solving the otherwise intractable problem of provenancing metals and, through their use, in advancing the aims of the British Academy Project. These advances could not have been made without the careful development of the lead isotopic analytical approach to provenancing which has taken place since the last Royal Society/British Academy symposium on archaeological science in 1969.

The important advances in archaeological lead isotope analyses which have taken place since the beginning of this subject are:

i) the recognition of the need for close definition of the archaeological problem whose solution is sought,

ii) the recognition of the importance of field work for examination of ore deposits and metallurgical remains,

iii) the mineralogical examination of possible ore sources, and the comparison of copper alloy artefacts not with lead/silver deposits but only with ore deposits which could anciently have yielded copper metal, etc.,

iv) the necessity of taking into account ore geology and isotope geochemistry together with the processes of extractive metallurgy,

v) ever more accurate mass spectroscopy and low blank chemical separative techniques, and

vi) more sophisticated data analysis and interpretation.

We hope that we have demonstrated that developments iii), v) and vi) are vital for differentiating ore deposits whose lead isotope compositions are close together, without which it is indeed not possible to assign artefacts to a single ore source.

9. Isotope archaeology

The use of lead isotopic analyses for provenancing metals is but one aspect of a broader subject. The technique of mass spectrometry can now advance archaeological science to such an extent that we believe that we can now speak of a new subject of isotope archaeology, just as about 30 years ago there began the then new subject of isotope geochemistry. Isotope geochemistry and geochronology brought about a revolution in the study of the Earth Sciences. Studies of variations in the isotopic composition of Pb, Sr, Nd, Hf, Ar etc. on the one hand allowed the construction of an absolute chronology (not hitherto available) stretching back for 4,500 million years. In another direction the isotope geochemistry of these and other elements (including Mg, Cr, Ag, Xe, Pu) allowed fundamental questions of petrogenesis and the mode of formation of ore deposits, the origin of the elements and the origin and evolution of the Solar System, etc, to be attacked (Wasserburg 1987; Allegre 1987). We believe that similar studies may have a similar impact upon archaeological science.

Table 1.   Mass Spectrometry In Archaeological Science

---

i) Gas Source Mass Spectrometry:

(a) C, N isotopic compositions for identification of burned or cooked food residues and for the construction of palaeodiets by the analysis of bone collagen: both can be used also to assess modern animal diets.

(b) C, N for tracing ivory back to source (with TIMS for Sr and Pb).

(c) S (with Sr) isotopes for provenancing objects made of Gypsum; S isotopes (ores/metal) to aid the provenancing of copper alloy objects.

(d) C, O, (with TIMS for Sr and Pb), for provenancing marble.

ii) Accelerator Mass Spectroscopy:

(a) Small sample C-14 dating in the range up to 50,000 years BP.

iii) Thermal Ionisation Solid Source Mass Spectroscopy:

(a) Pb isotopic compositions of metal ores and metal objects to trace the ore sources from which the metal was smelted to make metal objects; applicable principally to objects made of lead, silver, copper alloys, but also to some iron, tin and zinc objects.

(b) Pb isotopic compositions for provenancing (authenticating) glasses, glazes and pigments.

(c) Sr isotopic compositions for provenancing obsidian and gypsum.

(d) Sr (with Pb, Nd) isotopes (with C, N) for tracing ivory back to source.

(e) Cu isotopes may allow direct tracing of copper back to ore source.

(f) A combination of Sr, Nd, (Ca, Pb) isotopes may allow better provenancing of ceramics and marble.

(g) Mass spectrometric U, Th disequilibrium dating allows certain materials such as corals, speleothems (bones?; molluscs??) to be dated with a precision of 1% in the range 100 years to 400,000 years.

In applications both to geology and to archaeology there is a broad trichotomy, based on the type of mass spectrometer which has to be used, into gas mass spectroscopy, accelerator mass spectroscopy and thermal ionisation mass spectroscopy. To illustrate something of the scope of this approach Table 1 gives some examples of the applications to archaeological science. They embrace the provenancing of metals (this paper and Gale and Stos-Gale 1985), obsidian (Gale 1981), marble (Duke 1988; Roos *et al.* 1988), gypsum (Gale *et al.* 1988), glass (Brill *et al.* 1979), ivory and bone (van der Merwe *et al.* 1990; Vogel *et al.* 1990), pigments (Keisch and Callahan 1976), etc., dating using C-14 (Purser *et al.* 1982) and the uranium, thorium disequilibrium method (Lawrence Edwards *et al.* 1987), identification of food residues (DeNiro and Epstein 1981; Hastorf and DeNiro 1985), the reconstruction of prehistoric diets (Schoeninger and DeNiro 1984; Walker and DeNiro 1986 , van der Merwe 1982; Sealy *et al.* 1991), etc.

The importance to archaeological science of mass spectrometry and isotope archaeology is perhaps reflected in the papers presented to this discussion meeting, in that no less than 4 out of a total of 15 papers are involved with various aspects of this subject. The importance, and range of application, of isotope archaeology within modern archaeological science has led us to set up at Oxford, with the help of the Science and Engineering Research Council and the University, a new laboratory for research into this subject on a broad front.

Acknowledgements

This work would not have been possible without generous support from the Leverhulme Trust, the British Academy and the Science and Engineering Research Council, which we gratefully acknowledge. Our thanks are due to the Greek Ministry of Culture and to many colleagues in Greece and elsewhere, especially to Dr Hector Catling, Dr Yiannis Tsedakis, Dr Vassos Karageorghis, Professors Yiannis Sakellarakis, Georgios Korres, Klaus Kilian, Christos Doumas, John Coleman, P. Zuffardi and Ulrich Zwicker, Dr Katie Demakopoulou, Dr Fulvia Lo Schiavo, Dr Stavros Papastavrou, Dr A. Panayiotou, Dr Constantinides, Dr Panos Perlikos, Dr A. Leonardelli, Herr Walter Fasnacht, Kyrie Artemis Papastamataki, and many others.

References

Akishin, P.A., Nikitin, O.T. and Panchenkov G.M. 1957: A new effective ion emitter for isotopic lead analysis. *Geokimya* 5, 429–434.

Allegre, C.J. 1987: Isotope geodynamics. *Earth and Planetary Science Letters* 86, 175–203.

Amov, B. 1968: Thermionic emission of lead from refractory oxides and their application in the ion sources of mass spectrometers. *Isotopenpraxis* 9, 358–363.

Arden, J. and Gale, N.H. 1974: New electrochemical technique for the separation of lead at trace levels from natural silicates. *Analytical Chemistry* 46, 2–9.

Barnes, I.L., Murphy, T.J., Gramlich, J.W. and Shields, W.R. 1973: Lead separation by anodic deposition and isotope ratio mass spectrometry of microgram and smaller samples. *Analytical Chemistry* 45, 1881–1884.

Barnes, I.L., Gramlich, J.W., Diaz, M.G. and Brill, R.H. 1978: The possible change of lead isotope ratios in the manufacture of pigments. In Carter, G.F. (editor), *Archaeological Chemistry II* (Washington, American Chemical Society) 273–279.

Barnes, J.W. 1989: *Ores and Minerals: Introducing Economic Geology.* (Milton Keynes, Open University Press).

Bass, G.F. 1967: Cape Gelidonya: a Bronze Age shipwreck. *Transactions of the American Philosophical Society* 57/8. (Philadelphia).

Bass, G.F. 1986: A Bronze Age shipwreck at Ulu Burun (Kaş): 1984 campaign. *American Journal of Archaeology* 90, 269–296.

Bear, L.M. 1963: *The Mineral Resources and Mining Industry of Cyprus* (Nicosia, Ministry of Commerce and Industry).

Begemann, F., Schmitt-Strecker, S. and Pernicka, E. 1989: Isotopic composition of lead in early metal artefacts. In Hauptmann, A., Pernicka, E. and Wagner, G.A. (editors), *Old World Archaeometallurgy, Der Anschnitt Beiheft 7* (Bochum, Deutschen Bergbau-Museums) 269–278.

Bowman, R., Friedman, A.M., Lerner, J. and Milsted, J. 1975: A statistical study of the impurity occurrences in copper ores and their relationship to ore types. *Archaeometry* 17, 157–164.

Brill, R.H. 1970: Lead and oxygen isotopes in ancient objects. *Philosophical Transactions of the Royal Society of London* A269, 143–164.

Brill, R.H. 1988: The examination of some Egyptian glass objects. In Rothenberg, B. (editor), *The Egyptian Mining Temple at Timna* (London, Institute of Archaeometallurgical Studies) 217–223.

Brill, R.H., Barnes, I.L. and Adams, B. 1974: Lead isotopes in some ancient Egyptian objects. In Bishay, A. (editor), *Recent Advances in Science and Technology of Materials* 3 (New York, Plenum) 9–27.

Brill, R.H., Yamasaki, K., Barnes, I.L., Rosman, K.J.R. and Diaz, M. 1979: Lead isotopes in some Japanese and Chinese glasses. *Ars Orientalis* 11, 87–109.

Buchholz, H.G. 1959: Keftiubarren und erzhandel im zweiten vorchristlichen jahrtausend. *Prähistorische Zeitschrift* 37, 1–40.

Cameron, A.E., Smith, D.H. and Walker, R.L. 1969: Mass spectrometry of nanogram-size samples of lead. *Analytical Chemistry* 41, 525–528.

Camporeale, G. 1989: Gli Etruschi e le risorse minerarie: aspetti e problemi. In Domergue, C. (editor), *Mineria y Metalurgia en Las Antiguas Civilizaciones Mediterraneas y Europeas I* (Madrid, Ministerio de Cultura) 205–212.

Catanzaro, E.J., Murphy, T.J., Shields, W.R. and Garner, E.L. 1968: Absolute isotopic ratios of common, equal atom and radiogenic lead isotopic standards. *Journal of Research, National Bureau of Standards* 72A, 261–267.

Catling, H.W. 1964: *Cypriot Bronzework in the Mycenaean World* (Oxford, Clarendon Press).

Chernykh, E. 1966: *Istoriya Drevneischei Metallurgii Vostochnoi Evropi* (Moscow, A.N.).

Cleuziou, S. and Berthoud, Th. 1982: Early tin in the Near East: a reassessment in the light of new evidence from western Afghanistan. *Expedition* 25, 14–19.

Coles, J.M. 1982: The Bronze Age in northwestern Europe: problems and advances. In Wendorf, F. and Close, A.E. (editors), *Advances in World Archaeology I* (Orlando, Academic Press) 265–321.

Constantinou, G. 1982: Geological features and ancient exploitation of the cupriferous sulphide orebodies of Cyprus. In Muhly, J., Maddin, R. and Karageorghis, K. (editors), *Early Metallurgy in Cyprus* (Nicosia, Pierides Foundation) 13–24.

Cumming, G.L. and Richards, J.R. 1975: Ore lead isotope ratios in a continuously changing earth. *Earth and Planetary Science Letters* 28, 155–171.

DeNiro, M.J. and Epstein, S. 1981: Influence of diet on the distribution of nitrogen isotopes in animals. *Geochimica et Cosmochimica Acta* 45, 341–351.

Desch, C.H. 1928: Report on the metallurgical examination of specimens for the Sumerian Committee of the British Association. *British Association for the Advancement of Science,* Report of the 96th Meeting, 437–441.

Dodson, M.H. 1963: A theoretical study of internal standards for precise isotopic analysis by the surface ionisation technique. *Journal of Scientific Instruments* 40, 289–295.

Dossin, G. 1970: Archives de Sumu-iamam, roi de Mari. *Revue d'Assyriologie et d'Archéologie Orientale* 4, 17–26.

Duke, M.J. 1988: Combined INAA, O, C, and Sr isotopic analyses in determining the provenance of classical marbles. In Farquhar, R.M., Hancock, R.G.V. and Pavlish, L.A. (editors), *Proceedings of the 26th. International Archaeometry Symposium* (Toronto, Archaeometry Laboratory) 227–232.

Faure, G. 1986: *Principles of Isotope Geology* (New York, Wiley).

Gale, N.H. 1980: Some aspects of lead and silver mining in the Aegean. In Doumas, C. (editor), *Thera and the Aegean World II* (London, Thera and the Aegean World) 161–196.

Gale, N.H. 1981: Mediterranean obsidian source characterisation by strontium isotope analysis. *Archaeometry* 23, 41–51.

Gale, N.H. 1986: Lead isotope studies applied to provenance studies—a brief review. In Maniatis, Y. (editor), *Archaeometry: Proceedings of the 25th International Symposium, Athens 1986* (Amsterdam, Elsevier) 469–502.

Gale, N.H. 1989: Archaeometallurgical studies of late Bronze Age oxhide copper ingots from the Mediterranean region. In Hauptmann, A., Pernicka, E. and Wagner, G.A. (editors), *Old World Archaeometallurgy, Der Anschnitt Beiheft 7* (Bochum, Deutschen Bergbau-Museum) 247–268.

Gale, N.H. 1991: Lead isotope analyses applied to provenance studies. In Hughes, M.J. (editor), *Chemical Analysis of Art and Archaeological Objects* (New York, Wiley).

Gale, N.H. and Mussett, A.E. 1973: Episodic uranium-lead models and the interpretation of variations in the isotopic composition of lead in rocks. *Reviews of Geophysics and Space Physics* II, 37–86.

Gale, N.H. and Stos-Gale, Z.A. 1981a: Cycladic lead and silver metallurgy. *Annual of the British School at Athens* 76, 169–224.

Gale, N.H. and Stos-Gale, Z.A. 1981b: Lead and silver in the ancient Aegean. *Scientific American* 244(6), 176–192.

Gale, N.H. and Stos-Gale, Z.A. 1982: Bronze Age copper sources in the Mediterranean: a new approach. *Science* 216, 11–19.

Gale, N.H. and Stos-Gale, Z.A. 1985: Lead isotope analysis and Alashiya: 3. *Reports of the Department of Antiquities, Cyprus, 1985*, 83–99.

Gale, N.H. and Stos-Gale, Z.A. 1986: Oxhide ingots in Crete and Cyprus and the Bronze Age metals trade. *Annual of the British School at Athens* 81, 81–100.

Gale, N.H. and Stos-Gale, Z.A. 1987: Oxhide ingots from Sardinia, Crete and Cyprus and the Bronze Age copper trade: new scientific evidence. In Balmuth, M.S. (editor), *Studies in Sardinian Archaeology III: Nuragic Sardinia and the Mycenaean World* (Oxford, British Archaeological Reports International Series 387) 135–178.

Gale, N.H. and Stos-Gale, Z.A. 1989a: Bronze Age archaeometallurgy of the Mediterranean: the impact of lead isotope studies. In Allen, R.O. (editor), *Archaeological Chemistry IV. Advances in Chemistry Series 220* (Washington, American Chemical Society) 159–198.

Gale, N.H. and Stos-Gale, Z.A. 1989b: Some aspects of early Cycladic metallurgy. In Domergue, C. (editor), *Mineria y Metalurgia en Las Antiguas Civilizaciones Mediterraneas y Europeas* I (Madrid, Ministerio de Cultura) 21–38.

Gale, N.H., Gentner, W. and Wagner, G.A. 1980: Mineralogical and geographical silver sources of Archaic Greek coinage. In Metcalf, D.M. (editor) *Metallurgy in Numismatics I* (London, Royal Numismatic Society Special Publication 13) 3–50.

Gale, N.H., Stos-Gale, Z.A. and Davis, J.L. 1984: The provenance of lead used at Ayia Irini, Keos. *Hesperia* 53(4), 389–406.

Gale, N.H., Stos-Gale, Z.A. and Gilmore, G.R. 1985: Alloy types and copper sources for Anatolian copper alloy artefacts. *Anatolian Studies* XXXV, 143–173.

Gale, N.H., Einfalt, H.C., Hubberten, H.W. and Jones, R.E. 1988: The sources of Mycenaean gypsum. *Journal of Archaeological Science* 15, 57–72.

Griffitts, W.R., Albers, J.B. and Oner, O. 1972: Massive sulfide deposit of the Ergani Maden area, southeastern Turkey. *Economic Geology* 67, 701–716.

Gulson, B.L. 1986: *Lead Isotopes in Mineral Exploration*. (Oxford, Elsevier).

Hastorf, C.A. and DeNiro, M.J. 1985: Reconstruction of prehistoric plant production and cooking practices by a new isotopic method. *Nature* 315, 489–491.

Hermann, G. 1968: Lapis lazuli: the earliest phases of its trade. *Iraq* 30(1), 21–67.

Holmes, A. 1946: An estimate of the age of the earth. *Nature* 157, 680–684.

Hood, S. 1978: *The Arts in Prehistoric Greece* (Harmondsworth, Penguin Books).

Iakovides, S.E. 1974: The centuries of Achaian sovereignty. In Christopoulos, G.A. (editor), *History of the Hellenic World: Prehistory and Protohistory* (Athens, Ekdotike Athenon S.A.) 268–301.

Iakovides, S.E. 1982: The Mycenaean bronze industry. In Muhly, J.D., Maddin, R. and Karageorghis, V. (editors), *Early Metallurgy in Cyprus, 4000–500 B.C.* (Nicosia, Pierides Foundation) 213–232.

Junghans, S., Sangmeister, E. and Schroder, M. 1968: Kupfer und bronze in der frühen metallzeit Europas (Three vols.), *Studien zu den Anfangen der Metallurgie II* , (Berlin, Verlag Gebr. Mann)

Kanasewich, E.R. 1968: The interpretation of lead isotopes and their geological significance. In Hamilton, E.I. and Farquhar, R.M. (editors), *Radiometric Dating for Geologists* (New York, Wiley Interscience) 147–223.

Keisch, B. and Callahan, R.G. 1976: Lead isotope ratios in artist's lead white: a progress report. *Archaeometry* 18, 181–194.

Knapp, A.B. 1989: Science, statistics and Mediterranean archaeology: the British Academy Group Research Project. *Old World Archaeology Newsletter* 13(3), 10–12.

Knapp, A.B. and Cherry, J.F. 1990: The British Academy Group Research Project: an aspect of science and archaeology in Great Britain. *Society for Archaeological Sciences Bulletin* 13(1), 3–5.

Köppel, V. and Köstelka, L. 1976: The isotopic composition of ore lead from Bleiberg, Austria. *Abstracts, Fourth European Colloquium on Geochronology, Amsterdam.*

Köppel, V. and Grünenfelder, M. 1979: Isotope geochemistry of lead. In Jaeger, E. and Hünziker, J.C. (editors), *Lectures in Isotope Geology* (Berlin, Springer) 134–153.

Koukouli-Chrysanthaki, Ch. 1982: Die frühe eisenzeit auf Thasos. In *Südosteuropa zwischen 1600 und 1000 v. Christ (Prähistorische Archäologie in Südosteuropa, Bd. 1)* (Berlin) 119–143.

Lawrence Edwards, R., Chen, J.H. and Wasserburg, G.J. 1987: ^{238}U-^{234}U-^{230}Th-^{232}Th systematics and the precise measurement of time over the past 500,000 years. *Earth and Planetary Science Letters* 81, 175–192.

Macnamara, E.D., Ridgway, D. and Ridgway, F.R. 1984: *The Bronze Hoard from Santa Maria in Paulis, Sardinia* (London, British Museum Occasional Publication 45).

Marechal, J. 1966: Etat actuel des recherches sur la corrélation entre la paragénèse des gisements miniers et la composition des objets de métal par les méthodes chimiques et spectro-graphiques. *Actes du 91ème congrés des Sociétés Savantes*, Rennes, 295–324.

Muhly, J.D., Maddin, R. and Karageorghis, V. (editors) 1982: *Early Metallurgy in Cyprus, 4000–500 B.C.* (Nicosia, Pierides Foundation).

Pernicka, E. 1989: Erzlagerstätten in der Ägäis und ihre ausbeutung im altertum: geochimische untersuchungen zur herkunftsbestimmung ärchäologischer metallobjekte. *Jahrbuch des Römisch-Germanischen Zentralmuseums* 35, 607–714.

Pernicka, E. and Wagner, G.A. 1988: Thasos als rohstoffquelle für bunt-und edelmetalle im altertum. In Wagner, G.A. and Weisgerber, G. (editors), *Antike Edel-und Buntmetallgewinnung auf Thasos, Der Anschnitt Beiheft 6* (Bochum, Deutschen Bergbau-Museum) 224–231.

Pernicka, E., Seeliger, T.C., Wagner, G.A., Begemann, F., Schmitt-Strecker, S., Eibner, C., Öztunali, Ö. and Baranyi, I. 1984: Archäometallurgische untersuchungen in Nordwestanato-lien. *Jahrbuch des Römisch-Germanischen Zentralmuseums* 31, 533–599.

Pernicka, E., Begemann, F., Schmitt-Strecker, S. and Grimanis, A.P. 1990: On the composition and provenance of metal artefact s from Poliochni on Lemnos. *Oxford Journal of Archaeology* 9(3), 263–298.

Pigorini, L. 1904: Pani di Rame Provenienti dall'Egeo e Scoperti a Serra Ilixi in Provincia di Cagliari. *Bolletino Paletnologia Italiano* X, 91–107.

Pliny, C: *Natural History* (translation by Eichholz, D.E. 1962) (London, Heinemann).

Purser, K.H., Russo, C.J., Liebert, R.B., Gove, H.E., Elmore, D., Ferraro, R., Litherland, A.E.,

Kilius, L.R. and Lee, H.W. 1982: The application of electrostatic tandems to ultrasensitive mass spectrometry and nuclear dating. In Currie, L.A. (editor), *Nuclear and Chemical Dating Techniques: Interpreting the Environmental Record* (Washington, American Chemical Society) 45–74.

Reedy, C.L. and Reedy, T.J. 1988: Lead isotope analysis for provenance studies in the Aegean region: a re-evaluation. In Sayre, E.V., Vandiver, P., Druzik, J. and Stevenson C. (editors), *Materials Issues in Art and Archaeology* (Pittsburgh, Materials Research Society) 65–70.

Renfrew, A.C. 1972: *The Emergence of Civilisation* (London, Methuen).

Roos, P., Moens, L., Derudder, J., Dupaepe, P., van Hende, J. and Waelkens, M. 1988: Chemical, isotopic and petrographic characterisation of ancient white marble quarries. In Farquhar, R.M., Hancock, R.G.V. and Pavlish, L.A. (editors), *Proceedings of the 26th. International Archaeometry Symposium* (Toronto, Archaeometry Department) 220–226.

Rothenberg, B. 1988: Introduction to researches in the Arabah. In Rothenberg, B. (editor), *The Egyptian Mining Temple at Timna* (London, Institute of Archaeometallurgical Studies) 1–18.

Sarda 1949: La Sardegna: Miniere. In *Il Gruppo Elettrico Sardo e Gli Impianti dell'Alto Flumendosa* (Roma, Societa Elettrica Sarda) 59–101.

Sayre, E.V. 1975: *Brookhaven Procedures for Statistical Analysis of Multivariate Archaeometric Data.* (Brookhaven National Laboratory, New York; unpublished in-house report).

Sayre, E.V., Yener, K.A., Joel, E.C. and Barnes, I.L. 1990. Statistical analysis of the presently accumulated lead isotope data from the Near East. In Pernicka, E. and Wagner, G.A. (editors), Abstracts of the *International Symposium on Archaeometry, Heidelberg.*

Schoeninger, M.J. and DeNiro, M.J. 1984: Nitrogen and carbon isotopic composition of bone collagen from marine and terrestrial animals. *Geochimica et Cosmochimica Acta* 48, 625–639.

Sealy, J.C., van der Merwe, N.J., Sillen, A., Kruger, F.J. and Krueger, H.W. 1991: $^{87}Sr/^{86}Sr$ as a dietary indicator in modern and archaeological bone. *Journal of Archaeological Science* 18, 399–416.

Shareq, A. and Abdullah, S. 1977: *Mineral Resources of Afghanistan. United Nations Development Support Project AFG/74/12.* (Kabul, Ministry of Mines and Industries).

Slater, E.A. and Charles, J.A. 1970: Archaeological classification by metal analysis. *Antiquity* 44, 207–213.

Stacey, J.S. and Kramers, J.D. 1975: Approximation of terrestrial lead isotope evolution by a two-stage model. *Earth and Planetary Science Letters* 26, 207–221.

Stanton, R.L. and Russell, R.D. 1959: Anomalous leads and the emplacement of lead sulfide ores. *Economic Geology* 54, 588–607.

Stos-Gale, Z.A. 1985: Lead and silver sources for Bronze Age Crete. *Pepragmena tou E' Diethnous Kritologikou Sinedriou,* (1981) Tomos A' (Herakleion, Etairia Kritikon Istorikon Meleton), 365–372.

Stos-Gale, Z.A. 1988: An early Bronze Age copper smelting site on the Aegean Island of Kythnos. In Ellis-Jones, J. (editor), *Aspects of Ancient Mining and Technology, Acta of a British School at Athens Centenary Conference, Bangor 1986* (Bangor, University College of North Wales) 23–30.

Stos-Gale, Z.A. 1989: Cycladic copper metallurgy. In Hauptmann, A., Pernicka, E. and Wagner, G.A. (editors), *Old World Archaeometallurgy, Der Anschnitt Beiheft 7*, (Bochum, Deutschen Bergbau-Museum) 279–292.

Stos-Gale, Z.A. and Gale, N.H. 1982: The sources of Mycenaean silver and lead. *Journal of Field Archaeology,* 9, 467–485.

Stos-Gale, Z.A. and Gale, N.H. 1984: The Minoan Thalassocracy and the Aegean metal trade. *Skrifter Utgivna av Svenska Institutet i Athen* 32, 59–64.

Stos-Gale, Z.A. and MacDonald, C.F. 1991: Sources of metal and trade in the Bronze Age Aegean. In Gale, N.H. (editor), *Bronze Age Trade in the Mediterranean*, SIMA XC, 258–280.

Stos-Gale, Z.A., Gale, N.H. and Gilmore, G.R. 1984: Early Bronze Age Trojan metal sources and Anatolians in the Cyclades. *Oxford Journal of Archaeology* 3, 23–43.

Stos-Gale, Z.A., Gale, N.H. and Zwicker, U. 1986: The copper trade in the south-east Mediterranean region. Preliminary scientific evidence. *Report of the Department of Antiquities, Cyprus* 122–144.

Thompson, F.C. 1958: The early metallurgy of copper and bronze. *Man* 58, 1–7.

Todt, W., Cliff, R.A., Hanser, A. and Hofmann, A.W. 1984: ^{202}Pb -^{205}Pb double spike for lead isotopic analyses. Abstract J4, *Terra Cognita* 4, 209.

Tylecote, R.F., Ghaznavi, H.A. and Boydell, P.J. 1977: Partitioning of trace elements between ores, fluxes, slags and metals during the smelting of copper. *Journal of Archaeological Science* 4, 305–333.

van der Merwe, N.J. 1982: Carbon isotopes, photosynthesis and archaeology. *American Scientist* 70, 596–606.

van der Merwe, N.J., Lee-Thorpe, L.J., Thackeray, J.F., Hall-Martin, A., Kruger, F.J., Coetzee, H., Bell, R.H.V. and Lideque, M. 1990: Source-area determination of elephant ivory by isotopic analysis. *Nature* 346, 744–746.

Vogel, J.C., Eglington, B. and Auret, J.M. 1990: Isotope fingerprints in elephant bone and ivory. *Nature* 346, 747–749.

Wace, A.J.B. 1953: Mycenae, 1939–1952. *Annual of the British School at Athens* 48, 1–93.

Wagner, G.A., Öztunali, Ö. and Eibner, C. 1989: Early copper in Anatolia. In Hauptmann, A., Pernicka, E. and Wagner, G.A. (editors), *Old World Archaeometallurgy, Der Anschnitt Beiheft 7* (Bochum, Deutschen Bergbau-Museum) 299–306.

Walker, P.L. and DeNiro, M.J. 1986: Stable carbon and nitrogen isotope ratios in bone collagen as indices of prehistoric dietary dependence on marine and terrestrial resources in southern California. *American Journal of Physical Anthropology* 71, 51–61.

Warren, P. 1975: *The Aegean Civilisations* (London, Elsevier-Phaidon)

Wasserburg, G.J. 1987: Isotopic abundances: inferences on solar system and planetary evolution. *Earth and Planetary Science Letters* 86, 129–173.

Wasserburg, G.J., Papanastassiou, D.A., Nenow, E.V. and Bauman, C. 1969: A programmable magnetic field mass spectrometer with on-line data processing. *Reviews of Scientific Instruments* 40, 288–295.

Webster, R.K. 1960: Isotope dilution analysis. In Smales, A.A. and Wager, L.R. (editors), *Methods in Geochemistry* (London, Interscience) 199–210.

Yener, K.A., Özbal, H., Minzoni-Deroche, A. and Aksoy, B. 1989: Bolkardag: archaeometallurgy surveys in the Taurus Mountains, Turkey. *National Geographic Research* 5, 477–494.

Yener, K.A., Sayre, E.V., Joel, E.C., Özbal, H., Barnes, I.L. and Brill, R.H. 1991: Stable lead isotope studies of Central Taurus ore sources and related artifacts from Eastern Mediterranean Chalcolithic and Bronze Age sites. *Journal of Archaeological Science* 18, 541–577.

Proceedings of the British Academy, **77**, 109–110

New Views of Early Mining and Extractive Metallurgy

P. T. CRADDOCK

*Department of Scientific Research, British Museum, Great Russell Street,
London WC1B 3DG, UK.*

Summary. The technology of mining and smelting metals in antiquity
had received little serious study until quite recently. Now archaeological excavation coupled with detailed scientific examination from
production sites all over the world is building up a comprehensive
picture of the development of one of human society's key technologies. Mining and smelting sites present very different problems
and potentials from most ancient sites, and in this lecture some of the
archaeological and scientific methodology will be described. There
will also be an outline of the development of metallurgy based on
this approach, exemplified by sites in Britain, the Mediterranean and
India.

The subject matter of this lecture is well-covered in the following
publications:

General

Craddock, P. T. 1989: The scientific investigation of early mining and metallurgy. In Henderson,
    J. (editor), *Scientific Analysis in Archaeology* (Oxford, Oxford University Committee for
    Archaeology Monograph 9) 178–212.
Craddock, P. T. and Hughes, M. J. (editors) 1985: *Furnaces and Smelting Technology in Antiquity*
    (London, British Museum Occasional Paper 48).
Freestone, I. C. 1989: Refractory materials and their procurement. In Hauptman, A., Pernicka,
    E. and Wagner, G. A. (editors), *Old Word Archaeometallurgy, Der Anschnitt Beiheft 7*
    (Bochum, Deutschen Bergbau-Museum) 155–163.

Read 13 February 1991. © The British Academy 1992.

P. T. Craddock

Britain

Crew, P. and Crew, S. (editors) 1990: *Early Mining in the British Isles* (Maentwrog, Plas Tan y Bwlch Occasional Paper 1).

Mediterranean

Rothenberg, B. (editor) 1990: *The Ancient Metallurgy of Copper* (London, Institute of Archaeo-metallurgical Studies, University College London).

India

Craddock, P. T., Freestone, I. C., Gurjar, L. K., Middleton, A. and Willies, L. 1989: The production of lead, silver and zinc in Ancient India. In Hauptman, A., Pernicka, E. and Wagner, G. A. (editors), *Old World Archaeometallurgy, Der Anschnitt Beiheft 7* (Bochum, Deutschen Bergbau-Museum) 51–70.

Proceedings of the British Academy, **77**, 111–131

The Impact of Electron Microscopy on Ceramic Studies

M. S. TITE

Research Laboratory for Archaeology and the History of Art, University of Oxford, 6 Keble Road, Oxford OX1 3QJ, UK.

Summary. Scanning electron microscopy (SEM), in combination with quantitative elemental analysis, provides a powerful technique for studying the microstructure of ancient ceramics. The primary aim of such studies is to elucidate the production technology in terms of the raw materials used, the methods of decoration and the firing procedures. A similar approach can be used to extract information on metal production processes from the associated refractory ceramic debris (e.g., furnace linings, tuyeres, etc.).

To illustrate the power of the SEM, information thus obtained on production technology is presented for Greek Attic red-figure ware, Chinese blue-and-white porcelain and Iznik ware, as well as for glass and other vitreous materials such as faience and Egyptian blue. The role of transmission electron microscopy, which can reveal finer details of ceramic microstructures, is also briefly discussed, and the need to consider ceramic technology in its wider cultural context is emphasised.

1. Introduction

SEM with attached analytical facilities provides an extremely powerful technique for studying the microstructure of ceramics; that is, establishing the composition, identity, shape and distribution of the different crystalline and glassy phases present (Freestone and Middleton 1987).

The fundamental role of both microstructure and macrostructure in investigating ceramic technology derives from the fact that a central paradigm of materials science is that the selection and processing of materials

Read 13 February 1991. © The British Academy 1992.

gives rise to a particular structure which is the source of useful properties (Kingery 1987). Thus by studying the structure of ceramics, one aims to reconstruct what raw materials were used and how the ceramics were produced.

Such microstructural studies have been central to the investigation of metals since the examination of metal sections in reflected light by Sorby more than 100 years ago (Smith 1988, 167). However, the study of the microstructures of ceramics, both ancient and modern, has lagged severely behind that of metals. This is principally because optical microscopy is of limited use in resolving the very complex and fine-scale microstructures associated with ceramics and in particular those associated with traditional clay-based ceramics. Further, unlike the situation for metals the correlation between the microstructure and mechanical properties of ceramics is less clear-cut and therefore there was less motivation for pursuing the investigation of ceramic microstructure. Thus, it was only with the comparatively recent development of the scanning electron microscope (SEM) that it became possible to fully and easily investigate the microstructures of ceramics.

The study of the microstructure, as observed in the SEM, is thus now central to the investigation of the raw materials and their preparation, the methods of surface decoration and the firing procedures employed in the production of ancient ceramics. However, information on the methods used to form the ceramics (e.g., by modelling; from coils or slabs; by wheel throwing or moulding) can still best be obtained by careful visual examination of the macrostructure, supplemented by x-ray radiography.

In addition to providing information on *what* raw materials and production methods were used, the observed microstructure can help in assessing the physical properties both of the raw materials (e.g., plasticity, drying shrinkage, green strength) and of the finished ceramics (e.g., permeability, strength, thermal shock resistance). In turn, a knowledge and understanding of these physical properties can sometimes provide a technological explanation for *why* particular raw materials and production methods were used (Tite 1988a).

Scanning electron microscopy can also make some contribution to provenance studies and usage studies which are the two other main aims of science-based investigations of ancient ceramics. Provenance studies involve characterising and locating the natural sources of the raw materials used to make the ceramics and thus establishing the pattern of trade and exchange. In such studies, quantitative elemental analysis of the individual mineral inclusions (feldspars, pyroxenes, amphiboles) surviving in the fired clay can sharpen the information provided by optical petrography on the type and the source of the rock from which they were derived (Freestone 1982). Usage studies involve investigating the ways in which the ceramics were used. In this context, the physical properties of the ceramics, which can sometimes be inferred from the observed microstructure, can help in assessing the suitability of the ceramic for its hypothesised use.

However, the prime role of scanning electron microscopy in ceramic studies undoubtedly is the investigation of their production technologies. There is no doubt that the high quality microstructural images and compositional data provided by the analytical SEM has transformed such investigations. As a result, our understanding of ancient ceramic technology has begun to catch up with our understanding of ancient metallurgy and the general pattern of the development of ceramic technology in antiquity is now more-or-less established.

2. Experimental procedures

For the examination of ceramics in a SEM, polished sections from the surface into the body are normally prepared. The SEM is used in the magnification range x10 to x10,000 with a range x100 to x500 generally being most appropriate. A backscattered electron detector, rather than a secondary electron detector, is normally used. With this detector, the grey level of the image (from black to grey to white) depends on the atomic number of the phase being observed, with black through to white correlating with low to high atomic number. In this way, the different crystalline and glassy phases present can be easily distinguished. Normally, these phases can then be identified by qualitative elemental analysis using the attached x-ray spectrometer and their overall distribution pattern thus established. Fully quantitative analysis of both the bulk material (Table 1) and the individual phases is also possible using the x-ray spectrometer.

3. Case studies

In the overall history of ceramics, it is possible to identify three primary technologies, that is, earthenware, quartz-based ware and stoneware plus porcelain (Kingery and Vandiver 1986). In this paper, the role of SEM examinations in the investigation of each of these three primary technologies will be considered. The developments in earthenware and quartz-based ware technologies resulting from the efforts by Islamic and European potters to imitate Chinese porcelain will then be discussed briefly. In each case, examples will be presented of the reconstruction of the raw materials and production processes from a careful "reading" of the SEM microstructures.

Table 1. Typical bulk chemical compositions for case study ceramics

Ceramic type	Component	Oxide concentrations (per cent weight)[1]									
		SiO$_2$	Al$_2$O$_3$	Na$_2$O	K$_2$O	MgO	CaO	FeO	CuO	PbO	SnO$_2$
Greek Attic	Body	53.9	20.6	1.0	4.1	5.4	5.0	10.0	—	—	—
	Slip	47.7	31.6	0.4	3.2	1.8	0.5	14.8	—	—	—
Faience	Body	96.6	—	1.1	0.5	—	0.5	—	1.3	—	—
	Glaze	70.0	—	16.2	5.7	0.2	0.2	0.3	7.5	—	—
Egyptian blue frit	—	70.2	0.5	2.4	0.2	0.6	12.3	—	13.8	—	—
Egyptian blue frit	—	65.9	0.4	0.4	0.2	0.7	13.2	0.4	18.8	—	—
Pale blue frit	—	75.1	0.4	5.5	0.8	—	11.3	—	6.9	—	—
Porcelain stone	—	77.5	16.6	0.9	3.2	0.4	0.8	0.6	—	—	—
Yingqing porcelain	Body	78.3	15.9	0.8	3.3	0.2	1.0	0.5	—	—	—
	Glaze	67.0	14.9	0.8	2.5	0.4	13.9	0.5	—	—	—
Underglaze blue porcelain	Body	72.1	20.6	1.6	4.0	0.2	0.1	1.4	—	—	—
	Glaze	66.1	16.0	2.2	4.1	0.5	9.3	1.8	—	—	—
Ding porcelain	Body	64.7	28.4	0.7	2.0	1.4	2.0	0.8	—	—	—
	Glaze	69.8	18.7	0.9	2.3	2.7	4.9	0.7	—	—	—
Islamic-Abbasid	Body	48.0	12.6	2.0	1.0	7.0	21.4	6.7	—	—	—
	Glaze	68.1	2.4	8.1	5.0	2.4	6.4	0.9	—	2.0	1.8
Isnik ware	Body	88.7	2.6	2.2	0.8	1.0	2.1	0.9	—	1.7	—
	Slip	91.6	2.2	2.3	0.6	0.6	1.3	—	—	1.4	—
	Glaze	49.4	0.5	9.2	0.8	—	1.0	0.4	—	33.3	5.4

[1] Oxide concentrations normalised to 100 per cent.

3.1 Earthenware

Pottery made from low refractory earthenware clays was first produced on any significant scale in the Near East during the 7th millennium BC. Before the end of the 4th millennium BC, the technological repertoire associated with the production of *unglazed* earthenware (i.e., careful preparation of the clay, throwing on potter's wheel, slip and painted decoration, firing with controlled atmosphere and temperature) was more-or-less complete. Subsequently, various combinations of this overall technological repertoire continued to be used according to local requirements, but with no obvious steady technological progression, through to the Roman period and beyond.

In the investigation of earthenware technologies, the SEM is used to determine the bulk chemical composition of the body clay, to examine the surface decoration and to estimate the firing temperature.

In the context of bulk chemical composition, the alumina content provides a measure of the clay mineral content of the original body clay; the alkali content (potash and soda) determines the refractoriness of the clay; and the iron oxide content in conjunction with the firing atmosphere determines the colour of the body. The distinction between non-calcareous and calcareous clays (i.e., respectively less than or greater than 5 per cent fine textured, well-dispersed lime plus magnesia) is also important since the lime plus magnesia content affects both the firing properties of the clay and the resulting microstructure.

By examining a cross-section through the surface and into the body of the pottery, it is possible to distinguish burnishing from the application of clay slip, both of which can result in a high gloss surface finish. Also any mineral pigments (e.g., iron oxide, manganese oxide) used to decorate the pottery can be identified (Middleton 1987).

The firing temperature employed in the production of pottery can be estimated from the extent of vitrification in the body as revealed by the degree of interconnection between the mineral particles. For low fired pottery, individual mineral particles are readily distinguished and there is only limited grain-to-grain interconnection. With increasing firing temperature, a network of interconnecting glass/relict clay phases is formed between the non-plastic inclusions such as quartz, feldspars and micas (Figure 1). Subsequently, the extent of the glass phase increases and the porosity decreases. The pores then become isolated; trapped gases expand causing the formation of rounded vesicles (Figure 2) and finally at high temperatures, typically in the range 1100–1200°C, the body becomes molten with either slumping or massive bloating.

The temperatures at which these different vitrification stages are reached depends first on the chemical composition of the clay (Maniatis and Tite

M. S. Tite

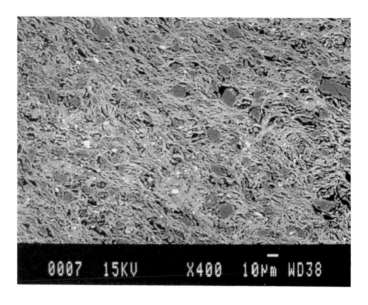

Figure 1. SEM photomicrograph of section through German stoneware sherd showing body which consists of scattered quartz (darker grey) in a fine network of interconnecting glass/relict clay phases.

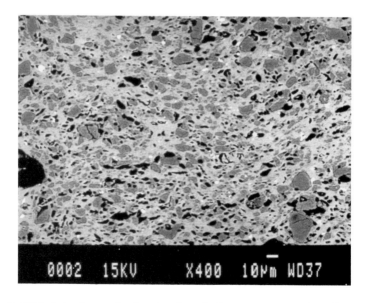

Figure 2. SEM photomicrograph of section through German stoneware sherd showing body which consists of continuous glassy matrix containing fine bloating pores (black) and unreacted quartz (darker grey).

1981). Therefore, in order to estimate firing temperatures, samples of the pottery must be refired in the laboratory at known temperatures until an increase in the extent of vitrification is observed. Further, since firing in a reducing atmosphere, rather than in an oxidising atmosphere, can lower the temperature at which a particular vitrification stage is achieved by between 50–100°C, the refiring atmosphere used in the laboratory should match the original firing atmosphere as closely as possible.

The same approach as that employed in estimating the firing temperatures of earthenwares can be applied to the study of the refractory ceramics (e.g., crucibles, tuyeres, furnace linings etc.) used in metal production and metal working. In this way, information is obtained on the operating conditions (firing temperature, time and atmosphere) used in the associated metallurgical process (Freestone and Tite 1986).

The results of the examination of Greek Attic black-figured and red-figured wares, produced from 7th to 4th centuries BC, provide an example of the information that can be obtained using the SEM (Tite *et al.* 1982). These results show that the bodies which are red in colour were made from iron-rich calcareous clays (approx 10 per cent FeO and 10 per cent CaO plus MgO). The characteristic black high gloss surface finish was produced by applying a fine textured iron-rich non-calcareous clay slip (approximately 15 per cent FeO and less than 3 per cent CaO plus MgO) approximately 10–20 μm in thickness and more-or-less free from non-plastic inclusions. Both the bodies and slips have relatively high potash contents (3–6 per cent K_2O) and therefore the clays used would have been rich in illite. Further, it is possible that both were prepared from a single clay with the unrefined clay being used for the body and the fine fraction for the slip. The bodies exhibit the open network of interconnecting glass/relict clay phases which is characteristic of calcareous clays fired in the temperature range 850–1050°C (Figure 3). In contrast, in the finer textured non- calcareous slip the glass/relict clay phases are essentially continuous with no obvious porosity.

On the basis of these data, it can be inferred that the observed differential oxidation-reduction between the red body and the black slip of Greek Attic ware was produced in a single firing involving an oxidising atmosphere during the heating up of the kiln, then a reducing atmosphere and finally an oxidising atmosphere again. At the end of the reducing phase, both the body and slip would have been black due to the formation of a magnetite-hercynite spinel (Fe_3O_4-$FeAl_2O_4$). Then during the final oxidising phase, the porous body would have been re-oxidised with the formation of haematite (αFe_2O_3) whereas the impermeable slip would have remained in its black reduced state.

It is apparent that the impermeable slip essential to the production of Greek Attic black-figured and red-figured wares has been achieved by careful selection of the clay. The illitic clay used is non-calcareous and has been

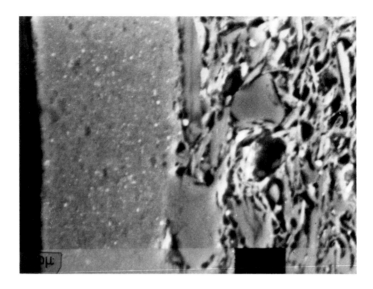

Figure 3. SEM photomicrograph of section through Greek Attic red-figured ware sherd showing high gloss surface slip which is essentially continuous and body which consists of open network of interconnecting glass/relict clay phases.

refined to remove non-plastic inclusions, both features that are necessary to ensure low porosity in the slip. Further, the high iron oxide content increases the extent of vitrification when fired in a reducing atmosphere and thus again tends to reduce the porosity.

3.2 Quartz-based ware

The second ceramic technology to evolve in antiquity was based on the use of a ground quartz or quartz sand body rather than a clay body. The materials first produced within this technology are normally referred to as faience or frit, depending on whether or not they are glazed (Tite 1987). Faience and frit were used in Egypt and the Near East from about the 4th millennium BC onwards to produce small objects such as beads, amulets, seals, figures and vessels. In the first instance, the great majority of faience and frit objects were coloured blue. It seems probable, therefore, that the driving force for the development of these materials was the desire to find a substitute for scarce and highly prized semi-precious stones such as lapis lazuli and turquoise.

The technology associated with faience and frit production is clearly related to that first used in making small objects of glazed stone such as steatite. In turn, the faience and frit technologies themselves provide the basis for the subsequent development of glass production in Egypt and the Near

East during 2nd millennium BC and, ultimately, for the development of the quartz-frit wares produced by Islamic potters from about 12th century AD onwards.

In the investigation of faience and frit technologies, the SEM is used to obtain information on the methods of production employed as well as to establish the technological relationship between the different materials.

In terms of microstructure as seen in the SEM (Figure 4), faience consists of a core of angular quartz grains bonded together by varying amounts of interstitial glass. Normally, the core is covered by a layer of quartz-free alkali-based glaze. Intermediate between the glaze and core, there is an interaction layer which was formed by the reaction between the glazing mixture and the quartz core and which consists of quartz embedded in a continuous matrix of glass. Replication in the laboratory of the three methods proposed for glazing the quartz body (i.e., direct application, cementation, efflorescence) has shown that the thickness of the glaze and interaction layers as well as the amount of interstitial glass in the core depends on which of these methods was used (Tite and Bimson 1986, Vandiver 1983).

When the glaze was applied in the form of a slurry of finely ground prefired glazing mixture (i.e., a mixture of quartz sand, lime, alkali and

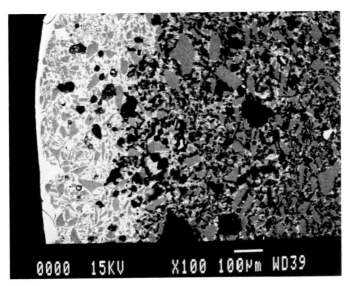

Figure 4. SEM photomicrograph of section through faience produced by efflorescence glazing method showing thin surface glaze layer; glaze-core interaction layer which consists of quartz in a continuous glass matrix; and quartz core which contains fairly extensive interstitial glass. The glaze and glass appear white compared to the quartz which appears grey.

copper), a thick surface glaze layer was formed during subsequent firing and the quartz core contained minimal interstitial glass. This microstructure reflects the fact that a reaction occurred only at the interface of the glazing mixture and the core and that there was no transport of alkali or copper colorant beyond the glaze-core interaction layer.

With the cementation glazing method, in which the quartz body was fired whilst buried in the glazing mixture, a thin irregular glaze layer was formed and the quartz core contained small amounts of interstitial glass. This microstructure reflects the fact that there was some initial transport of glazing components into the core but that this ceased with the formation of a protective glaze-core interaction layer.

Finally, with the efflorescence glazing method, in which the unfired glazing components were mixed with the moistened quartz body, a reasonably thick glaze layer was formed during subsequent firing and the quartz core contained extensive interstitial glass such that the core tended to merge into and could not always be readily distinguished from the glaze-core interaction layer (Figure 4). This microstructure reflects the fact that the glazing components were only partially carried to the surface during drying and a significant proportion remained in the core to form, on firing, the interstitial glass.

Frits, which by definition are unglazed, differ in bulk chemical composition from faience bodies in that their lime and copper oxide contents are significantly higher (i.e., 6–13 per cent CaO and 2–20 per cent CuO as compared with less than about 1.5 per cent for faience cores). Further, the relative concentrations of lime and copper oxide are of primary importance in determining the microstructure of the frits thus produced, as well as their colour, hardness and texture (Tite 1987).

If the copper oxide content exceeds the lime content, crystals of Egyptian blue (calcium-copper tetrasilicate $CaCuSi_4O_{10}$) are formed and the frit exhibits an intense blue colour that is characteristic of this phase. Such Egyptian blue frits consist of an intimate mixture of Egyptian blue crystals and unreacted quartz together with a glass phase (Figure 5), the amount of which increases with increasing bulk alkali content. The glass provides long range interconnection between the crystalline phases and therefore the hardness of the frit also increases with increasing alkali content. Further, the Egyptian blue frit can be classified as coarse- or fine-textured according to the size and degree of aggregation of the Egyptian blue crystals. Coarse-textured frit contains aggregates of large Egyptian blue crystals (Figure 5) which result in a dark blue colour whereas fine-textured frit contains small dispersed crystals (Figure 6) which result in a lighter but still intense blue colour.

On the basis of replication in the laboratory, it has been suggested that the coarse-textured Egyptian blue frit which normally occurs in the form of

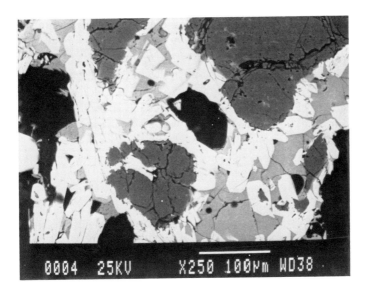

Figure 5. SEM photomicrograph of section through coarse-textured Egyptian blue frit showing aggregates of Egyptian blue crystals (white) and unreacted quartz (dark grey) embedded in glass matrix (light grey).

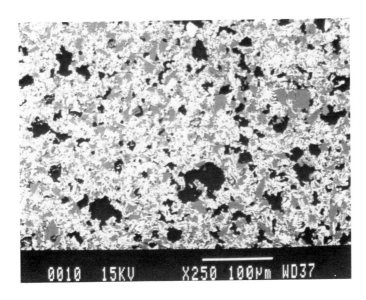

Figure 6. SEM photomicrograph of section through fine-textured Egyptian blue frit showing an intimate mixture of dispersed Egyptian blue crystals (white) and unreacted quartz (grey).

large blocks or small balls was produced by firing an intimate mixture of quartz, lime, copper and alkali at a temperature in the range of 900–1000°C (Tite *et al.* 1984a). In contrast, a two-stage firing cycle, with grinding and moulding to the required shape between the first and second firings, appears to have been used to produce small objects of fine-textured Egyptian blue frit. Thus the coarse-textured frit should probably be regarded as the 'raw material' for making small objects as well as for use as a pigment.

If, however, the lime content exceeds the copper oxide content, Egyptian blue crystals are not formed. Instead, the excess lime is precipitated from the glass as calcium silicate (wollastonite—$CaSiO_3$) and the copper remains dissolved in the glass to produce a characteristic pale blue colour. Such pale blue frits consist of extended areas of copper-rich glass containing unreacted quartz together with high concentrations of precipitated tridymite/cristobalite and wollastonite.

Thus, it can be seen that for frits, there is a clear inter-relationship between the raw materials (i.e., proportions of lime, copper and alkali), the processing (i.e., one- or two-stage firing cycle), the microstructure and the physical properties (i.e., colour, hardness and texture). Frits, therefore, provide an excellent example of the central materials science paradigm referred to in the introduction.

3.3 Stoneware and porcelain

Stoneware and porcelain production which represents the third primary ceramic technology can be regarded as a development from earthenware production. Stoneware is produced by firing high refractory clays to temperatures of about 1200°C such that well vitrified impermeable bodies are achieved. Stoneware was first produced in China during the 2nd millennium BC (Shang and Zhou dynasties) and associated with its early production was the development of high temperature glazes. Porcelain with its white translucent body requires a somewhat higher firing temperature, typically about 1300°C, and thus represents a development from stoneware. Again porcelain was first produced in China, in this case by about the 9th century AD (Tang dynasty) with large scale production occurring during the subsequent Song dynasty (AD 960–1279).

In the investigation of stoneware and porcelain technologies, the SEM provides information on the raw materials used to make the bodies and glazes as well as providing some indication of the firing temperatures employed.

For example, it has been possible using the SEM to significantly extend our understanding of the different raw materials used in the production of porcelain in southern and northern China. In terms of microstructure as seen in the SEM (Figure 7), the bodies of yingqing (also known as qingbai) and underglaze blue porcelain produced in Southern China during Song and Yuan dynasties consist typically of a continuous glassy matrix containing rounded partially-reacted quartz grains, ragged lath-shaped aggregates of mullite and glassy pools containing randomly-oriented mullite needles (Tite et al. 1984b).

An account of porcelain production at Jingdezhen in southern China, given in a letter written by Père d'Entrecolles in 1712, indicates that, at least by the early 18th century, porcelain bodies were made from a mixture of kaolin and porcelain stone ('petuntse'). Subsequent analyses have established that porcelain stone consists primarily of quartz and a fine-particled muscovite mica of the sericite variety (Wood 1984). In addition, depending on the degree of weathering of the quartz-feldspar rock from which it was formed, porcelain stone contains small amounts of feldspar and kaolinite. With this knowledge, the lath-shaped aggregates of mullite observed in the yingqing and underglaze blue porcelain microstructures can be interpreted as relict mica from the porcelain stone and the glassy pools as pseudomorphs of the feldspar in the porcelain stone. The bulk compositions, and in particular the alumina contents (15–18 per cent Al_2O_3), of Song dynasty yingqing porcelain bodies match those of typical kaolinised porcelain stones. Thus it seems

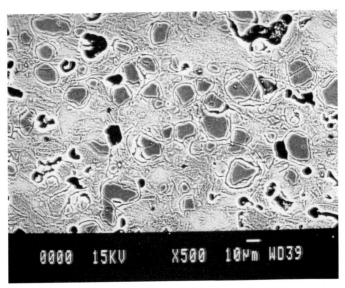

Figure 7. SEM photomicrograph of section through Song dynasty yingqing porcelain sherd showing body which consists of continuous glassy matrix containing partially-reacted quartz (darker grey), ragged lath-shaped aggregates of mullite and glassy pools containing randomly-orientated mullite needles.

probably that kaolinised porcelain stone was used by itself to produce porcelain bodies at this early period, with sericitic mica in the stone not only providing the flux (K_2O) but also, together with the kaolinite, contributing the necessary plasticity to the material. Similarly, the glaze compositions for these porcelains are consistent with their having been prepared by the addition of lime (in the form of glaze ash) to the same kaolinised porcelain stone as used for the bodies. In contrast, the alumina contents of Yuan dynasty underglazed blue porcelain bodies (19–22 per cent Al_2O_3) as well as Ming dynasty porcelain bodies (19–26 per cent Al_2O_3) are noticeably higher than those of both Song dynasty yingqing bodies and known porcelain stones (less than 20 per cent Al_2O_3). It therefore seems probable that these later porcelain bodies were made from a mixture of porcelain stone and kaolin as described in Père d'Entrecolles' letter. The kaolin was probably added in order to provide a finer textured body on which to apply the underglaze decoration. Again, the glaze compositions are consistent with the use of a mixture of lime and the same porcelain stone as used for the bodies but, in the case of the glazes, without the addition of kaolin.

Northern China does not have any deposits of porcelain stone and therefore the microstructure and composition of the associated porcelains differ from those of southern Chinese porcelains (Guo 1987). The bodies of the Ding porcelain produced in northern China during the Song dynasty consist of sparse partially-reacted quartz in a continuous glassy matrix containing a dense mass of fine mullite crystals (Figure 8). Their microstructures are thus more homogeneous than those observed for southern Chinese porcelain bodies. Further, the alumina contents of Ding porcelain bodies (27–33 per cent Al_2O_3) are significantly higher than those of southern Chinese porcelain bodies. Ding porcelain bodies also contain typically 1—2 per cent each of lime and magnesia whereas their concentrations in southern Chinese porcelain bodies are normally less than 0.5 per cent. These observations are consistent with the use of a comparatively pure kaolin to which small amounts of feldspar and dolomitic limestone were probably added as flux. The glazes also seem to have been prepared from a mixture of kaolin, feldspar and dolomitic limestone but with higher proportions of the two fluxing components than in the bodies.

In comparing European hard-paste porcelain with Chinese porcelain, it should be noted that the European porcelain bodies, after some initial experimentation, were made from a mixture of china clay (i.e., kaolin) and potassium feldspar (Kingery 1986). They therefore differ significantly from the southern Chinese porcelain bodies which they were attempting to imitate in that the southern Chinese bodies were micaceous rather than feldspathic. Instead, the European bodies are closer in composition to the Ding porcelain

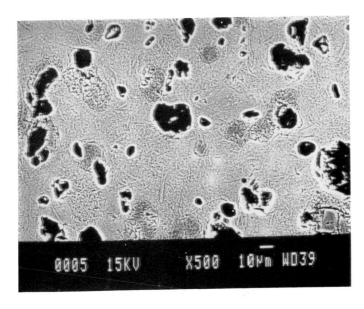

Figure 8. SEM photomicrograph of section through Song dynasty Ding porcelain sherd showing body which consists of sparse partially-reacted quartz (darker grey) in continuous glassy matrix containing dense mass of fine mullite crystals.

bodies although the European bodies contained a higher proportion of feldspar and no limestone.

3.4 Imitations of Chinese porcelains

The import of Chinese porcelains into the Islamic world from the 9th century AD onwards inspired a number of developments in the indigenous ceramic technologies (Watson 1987). These developments resulted from the attempts by the Islamic potters to replicate the hard white Chinese porcelain bodies without having either abundant supplies of the necessary white-firing clay or the associated high temperature technology. Subsequently, from the 15th century AD onwards Chinese porcelain, as well as the Islamic imitations, were imported into Europe where the attempts at replication resulted in the development first of Medici porcelain and ultimately of a wide range of both soft-paste and hard-paste porcelains.

SEM examination of both the Islamic and European imitations again provides information on the raw materials used and thus significantly extends our understanding of the means by which replication of the hard white Chinese porcelain was achieved (Tite 1988b).

During the Abbasid period (9th century AD) in Iraq, the Islamic potters continued to make their bodies from the locally available calcareous earthen-

M. S. Tite

ware clays (approx. 20 per cent CaO) which were iron rich (approx. 7 per cent FeO) and which fired to a buff colour. Their innovation was to achieve a white surface appearance by opacifying the glaze by the addition of tin oxide which formed clusters of particles up to 10 μm across (Figure 9). The glazes used were of the alkali-lime type containing up to about 2.5 per cent lead oxide. Their whiteness varied according to the tin oxide content which ranged from 1 per cent to 7 per cent. The pottery was decorated using a cobalt-blue pigment which was applied onto the powdery surface of the unfired glaze and which became fused into the glaze during firing. The bodies exhibit the open network of interconnecting glass/relict clay phases which is characteristic of calcareous clays fired in the temperature range 850–1050°C.

This method of decoration onto a tin-opacified glaze subsequently spread through the Near East and along North Africa reaching Europe by the 13th century AD where it was used in the production of Hispano-Moresque lustreware and Italian maiolica. It is interesting to note that calcareous clays were also used for both these European wares, most probably because calcareous clays have a number of technological advantages. First, the high thermal expansion of a calcareous clay body more closely matches that of a typical lead-alkali glaze and this reduces the risk of glaze crazing. Second, the vitrification structure of calcareous clays remains essentially unchanged over

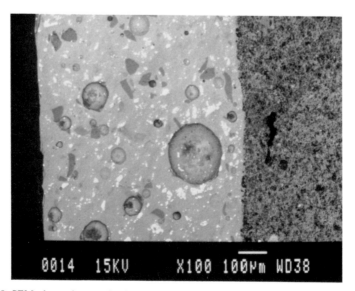

Figure 9. SEM photomicrograph of section through Abbasid blue-decorated sherd from Iraq showing glaze layer which contains tin oxide particles (white) and calcium- magnesium silicate crystals (darker grey) and body which consists of open network of interconnecting glass/relict clay phases.

the 850—1050°C firing temperature range and therefore the temperature control needed to achieve a consistent quality of body is less critical. Finally, even when they contain several per cent of iron oxide, calcareous clay bodies fire to a buff, rather than to a red, colour and this is more easily concealed by the tin-opacified glaze.

A second method of replicating Chinese porcelain which was widely used by Islamic potters from the 12th century AD onwards, involved reviving the quartz-based bodies employed in the Near East in the production of faience from 4th millennium BC through to the Roman period. Since these Islamic bodies were produced by the addition of glass frit to ground quartz or quartz sand, the resulting ceramics are normally referred to as quartz-frit wares.

A late, but technologically sophisticated, example of Islamic quartz-frit wares is Iznik ware which was produced in Ottoman Turkey during the late 15th and 16th centuries AD (Tite 1989). The Iznik ware bodies consist of angular quartz particles bonded together by a fairly extensive glass phase (Figure 10). The glass phase contains some 5—7 per cent each of alumina, alkali (soda plus potash) and lead oxide. On the basis of the composition and microstructure, it can be inferred that the Iznik ware bodies were made from ground quartz to which was added 5–10 per cent each of a white clay and an alkali-lead glass frit. The clay was presumably included in order to provide

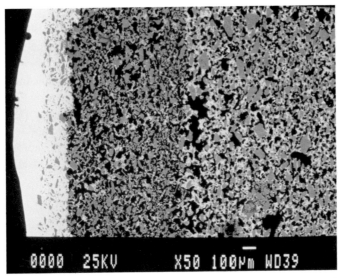

Figure 10. SEM photomicrograph of section through Iznik ware sherd showing glaze layer, fine-textured quartz-frit slip layer and quartz-frit body. The glaze and interstitial glass appear white compared to the quartz which appears grey.

the plasticity and green strength essential during the forming and subsequent handling of the unfired bodies.

The bodies are coated with quartz-frit slip layers which are typically 200–500 μm thick and which have a similar microstructure to those of the bodies. However, the quartz in the slip is finer textured (25 μm across as compared to 25–50 μm in the bodies) and the iron oxide content is lower (less than 0.3 per cent as compared to 1 per cent in the body). The glazes are of the lead-alkali type and contain some 4–7 per cent of tin oxide. However, the majority of the tin oxide is in solution so that it does not act as an opacifier. Therefore, the white surface appearance of Iznik ware is instead due to the very pure quartz-frit slip which coats the body. This fine-textured slip also provided an excellent ground for the mineral pigment decoration (e.g., cobalt, copper and chromium) which was applied under the glaze.

Although Iznik ware clearly falls within the general Islamic quartz-frit ware tradition, it differs technologically from related Islamic ceramics in a number of respects. First, the glass frits used to make both the bodies and slips are unusual in containing lead oxide as well as a alkali. Second, a slip has been applied to a body which itself already has a low iron content and is comparatively white. Third, although the tin oxide content is comparable to that in opaque Islamic lead-alkali glazes, the majority of the tin is in solution so that the glaze is transparent and the reason for adding the tin oxide remains something of a mystery. Thus, there does not appear to be any appropriate immediate antecedent for Iznik ware. Instead it seems possible that the Iznik potters, by careful choice of materials, successfully adapted existing Islamic ceramic technologies in order to meet the demands of the Ottoman court for pottery of a sufficiently high quality to match the Chinese porcelain reaching Turkey towards the end of the 15th century AD.

Thus it is seen that the Chinese imports resulted in significant developments in Islamic ceramic technologies. These developments provide an excellent illustration of the general principle proposed by Kingery (1984) that: "When a market for technology is established and recognised and technological innovations are rewarded, technological developments occur at a rapid rate." In other words, the level of the ceramic technology in the Islamic world rose to meet the market needs.

4. Future research

Having succeeded, I hope, in demonstrating the considerable power of the SEM examination of microstructures in elucidating the raw materials and processes used in the production of ancient ceramics, I now want to consider some of the possible directions for future research.

One important future development will be, I believe, the increasing use of image analysis techniques to obtain quantitative data on ceramic microstructures. In this context, the backscattered electron image is particularly appropriate since the different phases present can be distinguished by means of their grey level which changes progressively with the atomic number of the phase. Thus, it would be possible, for example, to quantify the extent of vitrification in the context of firing temperature estimates or to determine the proportions and particle size distributions of the different phases present in faience and frits.

Second, I expect to see some increase in the use of transmission electron microscopy (TEM). This instrument, with its increased resolution and capacity for crystallographic identification, can significantly extend the data on ceramic microstructure beyond that possible with scanning electron microscopy. For example, TEM examination has shown that the lustre decoration on 13th century Islamic lustre ware is associated with a high concentration of very small metallic silver particles (about 20 nm in diameter) in a thin surface layer in the glaze (Kingery and Vandiver 1986). Again, TEM examination has confirmed that the dichroism of the Lycurgus Cup, an outstanding late Roman cut-glass cage cup which appears wine-red in transmitted and pea-green in reflected light, is due to light scattering by silver-gold-copper colloid particles ranging from 50–100 nm in diameter and with average separation of the order of 10 μm (Barber and Freestone 1990). However, since sample preparation for TEM examination is much more difficult and the time needed to examine each sample at the associated high magnification is much greater, I would not expect the TEM to be used on a routine basis. Instead, transmission electron microscopy will normally be used to answer specific questions which require data beyond the resolution possible with scanning electron microscopy. As with the above examples, such questions will be concerned, typically, with trying to establish the physical basis for the external appearance of ceramics.

Third, I envisage considerable further application of the now more-or-less established SEM-microstructure approach to the study of ancient ceramic technologies. Such applications fall into two main categories. The first involves the investigation of the production technology of specific groups of ceramics. The second involves the investigation of specific technological innovations such as the introduction of glass production and its relationship to the preceding faience and frit technologies or the introduction of stoneware in China and other parts of the Far East and its relationship to the preceding earthenware technologies.

With either category of investigation a prime requirement must be for fully integrated projects involving both archaeologists and scientists in which the technology is studied within its wider social, economic and cultural context (Tite 1988a). Only in this way will it be possible to extend the answer to the question "Why were particular raw materials and production methods used?" beyond the sometimes rather simplistic technological reasons based on the observed or inferred physical properties of the raw materials and finished ceramics.

Acknowledgements

I wish to express my gratitude to Mavis Bimson and Dr Ian Freestone for the contributions that they have made, in their very different ways, to my understanding of the technology of ancient ceramics. Without the knowledge and insight that I gained from them during our period of collaboration together at the British Museum Research Laboratory, I would not have been in a position to write this review paper.

References

Barber, D.J. and Freestone, I.C. 1990: An investigation of the origin of the colour of the Lycurgus Cup by analytical transmission electron microscopy. *Archaeometry* 32, 33–45.

Freestone, I.C. 1982: Applications and potential of electron probe micro-analysis in technological and provenance investigations of ancient ceramics. *Archaeometry* 24, 99–116.

Freestone, I.C. and Middleton, A.P. 1987: Mineralogical applications of the analytical SEM in archaeology. *Mineralogical Magazine* 51, 21–31.

Freestone, I.C. and Tite, M.S. 1986: Refractories in the ancient and pre-industrial world. In Kingery, W.D. (editor), *Ceramics and Civilization 3* (Columbus, American Ceramic Society) 35–63.

Guo Y. 1987: Raw materials for making porcelain and the characteristics of porcelain wares in north and south China in ancient times. *Archaeometry* 29, 3–19.

Kingery, W.D. 1984: Interactions of ceramic technology with society. In Rice, P.M. (editor), *Pots and Potters: Current Approaches in Ceramic Archaeology* (Los Angeles, University of California, Monograph 24) 171–178.

Kingery, W.D. 1986: The development of European porcelain. In Kingery, W.D. (editor), *Ceramics and Civilisation 3* (Columbus, American Ceramic Society) 153–180.

Kingery, W.D. 1987: Microstructure analysis as part of a holistic interpretation of ceramic art and archaeological artifacts. *Archeomaterials* 1, 91–99.

Kingery, W.D. and Vandiver, P.B. 1986: *Ceramic Masterpieces* (New York, Free Press-Macmillan).

Maniatis, Y. and Tite, M.S. 1981: Technological examination of Neolithic-Bronze Age pottery from central and southeast Europe and from the Near East. *Journal of Archaeological Science* 8, 59–76.

Middleton, A.P. 1987: Technological investigation of coatings on some haematite-coated pottery from southern England. *Archaeometry* 29, 250–261.

Smith, C.S. 1988: *A History of Metallography* (Cambridge, Massachussetts Institute of Technology Press).

Tite, M.S. 1987: Characterisation of early vitreous materials. *Archaeometry* 29, 21–34.

Tite, M.S. 1988a: The study of ancient ceramic technologies: past achievements and future prospects. In Slater, E.A. and Tate, J.O. (editors), *Science and Archaeology 1987* (Oxford, British Archaeological Reports British Series 196) 9–25.

Tite, M.S. 1988b: Inter-relationship between Chinese and Islamic ceramics from 9th to 16th century AD. In Farquhar, R.M., Hancock, R.G.V. and Pavlish, L.A. (editors), *Proceedings of the 26th International Archaeometry Symposium*, (Toronto, University of Toronto) 30–34.

Tite, M.S. 1989: Iznik pottery: an investigation of the methods of production. *Archaeometry* 31, 115–132.

Tite, M.S. and Bimson, M. 1986: Faience: an investigation of the microstructures associated with the different methods of glazing. *Archaeometry* 28, 69–78.

Tite, M.S., Bimson, M. and Cowell, M.R. 1984a: Technological examination of Egyptian blue. In Lambert, J.B. (editor), *Archaeological Chemistry III* (Washington D.C., American Chemical Society Advances in Chemistry Series 205) 215–242.

Tite, M.S., Bimson, M. and Freestone, I.C. 1982: An examination of the high gloss surface finishes on Greek Attic and Roman Samian wares. *Archaeometry* 24, 117–126.

Tite, M.S., Freestone, I.C. and Bimson, M. 1984b: A technological study of Chinese porcelain of the Yuan dynasty. *Archaeometry* 26, 139–154.

Vandiver, P.B. 1983: The manufacture of faience. Appendix in Kaczmarczyk, A. and Hedges, R.E.M., *Ancient Egyptian Faience* (Warminster, Aris and Phillips) A1–137.

Watson, O. 1987: Islamic pots in Chinese style. *Burlington Magazine* 129, 304–306.

Wood, N. 1984: Chinese porcelain. *Ceramic Review* 89, 6–9.

Proceedings of the British Academy, **77**, 133–161

Geochemistry, Sources and Transport of the Stonehenge Bluestones

O. WILLIAMS-THORPE & R. S. THORPE*

Department of Earth Sciences, The Open University, Milton Keynes MK7 6AA, UK.

Summary. Stonehenge on Salisbury Plain, UK, is famous for its construction from large lintelled sarsen stones, and also because it has been proposed that some of its stones—the bluestones which are foreign to the solid geology of Salisbury Plain—were brought to the site by humans from a distant source in Preseli, South Wales. The bluestones include hard dolerites (mostly 'spotted') and rhyolites, and softer structurally unsuitable sandstones and basic tuffs. Chemical analysis of eleven dolerites and four rhyolite bluestones indicated that the dolerites originated at three sources in Preseli within a small area (*ca.* 2 km²), while the rhyolite monoliths are from four different sources including localities in northern Preseli and perhaps on the north Pembrokeshire coast, between 10 and 30 km apart. Opaque mineralogy of the dolerites supports the conclusion of a Preseli source, while modal analysis of a sandstone fragment excavated at Stonehenge shows that it is not from the Cosheston or Senni Beds of South Wales, as has been suggested. This variety of source implies selection of material from a mixed (glacial) source, not at a carefully human-chosen outcrop. Glacial erratic material from south-west Wales has been identified as far east as Cardiff, and early (Anglian) glaciation of the Bristol/Bath area is indicated by an erratic find and glacial landforms. The apparent lack of glacial erratics between Bristol and Stonehenge (except perhaps for the Boles Barrow boulder) and in rivers draining Salisbury Plain, is consistent with the irregular deposition of 'free' boulders at the edge

Read 13 February 1991. © The British Academy 1992.

*It is with very deep regret that we report the death of Dr. Richard Thorpe in August 1991.

of extensive ice sheets. Bluestone fragments on Salisbury Plain without clear archaeological context, and pieces incorporated, sometimes apparently accidentally, in monuments of Neolithic age onwards (some predating the bluestone erections at Stonehenge) may be remnants of erratics. Clearance of boulders from Salisbury Plain for agricultural purposes is clearly described by the geologist J.A. de Luc, and a boulder consistent in appearance with an erratic was found at Stonehenge in the 1920's.

It is concluded that the bluestones of Stonehenge were available locally to the builders, and were transported from south Wales not by humans, but by glacial activity of perhaps the Anglian period (*ca.* 400,000 years BP) or earlier. This conclusion has prompted re-examination of other suggestions of long-distance transport of megaliths. The sarsen stones at Stonehenge need not have been brought from 30 km to the north as has been suggested, since recent surveys show small concentrations of sarsens near Stonehenge, the remnant of boulders largely cleared during 18–19th centuries. Calculations of the manpower required to construct Stonehenge need to be re-assessed in view of the absence of long-distance stone transport. Other megaliths in Britain and in northern Europe show no evidence for stone transport of greater than *ca.* 5 km, and reveal a preference for use of erratics in some glaciated areas. In at least some cases the availability of stone has dictated the location of the monuments. It is therefore inappropriate to interpret the positions of megaliths in terms of social or economic territories without first examining the geological constraints on their siting.

1. Introduction

Stonehenge on Salisbury Plain is one of the most spectacular, and probably the most famous, of all British prehistoric monuments. It is unique partly because of its construction from huge lintelled sarsens, and also because it has been suggested that some of its stones—the 'bluestones' of the inner circle and horseshoe—were brought by humans from a distant source in south Wales, in a feat of endeavour unparalleled in British prehistory. The bluestones consist of a variety of igneous and sedimentary rock types which are foreign to the solid geology of Salisbury Plain, and their geological sources and mode of transport to Salisbury Plain—whether by humans or by natural (glacial) processes—have formed a subject of controversy for over 200 years. In 1923 H.H. Thomas suggested in a paper presented to the Society of Antiquaries that the distinctively spotted dolerite bluestones (the most common type at Stonehenge) could only originate in the Preseli Hills of south

Wales, and that these and the rhyolite bluestones were obtained from here, at and/or near the Carnmenyn outcrop, while the sandstone Altar Stone came from the Devonian Old Red Sandstone (Cosheston or Senni Beds) of south Wales. He further suggested that the stones could not have been moved to Salisbury Plain by glaciation but were transported the whole distance from south Wales by human action. This interpretation has dominated both academic and popular accounts of the Stonehenge bluestones for nearly 70 years.

The aim of our work has been to use geochemical and petrological analysis of samples of monoliths and of excavated fragments from Stonehenge to determine the location and number of sources of the bluestones. We use these data and a review of evidence for glaciation and recent boulder clearance on Salisbury Plain, to re-assess the mode of transport of bluestones to their present site.

Stonehenge and other megalithic monuments have been used to support hypotheses of social and technological organisation in British prehistory: such exercises are meaningful only if the geological constraints affecting the building and siting of such monuments are first considered.

Structural phases of Stonehenge referred to in this paper follow the outline summarised by Atkinson (1979). Dates are quoted as in data sources, following the convention of BC = calendar years; bc = uncalibrated carbon-14 years.

2. Bluestones at and around Stonehenge and elsewhere in the UK

The term "bluestone" is commonly used to refer to the non-sarsen monoliths at Stonehenge, and is also used loosely in much published literature to mean any apparently non-local stone similar to Stonehenge monoliths, found on or in the vicinity of Salisbury Plain.

The bluestone monoliths extant at Stonehenge include twenty-seven spotted dolerites (two broken in two pieces), three dolerites with no spots visible on the surface, five rhyolites (two lavas, two ignimbrites, one unknown type), five volcanic ashes or tuffs (composition unknown, possibly basic tuffs), and three micaceous sandstones (one of them the Altar Stone). All the volcanic ash and two of the sandstone monoliths are stumps no longer visible above ground. The monoliths, representing the remnants of perhaps eighty-two stones (*cf.* Atkinson 1979) are therefore of six distinct types, including hard durable rhyolite lavas and dolerites, and relatively soft, structurally poor volcanic ashes and sandstones. Burl (1987, 139–140) has summarised historical evidence which suggests that two stones each *ca.* 2 m high now in the High Street of the village of Berwick St. James 6 km south-west of Stonehenge are pieces of a monolith removed from Stonehenge during the 17th Century AD. These stones were examined by the authors in 1989 and, notwithstanding earlier reports that they are of sarsen (Engleheart 1933), they are in fact of peloidal packstone and packstone/grainstone, rare in the Lower Jurassic, and therefore perhaps from a Middle or Upper Jurassic source (R.C.L. Wilson, pers. comm.). Such rocks outcrop at many localities within southern England, and the nearest feasible source to Stonehenge is near Tisbury *ca.* 22 km to the south-west. This new evidence suggests the use of yet another type of rock for the Stonehenge monoliths.

Bluestones are found at Stonehenge in the form of fragments, including at least one weathered rounded boulder 13 × 20 cm, of sheared ignimbrite, unsuitable for working and consistent in appearance with a glacial erratic (G.A. Kellaway, pers. comm., following information from R.S. Newall). Other (non-bluestone) foreign stone fragments at Stonehenge are frequent and varied, and include limestone, schist, varied sandstones, quartzite and shale (Hawley 1922; 1925; Howard 1982; Evens *et al.* 1962; summary in Clough and Cummins 1988). Some of these could be from implements, finds of which include rhyolite (Howard 1982) and dolerite (Implement Petrology Group XVIII (Whin Sill); I.F. Smith pers. comm. 1990), and axes of greenstone (Groups I, Ia, III), tuff (Group VI) and sandstone (Clough and Cummins 1988). Bluestone was present at Stonehenge I, *ca.* 3000 BC (glauconitic sandstone found in the packing of Stone 97 (Howard 1982)) before its first use as monoliths in Stonehenge II.

Bluestone fragments are frequently reported in association with other archaeological monuments on and near Salisbury Plain (summaries in Howard 1982 and Thorpe *et al.* in press). It is noteworthy that these are recovered from a wide variety of monuments of disparate periods (round and long barrows, henge, cursus; e.g., Ashbee 1978; Cunnington 1924; J. Richards pers. comm. 1989; Stone 1948), and always from surface or fill soil (i.e., not deposited within burials as valued objects). Stray finds of rhyolite from near Avebury (find in Salisbury Museum, no. p.1.494. 5/1917–18) and spotted dolerite from Lake (Kellaway 1971) have no recorded archaeological context. A piece of rhyolite from a Neolithic pit may be dated to *ca.* 2500 BC (J. Richards pers. comm. 1989), and a 340 kg spotted dolerite boulder was incorporated in the long barrow at Heytesbury (Boles Barrow; Cunnington *op. cit.*) probably hundreds of years before the erection of Stonehenge II bluestones (the Boles Barrow boulder is compositionally identical with two of the bluestone monoliths; see source discussion below). The impression is therefore of frequent and unremarked presence of fragments and larger boulders of varied bluestones on Salisbury Plain incorporated, perhaps sometimes by accident, in monuments from the Neolithic period onwards.

This scenario is supported by the wide variety of other foreign (non-bluestone) stones found in other Wessex monuments. Amesbury Barrow 39 contained fragments of quartz diorite, hornblende diorite and granodiorite (Ashbee 1981), a combination of types found also in glacial assemblages in south Wales (cf. Strahan et al. 1914). Briggs (1976, 12) has also pointed out the similarity of foreign stone assemblages at Windmill Hill to those at Stonehenge.

Elsewhere in Britain there is no evidence that the main bluestone type used at Stonehenge—spotted dolerite—was particularly valued or preferentially used. Even within south Wales, near to the presumed Preseli source of the spotted dolerite, a survey by the authors (details in Thorpe et al. in press) has shown that of twenty-six megalithic monuments of Neolithic to Bronze Age date (including five stone circles, four of which may be dated to around 2000 BC, near the date of Stonehenge II), only one monument, Gorsfawr stone circle, is built of spotted dolerite similar in appearance to that at Stonehenge. In every single case, the monuments were built of stones readily available at the site of construction or within ca. 1 km of it, either in outcrop, or more frequently, as glacial erratic boulders; Gorsfawr for example lies in a field littered with spotted dolerite erratics.

Axes of spotted dolerite (Implement Petrology Group XIII) are a rare type (total number no more than thirty finds, Clough and Cummins 1988; Thorpe et al. in press), have no known factory site (cf. Drewett 1987), while their distribution (Clough and Cummins op. cit.; Thorpe et al. op. cit.) may be at least partially interpreted as use of glacial erratics removed from the source area and naturally dispersed eastwards (cf. below). It is thus necessary to invoke limited human traffic only for examples reported from north Wales and for the small number found in (presumed unglaciated) parts of eastern and south coast England (cf. Briggs 1989 on use of erratics for axes). Group XIII axes are not therefore evidence for direct links between Preseli and Wessex in the Late Neolithic/Early Bronze Age periods, or for knowledge of or interest in the Preseli area.

3. Sampling and description of bluestones

Fifteen bluestone monoliths at Stonehenge were sampled on the afternoon of October 15th 1987, including eleven dolerites (eight spotted, three unspotted) and all four rhyolites now above ground (Figure 1). Ten samples were removed by drilling with a 1 inch diameter diamond drill to a depth of ca. 5 cm and removing cores whole. Five samples were removed as chips from the surface of the stones. Samples were typically 50–100 g in weight. The Altar stone was examined macroscopically in situ only. Monolith samples were

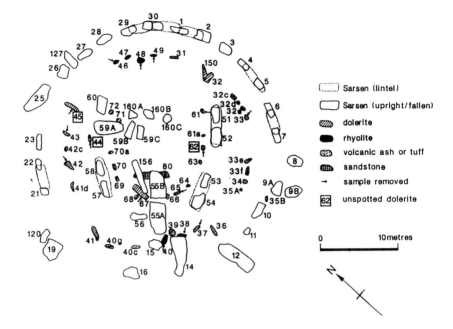

Figure 1. Plan of central stone settings at Stonehenge, after Newall (1959), Chippindale (1987), Atkinson (1979) and authors' observations, showing petrology of the stones and locations of samples removed for this work. Stone types are defined on the diagram. All dolerites are spotted except for stones 44, 45, and 62. Stone numbering is after Atkinson (1979) except for stone 61a which is our number (stump noted by Cunnington (1884), now above ground). From Thorpe *et al.* (in press).

numbered as the stones from which they were taken (numbering system after Petrie 1880 and Atkinson 1979) with the addition of prefix SH.

Excavated fragments of bluestone from Stonehenge were examined at the Salisbury and South Wiltshire Museum, Salisbury, and twenty-three (numbered OU1 to OU12, OU14 to OU24) selected for further study, including nine pieces of dolerite, thirteen of rhyolite, and one of sandstone (noted in museum record as 'Cosheston Beds?'). These include pieces found in Aubrey Holes 1, 5, 10, 11, 15, 16, 17, 21 and 22, the Heelstone ditch, Holes Y6 and Z6, and the Avenue. In addition, the Boles Barrow boulder, also housed in the Salisbury and South Wiltshire Museum, was sampled to remove 23g.

The dolerite samples are typically composed of clinopyroxene and plagioclase showing ophitic texture and variable alteration. The whitish spots, typically 2 mm—10 mm, which are the most distinctive feature of the spotted dolerites are formed by metamorphism resulting in small-scale element migration, and are not distinctive in thin section. The rhyolite samples have alkali feldspar plus or minus plagioclase in a fine grained to cryptocrystalline matrix, with *fiamme* visible in ignimbritic samples (two monoliths and two fragment samples). Full sample descriptions are given in Thorpe *et al.* in press.

4. Analytical methods

All monolith samples and fragment samples except for OU9 (sandstone) were analysed for major and twelve trace elements using X-Ray Fluorescence analysis at the Open University (following the procedure of Potts *et al.* 1984), and the Universities of Keele and Southampton. Precision at 1 sigma is typically below 1% relative for major elements and below 5% relative for many traces. Accuracy, measured by comparison of our data for international reference materials QLO-1, BE-N and BHVO-1 with recommended values (Gladney and Roelandts 1988) is comparable to precision values. Standard petrological thin sections were prepared for all samples, and modal analysis of one sample (OU9, sandstone) determined by point counting (R.G. Thomas, University of Calgary, Canada). A polished thin section of monolith sample SH61 (spotted dolerite) was prepared for examination of opaque mineralogy in reflected light (R.A. Ixer, University of Birmingham).

In addition to analysis of archaeological samples, forty new geological samples from outcrops of dolerite and rhyolite in the Preseli area and six of glacial erratics in Preseli and near Lampeter Velfrey (Figure 6) were collected and analysed as described above. Analysis of six samples of igneous erratics from near Cardiff (Pencoed, Figure 6) are given in Donnelly *et al.* (in preparation). Selected data are given in Tables 1 and 2 and full data are available in Thorpe *et al.* (in press) and from the authors on request.

5. Potential source areas of the bluestones

The distinctive spotted texture of most of the Stonehenge dolerites was noted by Thomas (1923) to occur only within the Preseli Hills of south Wales, and this remains the case today. Therefore in this paper we examine the Stonehenge samples in relation to rocks from this area. We also consider rocks of andesite, dacite and rhyolite composition in the Mendip Hills (Figure 2) since this forms a proximal occurrence of igneous rocks to Stonehenge and also lies close to the route proposed for human transport. It should be borne in mind that our study involved only fifteen monolith samples, and sourcing of these (below) to south Wales may not necessarily be the case for all other (unsampled) Stonehenge monoliths.

Igneous rocks occur in south Wales within extensive Ordovician and

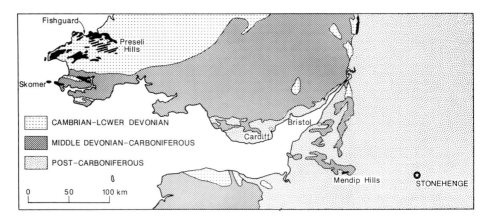

Figure 2. Geological map of south Wales and south-west central England showing the distribution of major stratigraphic units (*cf.* key) and Precambrian—Lower Palaeozoic intrusive
and extrusive igneous rocks (in black). The stratigraphic units and the igneous rocks include
the possible sources for Stonehenge bluestones discussed in text sections 5 and 6 (*cf.* Figures 3
and 4).

(more limited) late Precambrian outcrops, shown on Figure 2 and discussed
by, particularly, Bevins *et al.* (1984), Kokelaar *et al.* (1984), Leat *et al.* (1986)
and Leat and Thorpe (1986a; 1986b) and Thorpe *et al.* (1989). The
Ordovician rocks comprise chemically varied basalt-andesite and bimodal
basalt-subalkaline/peralkaline rhyolite provinces in which lavas have
volcanic arc or transitional volcanic arc/within-plate chemical characteristics.

Intermediate to acid composition lavas and ignimbrites occur within this
province in the Roch, Trefgarn and Sealyham groups (Thomas and Cox
1924; Evans 1945), Ramsey Island (Kokelaar *et al.* 1985), and within the
Fishguard Volcanic Group (e.g., Bevins 1982). Dolerite intrusions are extensive on the coast near and to the north of St. Davids Head (Figures 2 and 6)
and within the Fishguard Volcanic Group (Evans 1945). Spotted dolerites are
restricted to outcrops within the eastern part of the Fishguard Volcanic
Group in the eastern Preselis (Figure 5). The concentration of spots varies
within one outcrop from less than 5% to approximately 15% of the visible
surface. Samples from within these outcrops are petrographically identical to
the Stonehenge spotted dolerites. The rhyolites are less distinctive and petrographic features cannot be used to suggest sources of the Stonehenge rhyolites. Chemical analyses of these volcanics are given in Bevins (1979; 1982)
and Bevins *et al.* (1989), and new data from the present authors. Geochemical
characteristics of the groups are summarised in the discrimination graphs
below (Figures 3(a) and 4).

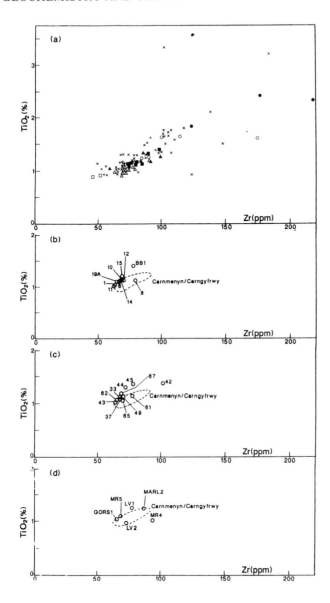

Figure 3. Graph of TiO$_2$ against Zr for (a) dolerites from the Preseli Hills, (b) excavated fragments from Stonehenge, (c) Stonehenge monolith samples and (d) glacial erratics. The symbols for the geological samples are as follows: open triangles = Carnmenyn/Carngwyfry; open squares = Carnbica; filled triangles = Carnbreseb; horizontal crosses = Carngeodog; filled squares = Cerrigmarchogion; open circles = Carnalw; filled circles = Foeldrygarn; oblique crosses = undifferentiated intrusions. SH and OU sample prefixes are omitted on the diagram. From Thorpe *et al.* (in press).

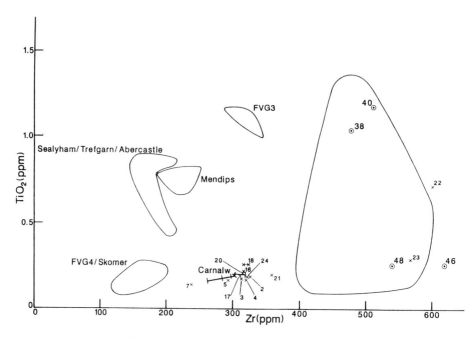

Figure 4. Graph of TiO_2 against Zr for andesite-rhyolite groups from Pembrokeshire and the Mendip Hills, showing excavated fragments from Stonehenge (crosses) and Stonehenge monolith samples (circles with dots in the middle). SH and OU prefixes are omitted on the diagram. Roch group not plotted (Y = < 3 ppm, Thorpe *et al.* in press). Duplicate analyses plotted for OU18. From Thorpe *et al.* (in press).

6. Results and provenancing of samples

6.1 Chemical analysis

The Precambrian and Ordovician volcanic rocks of south Wales have undergone chemical alteration as a result of burial and regional metamorphism (Bevins and Rowbotham 1983), hydrothermal alteration, and low temperature hydration of glassy rocks. These processes have caused mobility of most major elements and several trace elements (see, for example, Macdonald *et al.* 1987) on a large (outcrop) scale, and smaller scale migration of Al_2O_3, CaO and Sr into "spots" from surrounding rock. It is therefore important to use representative samples particularly of spotted dolerites, and to use variation diagrams based on elements unaffected by such alteration, in particular the high field strength elements Ti, Zr, Nb and Y.

Homogeneity within a single sample of *ca.* 1000 cm^3 was shown to be within 10% relative and mainly within precision (Thorpe *et al.* in press). Within an outcrop of *ca.* 900 m^2 (Carngyfrwy, Figure 5), variation of 10x precision was observed for some major elements, and of 2–6x precision for

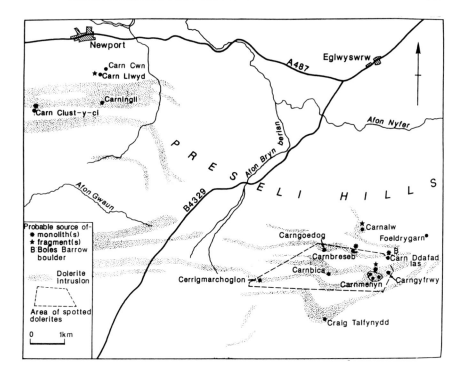

Figure 5. Sketch map of the Preseli Hills showing location of important outcrops mentioned in the text. The three outcrops surrounded by a dotted line are all part of the Carnmenyn outcrop. The dashed line shows the approximate extent of spotted dolerite, after Evans (1945). Map base is after Evans (*op. cit.*) and Bevins *et al.* (1989). Some dolerite areas contain small rhyolite occurrences, for example at Carnalw and Carningli. Probable sources of Stonehenge monolith and fragment samples, and of the Boles Barrow sample, are indicated. From Thorpe *et al.* (in press).

some traces, with Nb, Y and Zr among those elements showing least variation (Thorpe *et al.* in press, Table 7).

Figure 3(a) summarises the chemical variation of TiO_2 and Zr in Preseli dolerites (SiO_2 *ca.* 45–49%), (representative analyses in Table 1(a)). The good positive correlation between TiO_2 and Zr confirms the immobile behaviour of these elements, while greater scatter of TiO_2 at high Zr values may reflect accumulation/loss of Fe-Ti oxide. The graph also shows some regional variation within Preseli outcrops: for example, the Carnmenyn—Carngyfrwy, Carnalw and Foeldrygarn intrusions show restricted chemical ranges within the Preseli field. Excavated dolerite fragment samples are plotted on Figure 3(b) and, except for BB1 (Boles Barrow sample), show similar compositions to the Carnmenyn-Carngyfrwy field which also contains samples from Carnbreseb, Carngoedog and Cerrigmarchogion (within *ca.* 4 km of Carnmenyn) and other chemically undifferentiated dolerites studied by

Bevins *et al.* (1989). Monolith samples (Figure 3(c)) have the same restricted chemistry except for SH42, and SH44 and 45 (the last two identical to each other for unaltered elements), which may therefore come from different intrusions. Examination of all elements analysed (*cf.* Tables 1(a), 2(a) and compare Thorpe *et al.* in press Table 11) shows that most of the monolith samples and fragments have chemical characteristics consistent with an origin within the Carnmenyn-Carngyfrwy or Cerrigmarchogion and Carn-goedog intrusions, while SH44, SH45 and BB1 are similar within or near precision to Carn Ddafad-las *ca.* 550 m north of Carnmenyn, and SH42 similarly matches a high Y and Zr dolerite from Carnbreseb. Figure 3(d) shows analyses of glacial erratics from the Lampeter Velfrey area and from near the Gorsfawr stone circle (*ca.* 3 km south-west of Carnmenyn), and these also derive from the same restricted area as most of the monolith and fragment samples. Thus the chemical evidence for the dolerites does not clearly distinguish between selection from *in situ* outcrop or from a glacial deposit.

Figure 4, again using TiO_2 plotted against Zr, exemplifies the variations within andesite—rhyolite sources in south Wales and Mendip (*cf.* Table 1(b)). Of the rhyolite fragments analysed, most are chemically identical (including OU3, quoted in Table 2(b)) and plot with the Carnalw source in eastern Preseli. Three fragments, nos. OU7, OU22 and OU23 are chemically different and therefore originate at different sources. The four Stonehenge monolith rhyolite samples are all different from each other (*cf.* Table 2(b)), and all lie within or near to the high-Zr field which forms part of the Fishguard Volcanic Group (chemically differentiated here into four groups: Carnalw, Fishguard Volcanic Groups (FVG) 3 and 4, and high-Zr samples; *cf.* Bevins *et al.* 1989; Thorpe *et al.* in press), which contains outcrops in eastern Preseli, north Preseli and on the north Pembrokeshire coast near Strumble Head west of Fishguard (compare Figures 2 and 6). Monolith sample SH38 is identical in chemical composition to the outcrop of Carn Clust-y-ci in northern Preseli (RGR14, Table 1(b)), and SH46 and SH48 are characterised by very high Y and Zr and may be parallelled in similarly siliceous rocks on the north Pembrokeshire coast (see, for example, SP2, Table 1(b)); however no exact source match could be found for these. No source parallel was found for SH40, and while its characteristics are generally consistent with a Pembrokeshire origin it should be noted that similar ignim-brites also occur in north Wales (*cf.* Howard 1982). Fragment 23 is identical to monolith sample SH48, while fragment 22 is chemically identical to Carn Llwyd in northern Preseli (RGR16, Table 1(b)). No source was found for fragment 7.

The rhyolite samples were also compared with glacial erratics analysed by

Table 1(a).   Chemical analyses of dolerites from the Preseli Hills, south Wales

Sample G.R. Location	CM1 SN 143325 Carnmenyn	CM10 SN 146325 Carngyfrwy	CM12 SN 148329 Carn Ddafas las	CBR1 SN 136332 Carnbreseb	CB1 SN 130326 Carnbica	PFT53 SN 15613340 Foeldrygarn
SiO$_2$%	47.61	47.75	45.98	48.05	44.77	49.05
TiO$_2$	1.02	1.06	1.32	1.27	0.89	1.85
Al$_2$O$_3$	18.93	19.11	17.20	16.29	19.98	14.94
Fe$_2$O$_3$	8.40	8.70	10.25	10.38	9.46	0.26
FeO	–	–	–	–	–	10.24
MnO	0.15	0.14	0.17	0.17	0.14	0.21
MgO	6.49	6.59	8.85	7.34	7.28	6.76
CaO	10.29	10.87	10.03	10.92	10.50	10.04
Na$_2$O	2.71	3.08	2.35	2.33	2.66	1.95
K$_2$O	0.83	0.44	0.31	0.79	0.45	0.08
P$_2$O$_5$	0.10	0.11	0.13	0.14	0.06	0.16
H$_2$O$^+$	–	–	–	–	–	4.12
LOI	2.82	2.88	3.41	2.75	4.22	–
TOTAL	99.35	100.73	100.00	100.43	100.41	99.66
Ba ppm	326	204	306	150	167	–
Cr	213	285	195	295	320	189
Cu	60	56	49	33	63	60
Nb	3	3	4	5	3	2
Ni	29	33	118	34	120	40
Rb	19	15	9	17	12	2
Sr	276	318	276	249	303	343
Th	1	1	2	2	1	–
V	190	190	202	235	198	325
Y	20	18	20	28	16	32
Zn	68	64	79	72	68	96
Zr	68	70	73	99	45	123

Notes: LOI, Loss on ignition, included in totals; — not determined; iron as Fe$_2$O$_3$ total iron except PFT53 (FeO and Fe$_2$O$_3$); data from Thorpe *et al.* in press (PFT53 from Bevins *et al.* 1989).

O. Williams-Thorpe & R. S. Thorpe

Table 1(b). Chemical analyses of andesites and rhyolites from south Wales and Mendip

Sample	RGR14	SP2	CA2	RGR16	SW16	MH3
G.R.	SN 0419702	SM 88704058	SN 13903375	SN 0624380 5	SM 72260894	ST 666464
Location	Carn Clust-y-ci	Strumble Head	Carnalw	Carn Llwyd (Nr Carningli)	Skomer	Moons Hill
Group	High Zr	High Zr	Carnalw	High Zr	Skomer	Mendip
SiO_2 %	65.63	76.90	78.70	67.28	75.74	66.82
TiO_2	1.01	0.50	0.19	0.56	0.12	0.77
Al_2O_3	13.97	12.40	10.06	13.86	12.61	14.92
Fe_2O_3	1.62	1.87	2.74	3.91	3.52	4.42
FeO	4.12	–	–	2.09	–	–
MnO	0.06	0.03	0.02	0.13	0.02	0.03
MgO	3.05	0.64	0.37	0.70	0.66	1.90
CaO	1.53	0.99	0.22	2.13	0.12	1.97
Na_2O	4.34	2.80	1.15	4.73	3.56	4.49
K_2O	2.74	2.79	6.04	2.32	3.62	3.52
P_2O_5	0.22	0.07	0.03	0.13	0.04	0.16
H_2O^+	2.39	–	–	1.61	–	Cl+S 0.02
LOI	–	0.90	0.72	–	–	–
TOTAL	100.68	98.99	100.24	99.44	100.01	99.02
Ba ppm	–	–	1004	600	–	–
Cr	3	–	14	n.d.	10	–
Cu	5	–	1	4	–	14
Nb	13	29	20	17	–	11
Ni	7	–	3	10	–	8
Rb	35	34	110	37	8	61
Sr	89	135	75	193	101	304
Th	–	–	13	6.14	139	8
V	84	–	4	15	–	–
Y	76	85	97	104	42	23
Zn	68	–	63	124	–	29
Zr	481	553	300	613	150	234

Notes: LOI, Loss on ignition, included in totals except in SP2; — not determined; iron as Fe_2O_3 total iron except RGR14 and RGR16 (FeO and Fe_2O_3); n.d. not detected; data from Thorpe *et al.* in press (MH3, CA2, RGR14, RGR16), Hughes 1977 (SW16), and Bevins 1979 (SP2).

Table 2(a). Chemical analyses of selected dolerite samples from Stonehenge monoliths and excavated fragments, and of the Boles Barrow boulder

Sample Location	SH33 Stone 33	SH42 Stone 42	SH44 Stone 44	SH45 Stone 45	SH61 Stone 61	OU6 Aubrey Hole 10	BB1 Boles Barrow boulder
SiO_2%	47.89	48.07	48.10	48.34	47.70	46.55	47.46
TiO_2	1.15	1.37	1.30	1.37	1.17	1.11	1.40
Al_2O_3	17.77	17.79	15.76	15.51	18.11	16.14	17.66
Fe_2O_3	9.29	9.17	11.82	10.22	9.05	9.91	10.33
MnO	0.16	0.15	0.19	0.22	0.14	0.17	0.17
MgO	6.99	5.73	8.37	8.58	6.17	9.42	6.07
CaO	11.30	11.53	9.06	9.24	11.92	10.15	11.20
Na_2O	2.85	3.31	2.17	2.91	2.69	1.97	3.33
K_2O	0.18	0.15	0.42	0.08	0.18	0.76	0.07
P_2O_5	0.11	0.22	0.12	0.10	0.11	0.11	0.13
LOI	2.80	2.87	3.30	3.62	2.90	3.21	2.65
TOTAL	100.49	100.36	100.61	100.19	100.14	99.50	100.47
Ba ppm	120	123	225	232	114	184	119
Cr	479	279	216	262	258	277	257
Cu	52	46	70	81	80	47	53
Nb	6	7	7	6	6	4	4
Ni	45	29	70	111	38	124	31
Rb	10	8	12	7	8	16	7
Sr	225	235	235	273	217	328	244
Th	2	1	n.d	n.d	n.d	1	3
V	210	213	240	237	208	209	251
Y	21	31	23	24	22	20	23
Zn	72	69	91	82	76	69	96
Zr	67	101	71	77	77	66	77

Notes: LOI, Loss on ignition, included in totals; n.d., not detected: iron is total Fe as Fe_2O_3%; number of separate analyses averaged in these figures are: majors—n = 2 for SH33, SH45, SH61, n = 3 for SH44, n = 1 for SH42, OU6, BB1; traces—n = 2 for all samples; samples SH44 and SH45 are from unspotted dolerites, remainder are spotted dolerites; data from Thorpe et al. in press.

Table 2(b). Chemical analyses of rhyolite samples from Stonehenge monoliths and selected excavated fragments

Sample Location	SH38 Stone 38	SH40 Stone 40	SH46 Stone 46	SH48 Stone 48	OU3 Hole Z6	OU22 Aubrey Hole 16	OU23 Aubrey Hole 11	OU7 Aubrey Hole 17
SiO_2%	66.74	67.16	74.63	75.42	77.23	68.80	74.31	83.13
TiO_2	1.04	1.09	0.26	0.26	0.18	0.72	0.29	0.14
Al_2O_3	13.36	12.78	12.16	11.48	11.11	14.32	12.05	9.13
Fe_2O_3	6.10	7.43	3.35	3.40	1.78	5.31	3.73	0.80
MnO	0.11	0.19	0.08	0.11	0.01	0.07	0.12	n.d
MgO	2.43	2.13	0.68	0.51	0.10	1.66	0.68	0.07
CaO	2.04	1.68	0.35	0.89	0.52	0.89	0.57	0.26
Na_2O	4.86	4.49	3.93	3.92	4.46	6.20	3.95	3.52
K_2O	1.36	0.83	2.77	2.94	3.13	0.06	3.06	2.69
P_2O_5	0.24	0.37	0.03	0.03	0.03	0.21	0.03	0.02
LOI	2.15	2.24	1.35	1.50	0.56	1.65	1.02	0.39
TOTAL	100.43	100.39	99.59	100.46	99.11	99.89	99.81	100.15
Ba ppm	415	837	592	544	549	69	576	572
Cr	64	1	6	8	28	n.d	12	24
Cu	8	7	1	n.d	1	3	1	n.d
Nb	15	19	31	24	15	17	25	13
Ni	12	7	8	7	3	3	3	2
Rb	24	22	46	43	67	8	45	51
Sr	236	579	158	47	52	459	48	55
Th	1	3	8	8	13	6	8	10
V	100	50	14	15	13	5	13	4
Y	75	89	155	105	84	114	116	80
Zn	71	127	135	109	24	107	88	21
Zr	478	510	621	539	312	601	566	237

Notes: LOI, Loss on ignition, included in totals; n.d., not detected; iron is total Fe as Fe_2O_3 %; number of separate analyses averaged in these figures are: n = 2 for all except majors in OU3, 22, 23, 7 (n = 1). Samples SH38, SH40 and OU22 are ignimbritic, others are lavas; data from Thorpe *et al.* in press.

Donnelly *et al.* (in prep.), from Pencoed near Cardiff (Figure 6) but no chemical parallel for any was found in this assemblage.

The Stonehenge dolerites thus come from three sources chemically consistent with an origin within the Preseli Hills; the rhyolites come from a further seven sources (four for the monoliths, a further three for the fragments). These source areas are shown on Figures 5 and 6, and it is clear that the sources are both numerous and widespread, separated by distances of at least 10 km and perhaps over 30 km.

6.2 Opaque mineralogy of monolith sample SH61

One sample, from monolith SH61, was examined in polished thin section in reflected light by R.A. Ixer at the University of Birmingham, for comparison with Carnmenyn samples of dolerites. SH61 is characterised by heavily altered titanomagnetite and ilmenite, with minor amounts of altered pyrrhotite, chalcopyrite and pyrite, and trace amounts of spinel and violarite. With the single exception of violarite, these features are also encountered in Carnmenyn samples examined in the same way, and in addition the identical alteration history implied for both SH61 and for the Carnmenyn samples by the textures of the iron-titanium oxides (titanomagnetite and ilmenite) and the presence of metamorphic minerals surrounding aggregates of chalcopyrite, pyrrhotite and pyrite, suggest a common origin for all the samples. (A full list of the mineralogy of the samples is in Thorpe *et al.* in press). This supports the chemical provenancing of most of the monolith samples to the Carnmenyn—Carngyfrwy (or Carngoedog—Carrigmarchogion) area of Preseli.

6.3 Provenance evidence from sandstones at Stonehenge

Sandstone fragment OU9 excavated from Aubrey Hole 1 was examined in petrological thin section by R.G. Thomas of the University of Calgary, and modal analysis carried out by point counting, for comparison with Cosheston Group and other Lower Devonian sandstones of south Wales (Thomas 1978). Sample OU9 was found by Col. Hawley in the 1920's and its labelling as 'Cosheston Beds?' reflects an assumption of origin probably based on H.H. Thomas' provenancing of the Altar stone to the Cosheston or Senni Beds of south Wales in 1923 (*cf.* above). OU9 is characterised by pervasive pressure solution cleavage and paucity of rock fragments, features which indicate that it did not originate in either the Lower Devonian Cosheston or Senni Beds (full modal analysis in Thorpe *et al.* in press). It is more likely to be derived from a Silurian or older Lower Palaeozoic formation (*cf.* Figure 2) exposed in the Caledonian foldbelt of south-west Wales, or possibly from a Lower Devonian sandstone in westernmost Pembrokeshire, where such cleavage as is seen in OU9 has developed.

No sample was obtained from the Altar stone, and examination of this was based on macroscopic features. R.G. Thomas makes the comment that since it is more highly micaceous than OU9 it is not derived from the same unit. The Altar stone may be from the Senni Beds which form part of the Lower Devonian, approximately stratigraphically equivalent to the Cosheston Beds (Milford-Neyland-Cosheston districts) but cropping out to the east of Carmarthen Bay, from Kidwelly as far as the Abergavenny district *ca.* 90 km to the east. The evidence from the sandstones thus adds two more source areas for the Stonehenge bluestones, and shows that previous assumptions of source are unjustified in the case of OU9.

7. Review of evidence for glaciation and boulder clearance on Salisbury Plain

Controversy concerning the possible glaciation of Salisbury Plain has been a central factor in discussion concerning mechanisms of bluestone transport to Stonehenge. The main arguments against such glaciation have included the apparent lack of erratics on Salisbury Plain, and the absence of glacial material in Pleistocene river gravels draining Salisbury Plain, analysed by Green (1973). It can now be shown that neither of these arguments is as significant as previously suggested. Figure 6 illustrates the glacial movements referred to in this section.

Glaciation of south Wales including Pembrokeshire is well documented,

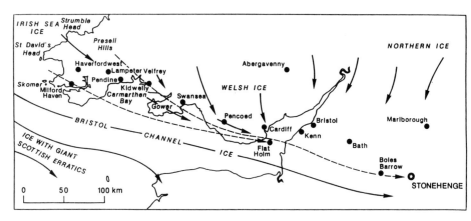

Figure 6. Map of south Wales and south-west central England showing generalised directions of ice movement (based on distribution of erratics) inferred for the Anglian glaciation (*cf.* Kellaway, 1971; Figure 2), and localities discussed in the text.

from early (Anglian or pre-Anglian; *ca.* 400 ka BP or earlier) features described by Bowen and Sykes (1988), Bowen (1982; 1989) and John (1970a; 1970b), through Wolstonian (*ca.* 150 ka BP) ice moving from the Irish Sea over Pembrokeshire into the Bristol Channel (e.g., Synge 1970; Kellaway 1971), to more recent (Devensian; *ca.* 20 ka BP) ice of more limited extent. Further east, glaciation of the Severn Estuary and the Bristol-Bath area is indicated by a relict till near Nunney (Kellaway 1971) and an erratic boulder at Kenn pier (Hawkins and Kellaway 1971), while amino acid racemisation dating of deposits at Kenn gives an age exceeding 400–600 ka (i.e., Anglian or pre-Anglian) for these features. Recent studies by Kellaway (pers. comm. and 1991) propose movement of northern ice (i.e., from Scotland and north Wales, not crossing south Wales) onto Salisbury Plain during a glaciation of *ca.* 500 ka BP (Beestonian) or earlier.

Igneous boulders were transported glacially south and eastwards from south-west Wales to the Haverfordwest area where they reach 4 m (Strahan *et al.* 1914), to *ca.* 20 km south-east of Carnmenyn (Lampeter Velfrey, Figure 6) where they reach over 2 m in size (Strahan *et al. op. cit.*; Thorpe *et al.* in press), and to near Carmarthen Bay *ca.* 2 km north of Pendine (spotted dolerite reported by Strahan *et al. op. cit.*, 218, Figure 20). Varied igneous erratics presumed to be from Scotland, Ireland and/or south-west Wales are described in Gower by George (1933) and Jenkins *et al.* (1985), and erratic boulders from Pencoed (Figure 6) near Cardiff analysed by Donnelly *et al.* (in prep.) include material from the St. Davids Head area and Skomer island (Figure 6). Igneous erratics on Flatholm island in the Severn Estuary (Figure 6) have been deduced to be from the Lake District and north and south Wales (Kellaway 1971) and erratics on the east side of the Severn estuary include a striated Carboniferous limestone boulder (*cf.* above; Hawkins and Kellaway 1971).

Between the Bristol area and Stonehenge (*ca.* 68 km) there is an apparent absence of glacial erratics. The Boles Barrow boulder (*ca.* 19 km west of Stonehenge on the proposed route of glacial movement; *cf.* Figure 6) appears unworked and is consistent with an erratic in appearance, and its likely early date of use (*cf.* above) suggests that it was obtained independently of the Stonehenge bluestones; as such the most obvious explanation for its presence is as a locally available erratic. Other fragments of bluestone on Salisbury Plain without secure archaeological context were noted above.

There is also evidence for removal of erratics from Salisbury Plain during intensification of agriculture in the 18th—19th centuries. De Luc (1811) (reported by Bartenstein and Fletcher 1987 and Thorpe *et al.* in press) made geological observations of the area between 1777 and 1809 and reported "masses of granulated quartz (sarsen? authors' comment) ...... associated with blocks of granite and of trap" (igneous rocks? authors' comment) (de

Luc 1811, 471). He commented on October 11 1809 that "as I approached *Marlborough*, I took particular notice of the state of the agriculture; and I was surprised at seeing what progress it had made since 1805, when last I had passed this way; the ground was all enclosed, and the blocks of *granulated quartz* had entirely disappeared. It will therefore be of advantage for future geologists and especially to those who may pay any attention to Stonehenge, that an account has been given of these blocks still scattered here not more than thirty years ago, and of the progress made since that time, by agriculture, which has thus occasioned their disappearance" (de Luc 1811, 501; original emphasis).

Geinitz (1886) describes similar removal of erratics in Germany, where, he says, the local inhabitants dispose of the stones partly through burial in pits; such a method of disposal may account for the rarity of sarsens in buildings on Salisbury Plain (*cf.* Atkinson 1979, 116). In the Drenthe Plateau of the Netherlands, Bakker and Groenman-van Waateringe (1988) note the difficulty in determining the original distribution of erratics "because the country was stripped of its boulders in historic times" (Bakker and Groenman-van Waateringe *op. cit.*, 146).

Deposition of boulders by an extensive ice sheet such as is proposed for Anglian glaciation of Britain is often sporadic and discontinuous, particularly at the margins of such ice sheets. Thus, for example, the distribution of Scandinavian erratics in the east of England is irregular, with concentrations at Cromer, Norwich and Cambridge (Norwich to Cambridge, *ca.* 100 km) (Phemister 1926, Figure 1; Charlesworth 1957, Figure 129), while North American ice in Dakota has left boulders so dispersed that "in some areas in the outermost, western part of the region (i.e., nearer to the limit of glaciation; authors' comment) one can travel several miles between boulders" (Flint 1955, 85). Such boulders may be deposited without accompanying fine material, (*cf.* Green 1973) as "free boulders" (Flint 1957, 129–130), either derived from nunataks or deposited from clean glacier ice (Flint 1955 in Flint 1957, 129).

In view of this evidence regarding behaviour of ice sheets in erratic dispersal, and of boulder clearance on Salisbury Plain, neither the "gap" in erratics between Bristol and Stonehenge, nor the absence of glacial material in river gravels can be used as evidence against the glaciation of Salisbury Plain.

8. Discussion of evidence for the mode of transport of the bluestones to Stonehenge

We have presented evidence above for the variety of rock types forming the

Stonehenge monoliths, originating at at least eight outcrops (including the Altar stone) dispersed over a distance of at least 10 and perhaps 30 km in south-west Wales. This does not imply selection at a carefully chosen *in situ* source but exploitation of an (already glacially) mixed deposit. The presence of monoliths of structurally poor rock types, the possibility of on site (i.e., at Stonehenge) working of bluestones (*cf.* Judd 1902), the availability of more durable rocks along the proposed human transport route from Wales to Stonehenge (e.g., Mendip, Bath) and the complete absence of evidence for valuing of bluestone in the source area of south Wales all argue against human transport. Antiquarian accounts (de Luc *op. cit.*) indicate the existence of glacial erratics on Salisbury Plain, now removed through agricultural clearance. The presence of bluestone fragments in a wide range of archaeological monuments of varied dates (incorporated casually, not as valued objects) and their finding without clear archaeological context also argue for their local availability as erratics. There is evidence of pre-Wolstonian glaciation at least as far as the Bristol-Bath area, and the present absence (or sporadic occurrence e.g., Boles Barrow) of erratics over the small (68 km) distance between Bristol and Stonehenge is consistent with the irregular dispersal of (free) boulders at the edge of an extensive ice sheet. Glacial erosion also removes preferentially hard, well-jointed rocks such as dolerite (Flint 1957), and this is also reflected in the predominance of dolerites at Stonehenge. All these arguments militate strongly in favour of glacial transport.

In contrast, the evidence in favour of human transport is limited to the account of Geoffrey of Monmouth, which Burl has suggested reflects contemporary knowledge of Irish megaliths rather than a folk memory of bluestone transport (Burl 1985a), and the proposed traffic in axes and Irish metals from or passing near the Preseli source area (*cf.* Atkinson 1979). These (tenuous) links are insufficient evidence for the unique feat of megalith transport proposed.

We conclude from our evidence therefore that the bluestones of Stonehenge were transported to Salisbury Plain by glaciation of the Anglian (*ca.* 400 ka BP) period or earlier.

9. Comment on the sources of the sarsen stones at Stonehenge

Sarsens are the silicified remnants of formerly extensive Cenozoic sedimentary cover within southern England. It has been proposed that the source of the Stonehenge sarsen monoliths lies in the Marlborough Downs some 30 km north of Stonehenge, and this proposal is still widely accepted (e.g., Atkinson 1979, 116; English Heritage Guide to Stonehenge (text by R.J.C. Atkinson)

1987), and elaborate models for the stone transport have been developed (Atkinson 1979, 116–120). Since 16th century writers propose a Marlborough source, (e.g., Lambarde 1580; *cf.* Harington, 1591; reported by Chippindale 1987, 36–37), it seems that at that period large sarsens were not common on Salisbury Plain. Aubrey (1665–1693) also proposes a Marlborough source, noting this area as "being scattered over with them (i.e., sarsens, authors' comment) ..... for about 20 miles in compass" (he does not say in which direction they are scattered). Early illustrations of Stonehenge may be unreliable as factual guides, but the 16th century illustrator 'R.F.' shows boulders around Stonehenge, as do early 19th century artists Fielding and Constable (reproduced in Chippindale 1987, Figure 22, plates VI and VII respectively).

Recent surveys of sarsens in southern England (Bowen and Smith 1977; Summerfield and Goudie 1980) show that there are examples near Stonehenge, including a concentration near Amesbury. These may not now contain stones as large as those in Stonehenge, but neither do the Marlborough deposits (*cf.* Chippindale 1987, 40). The presence at Stonehenge of one sarsen monolith clearly smaller than the others (stone 11) may imply that the builders were indeed exploiting a very limited, almost worked out, supply of large stones.

Summerfield and Goudie (*op. cit.*, 72) note that "the present distribution of sarsens reflects, to a large extent, their removal by man, and those remaining are only a vestige of the numbers in existence prior to man's arrival in Britain". This is consistent with the observations of de Luc noted above, reporting clearance of sarsen ('granulated quartz') boulders from Salisbury Plain in the late 18th and early 19th centuries. No chemical study of the Stonehenge sarsens has yet been done, but heavy mineral analysis carried out by Howard (1982, 119–123) on 5 excavated pieces of sarsen from Stonehenge showed mineralogical differences between these and two pieces from Piggledean in the Marlborough Downs. However, Howard also notes distinctions in thin section between material from two deposits in the Marlborough Downs, so that full interpretation of her data require further sampling, especially of the source material.

The evidence summarised, in particular the widespread occurrence of sarsen in southern England, and accounts of field clearance, suggests that sarsens were locally available for use in Stonehenge. While the tooling and erection of the sarsens gives Stonehenge its predominance in British prehistory, labour-intensive transport of sarsens from the Marlborough Downs was not required.

10. Implications of local availability of the bluestones and sarsens, for Stonehenge and other megalith studies

The conclusion that all the stones of Stonehenge, both bluestones and sarsens, were locally available at or close to the site of monument, necessitates a re-appraisal of estimates of the labour involved in the construction of Stonehenge II and IIIa, for which existing calculations are weighted heavily by assumptions of labour-intensive transport from remote sources (see, for example, Atkinson 1979, 121). The manpower required to build Stonehenge has also been used in the construction of monument 'hierarchies' within prehistoric Wessex (e.g., Renfrew 1983, 12; Startin and Bradley 1981: 292). Renfrew (*op. cit.*) suggests a total input of 30 million man-hours for 'Stonehenge', while Startin and Bradley propose that Stonehenge II required 360,000 man-hours, and Stonehenge IIIa, 1.75 million man-hours. Startin and Bradley (*op. cit.*) note that "we know the approximate source areas for the different stones used at Stonehenge" (*op. cit.*, 290) and this appears to imply that the factor of stone transport is incorporated in their figures. Such estimates now require revision to determine whether the construction of Stonehenge II and IIIa *without* stone transport from remote sources still requires more labour than that needed for monuments e.g., the larger henges.

Long distance transport of stones used in prehistoric megalith construction has been proposed for a number of other sites in the UK (although in no case does the distance proposed approach the 240 km suggested for the Stonehenge bluestones). For example, in the absence of geological study, human transport of *c.* 20 and 10 km has been assumed for the standing stones of Rudston and Boroughbridge (Devils' Arrows) in Humberside and North Yorkshire respectively (e.g., Burl 1979, 286; Dymond 1966). Similarly, transport over 11 km has been suggested for the stone circles of monoliths at Brogar and Stenness in Orkney (*cf.* Collins 1976). Ready acceptance of such proposals may have been influenced by the apparent existence of a parallel at Stonehenge. However, since this parallel can no longer be accepted, the present authors were prompted to re-assess evidence for transport of other megaliths such as those cited above.

This study (full details in Thorpe and Williams-Thorpe 1991) draws evidence from glaciated areas of the UK, Scandinavia, northern Germany and the Netherlands, and non-glaciated areas of France. The use of glacial boulders for megalith construction has been noted in south Wales (Thorpe *et al.* in press), in Ireland (O'Riordain 1965), in England (Thomas 1976), and in southern Scandinavia and northern Germany (Kaelas 1983; Geinitz 1886). In particular, Bakker and Groenman-van Waateringe (1988) point out the correlation between the distribution of Funnel-Necked Beaker (TRB) period megaliths (*hunebedden/hunebeds*) and the glacial boulders of the Drenthe Plateau in the Netherlands. Use of glacially transported blocks, and of locally quarried slabs, can be shown respectively for the Rudston and Borough-bridge stones (Thorpe and Williams-Thorpe 1991), and for the Stenness and Brogar megaliths (*cf.* Collins 1976, 45; Renfrew 1979, 41). Evidence present-ed by Burl (1985b) for Britanny (non-glaciated) shows that stones were transported no more than *ca.* 5 km, and in most cases much less. Evidence from France is extended by the comprehensive study of Mohen (1989) in which the maximum transport recorded is *ca.* 5 km.

Thorpe and Williams-Thorpe (1991) conclude therefore that European megaliths were built of readily available materials and that there is no evidence for megalith transport exceeding *ca.* 5 km, though the form of some monuments requires small scale (1–2 km) re-arrangement of stones (e.g., within the West Kennet Avenue, 2 km in length).

The distribution of megaliths in Arran and Orkney (Rousay) has been used by Renfrew to develop a hypothesis of segmentary society based on territories, each signalled by a megalithic tomb and delimited by Thiessen polygons drawn around that tomb (e.g., Renfrew 1973, 146–156; 1983). Renfrew maintains that 'the construction of these monuments represents a *serious, coherent, indeed patterned activity*' (Renfrew 1983, 9; original emphasis). However, evidence presented above suggests that the siting of megaliths is closely related to or even dictated by, the availability of stone. Bakker and Groenman-van Waateringe (1988, 155) note that for the TRB megaliths of Drenthe 'the presence of boulders dictated the place of the tombs' (*cf.* also O'Riordain 1965, 73: "The availability of suitable building material—especially a great glacial erratic to provide the capstone—without the necessity of long transport could have exercised an influence on the siting of individual tombs"). Bakker and Groenman-van Waateringe (*op. cit.*, 174) also conclude that "nothing was found to show that *hunebeds* lay in the centre of the territories of local communities (as Renfrew suggested for other megalithic landscapes)". It is therefore clear that socio-spatial analysis based on megaliths must be preceded by analysis of the geological sources of the stones and their mechanisms of transport, and consideration of the possible influence of these factors on megalith siting.

11. Conclusions

Chemical analysis of fifteen samples from bluestone monoliths at Stonehenge shows that they derive from seven different outcrops in Preseli (including Carnmenyn) and other parts of south-west Wales, up to 30 km apart. Twenty-two excavated fragments of dolerite and rhyolite from Stonehenge were also analysed, and include some which originate at a further three sources. A sandstone fragment originated not in the Senni or Cosheston Beds, but probably from a Lower Palaeozoic exposure in the Caledonian foldbelt in south-west Wales, while the Altar Stone may derive from the Senni Beds. This variety of source suggests selection from a mixed (glacial) deposit. Igneous rock erratics from south-west Wales have been identified near Cardiff, and other erratics are present in the Bristol Channel (Flatholm) and near Bristol. The apparent gap in erratic distribution between Bristol and Stonehenge is consistent with irregular dispersal of (free) boulders at the edge of ice sheets, and with intensive agricultural clearance of such boulders reported in historical times. This evidence, together with the presence at Stonehenge of structurally poor monoliths, suggests that the bluestones were glacially transported to the present site of Stonehenge, and were not transported by humans. A review of evidence for sarsen distributions and clearance in southern England suggests that these also were available locally, and did not need to be transported from the Marlborough Downs as has been proposed. The conclusion that all the Stonehenge monolith stones were available locally necessitates re-assessment of calculations of the labour required for the construction of the monument. A study of other European megaliths shows that there is no evidence for transport of any megalith stone over more than *ca.* 5 km, and the availability of stone, particularly as erratics, may influence the siting of megaliths. This means that hypotheses of social organisation based on megalith distribution are not meaningful unless the geological constraints on their siting are first considered.

Acknowledgements

The work on the Stonehenge bluestones was supported by Open University Research Committee Grant HG60 1601 343 which we gratefully acknowledge. Fieldwork in Wales was supported by the Department of Earth Sciences, Open University. We thank English Heritage, Department of the Environment, for permission to sample bluestones at Stonehenge, and Mr. Brian Davison, Professor M. Tite and Dr. C. Price for their help with this. Sampling was carried out by Mr. Ian Chaplin and an English Heritage stonemason. We thank Dr. J. Richards for unpublished information on bluestone finds on Salisbury Plain. For helpful comment and information on archaeological aspects of the work we thank Professor R.J.C. Atkinson, Professor R. Bradley, Dr. S. Briggs, and Dr. P. Drewett. Dr. G.A. Kellaway kindly allowed us to use unpublished information on bluestone finds at Stonehenge. Dr. H. Kars drew our attention to the work of Bartenstein and Fletcher and hence to de Luc. Dr. R.A. Ixer and Dr. R.G. Thomas respectively provided valuable opaque mineralogical and point counting analyses of Stonehenge dolerite and sandstone samples. For access to samples of excavated material from Stonehenge and the Boles Barrow boulder, we thank Miss Conybeare of the Salisbury and South Wiltshire Museum. For discussion and helpful comment on glaciological aspects of the work we thank Dr. B. John, Professor G.S. Boulton, Dr. C. Turner, Dr. G.A. Kellaway, and Dr. G. Gaunt. Dr. Kellaway also allowed us to refer to unpublished work on glaciation of the southern U.K. Dr. R. Bevins provided unpublished data on the Preseli Hills. Chemical analyses were carried out at the Open University and Universities of Southampton and Keele, and we thank Mr. J.S. Watson, Dr. P.C. Webb, Dr. I. Croudace and Dr. G. Lees for these. For helpful comment on the part of this paper dealing with megaliths outside Salisbury Plain we are grateful to Dr. A. Burl, Professor R. Bradley and Dr. G.D Gaunt. We also thank the anonymous referee for useful comments on the text. Mr. John Taylor and Mr. Andrew Lloyd drew the diagrams, and Mrs. Marilyn Leggett typed the manuscript. All opinions and conclusions expressed in the paper are the responsibility of the authors.

References

Ashbee, P. 1978: Amesbury Barrow 51: Excavations in 1960. *Wiltshire Archaeological and Natural History Magazine* 70/71, 1–60.

Ashbee, P. 1981: Amesbury Barrow 39: Excavation 1960. *Wiltshire Archaeological and Natural History Magazine* 74/75, 3–34.

Atkinson, R.J.C. 1979: *Stonehenge* (Harmondsworth, Penguin).

Aubrey, J. 1665–1693: *Monumenta Britannica* (Sherborne, Dorset Publishing Company) (published 1980).

Bakker, J.A. and Groenman-van Waateringe, W. 1988: Megaliths, soils and vegetation of the Drenthe Plateau. In Groenman-van Waateringe, W. and Robinson, M. (editors), *Man-made Soils* (Oxford, British Archaeological Reports International Series) 143–181.

Bartenstein, H. and Fletcher, B.N. 1987: The Stones of Stonehenge—an ancient observation on their geological and archaeological history. *Zeitschrift für Deutsche Geologische Gesellschaft* 138, 23–32.

Bevins, R.E. 1979. *The Geology of the Strumble Head—Fishguard Region, Dyfed* (Keele, University of Keele PhD Thesis).

Bevins, R.E. 1982: Petrology and geochemistry of the Fishguard Volcanic Complex, Wales. *Geological Journal* 17, 1–21.

Bevins, R.E. and Rowbotham, G. 1983: Low-grade metamorphism within the Welsh sector of the paratectonic Caledonides. *Geological Journal* 18, 141–168.

Bevins, R.E., Kokelaar, B.P. and Dunkley, P.M. 1984: Petrology and geochemistry of lower to middle Ordovician igneous rocks in Wales: a volcanic arc to marginal basin transition. *Proceedings of the Geologists' Association* 95, 337–347.

Bevins, R.E., Lees, G.J. and Roach, R.A. 1989: Ordovician intrusions of the Strumble Head-Mynydd Preseli region, Wales: lateral extensions of the Fishguard Volcanic Complex. *Journal of the Geological Society of London* 143, 113–123.

Bowen, D.Q. 1982: Pleistocene deposits and fluvioglacial landforms of north Preseli. In Bassett,

M.G. (editor), *Geological Excursions in Dyfed, south-west Wales* (Cardiff, National Museum of Wales) 289–296.

Bowen, D.Q. 1989: Amino acid geochronology of landform development in Britain. *Abstracts of the International Geological Congress Washington*, I-186, I-187.

Bowen, D.Q. and Sykes, G.A. 1988: Correlation of marine events and glaciations on the north-east Atlantic margin. *Philosophical Transactions of the Royal Society of London* B318, 619–635.

Bowen, H.C. and Smith, I.F. 1977: Sarsen stones in Wessex: The Society's first investigations in the Evolution of the Landscape project. *The Antiquaries Journal* 57, 185–196.

Briggs, C.S. 1976: Cargos and field clearance in the history of the English Channel. *Quaternary Research Association Newsletter* June 19, 10–16.

Briggs, C.S. 1989: Axe-making traditions in Cumbrian stone. *Archaeological Journal* 146, 1–43.

Burl, A. 1979: *The Stone Circles of the British Isles* (New Haven, Yale University Press).

Burl, A. 1985a: Geoffrey of Monmouth and the Stonehenge bluestones. *Wiltshire Archaeological and Natural History Magazine* 79, 178–183.

Burl, A. 1985b: *Megalithic Brittany* (London, Thames and Hudson).

Burl, A. 1987: *The Stonehenge People* (London, Dent and Sons).

Charlesworth, J.K. 1957: *The Quaternary Era* (2 volumes) (London, Edward Arnold).

Chippindale, C. 1987: *Stonehenge Complete* (London, Thames and Hudson).

Clough, T.H. McK. and Cummins, W.A., 1988: *Stone Axe Studies, Volume 2* (London, Council for British Archaeology Research Report 67).

Collins, G.H. 1976: Appendix 5—Geology of the Stones of Stenness, Orkney. In Ritchie, J.N.G., The Stones of Stenness, Orkney. *Proceedings of the Society of Antiquaries of Scotland* 107, 44–45.

Cunnington, B.H. 1924: The 'Blue Stone' from Boles Barrow. *Wiltshire Archaeological and Natural History Magazine* 42, 431–437.

Cunnington, W. 1884: Stonehenge notes: the fragments. *Wiltshire Archaeological and Natural History Magazine* 21, 141–149.

De Luc, J.A. 1811: *Geological Travels. Volume III. Travels in England* (London, F.C. and J. Rivington).

Donnelly, R., Bevins, R.E. and Thorpe, R.S. In prep.: The Storrie erratic collection: A reappraisal of the status of the Pencoed 'Older Drift' (south Wales).

Drewett, P.L. 1987: An archaeological survey of Mynydd Preseli, Dyfed. *Archaeology in Wales* 27, 14–16.

Dymond, D.P. 1966. Ritual monuments at Rudston, E. Yorkshire, England. *Proceedings of the Prehistoric Society* 32, 86–95.

Engleheart, G. 1933: A second Stonehenge 'Altar' stone? *Wiltshire Archaeological and Natural History Magazine* 46, 395–397.

English Heritage 1987: *Stonehenge and Neighbouring Monuments* (London, English Heritage).

Evans, W.D. 1945: The geology of the Prescelly Hills, north Pembrokeshire. *Quarterly Journal of the Geological Society of London* 101, 89–110.

Evens, E.D., Grinsell, L.V., Piggott, S., and Wallis, F.S. 1962: Fourth report of the sub-committee of the South-Western Group of Museums and Art Galleries on the petrological identification of stone axes. *Proceedings of the Prehistoric Society* 28, 209–266.

Flint, R.F. 1955: *Pleistocene Geology of eastern South Dakota* (United States Geology Survey Professional Paper 262).

Flint, R.F. 1957: *Glacial and Pleistocene Geology* (New York, John Wiley and Sons).

Geinitz, E. 1886: Der Boden Mecklenburgs. In Lehmann, R.C. (editor), *Forschungen zur Deutschen Lands-und Volkskunde, Volume I* (Stuttgart, J. Engelhorn), 1–32.

George, T.N. 1933: The glacial deposits of Gower. *Geological Magazine* 70, 208–232.

Gladney, E.S., and Roelandts, I. 1988: 1987 compilation of elemental concentration data for

USGS BHVO-1, MGA-1, QLO-1, RGM-1, SCo-1, SDC-1, SGR-1, and STM-1. *Geostandards Newsletter* 12, 253–362.

Green, C.P. 1973: Pleistocene river gravels and the Stonehenge problem. *Nature* 243, 214–216.

Harington, J. 1591: *Orlando Furioso in English Heroical Verse* (London, Richard Field).

Hawkins, A.B., and Kellaway, G.A. 1971: Field meeting at Bristol and Bath with special reference to new evidence of glaciation. *Proceedings of the Geologists Association* 82, 267–291.

Hawley, W. 1922: Second report on the excavations at Stonehenge. *Antiquaries Journal* 2, 36–51.

Hawley, W. 1925: Report on the excavations at Stonehenge during the season of 1923. *Antiquaries Journal* 5, 21–50.

Howard, H. 1982: A petrological study of the rock specimens from excavation at Stonehenge, 1979–1980. In Pitts, M.W., On the road to Stonehenge: report on investigations beside the A344 in 1968, 1979 and 1980. *Proceedings of the Prehistoric Society* 48, 104–126.

Hughes, D.J. 1977: *The Petrochemistry of the Ordovician Igneous Rocks of the Welsh Basin* (Manchester, University of Manchester PhD Thesis).

Jenkins, D.G., Beckinsale, R.D., Bowen, D.Q., Evans, J.A., George, G.T., Harris, N.B.W., and Meighan, I.G. 1985: The origin of granite erratics in the Pleistocene Patella beach, Gower, south Wales. *Geological Magazine* 122, 297–302.

John, B.S. 1970a: The Pleistocene drift succession at Porth-Clais, Pembrokeshire. *Geological Magazine* 107, 439–457.

John, B.S. 1970b: Pembrokeshire. In Lewis, C.A. (editor), *The Glaciations of Wales and Adjoining Regions* (London, Longman) 229–265.

Judd, J.W. 1902: Note on the nature and origin of the rock-fragments found in the excavations made at Stonehenge by Mr. Gowland in 1901. In Gowland, W., Recent excavations at Stonehenge, *Archaeologia* 58, 106–118.

Kaelas, L. 1983: Megaliths of the Funnel Beaker culture in Germany and Scandinavia. In Renfrew, C. (editor), *The Megalithic Monuments of Western Europe* (London, Thames and Hudson) 77–91

Kellaway, G.A. 1971: Glaciation and the stones of Stonehenge. *Nature* 232, 30–35.

Kellaway, G.A. (editor) 1991: *Hot Springs of Bath; investigations of the thermal waters of the Avon Valley* (Bath, Bath City Council).

Kokelaar, B.P., Howells, M.F., Bevins, R.E., Roach, R.A., and Dunkley, P.N. 1984: The Ordovician marginal basin of Wales. In Kokelaar, B.P. and Howells, M.F. (editors), *Volcanic and Associated Sedimentary and Tectonic Processes in Modern and Ancient Marginal Basins* (Geological Society of London Special Publication 16) 245–269.

Kokelaar, B.P., Bevins, R.E. and Roach, R.A. 1985: Submarine silicic volcanism and associated sedimentary and tectonic processes, Ramsey Island, south-west Wales. *Journal of the Geological Society of London* 142, 591–613.

Lambarde, W. 1580. *Angliae Topographicum et Historiarum* (London, F. Gyles). (published 1730 from a manuscript of 1580).

Leat, P.T. and Thorpe, R.S. 1986a: Geochemistry of an Ordovician basalt-trachybasalt-subalkaline/peralkaline rhyolite association from the Lleyn Peninsula, N. Wales, U.K. *Geological Journal* 21, 29–43.

Leat, P.T. and Thorpe, R.S. 1986b: Ordovician volcanism in the Welsh borderland. *Geological Magazine* 123, 129–140.

Leat, P.T., Jackson, S.E., Thorpe, R.S. and Stillman, C.J. 1986: Geochemistry of bimodal, basalt-subalkaline/peralkaline rhyolite provinces within the southern British Caledonides. *Journal of the Geological Society of London* 143, 259–273.

Macdonald, R., Davies, G.R., Bliss, C.M., Leat, P.T., Bailey, D.K., and Smith, R.L. 1987: Geochemistry of high-silica peralkaline rhyolites, Naivasha, Kenya Rift Valley. *Journal of Petrology* 28, 978–1008.

Mohen, J-C. 1989: *The World of Megaliths* (London, Cassell).

Newall, R.S. 1959: *Stonehenge* (London, Her Majesty's Stationery Office).

O'Riordain, S.P. 1965: *Antiquities of the Irish Countryside* (London, Methuen).

Petrie, W.M.F. 1880: *Plans, Description, and Theories* (re-published London, Histories and Mysteries of Man Ltd. 1989).

Phemister, J. 1926: The distribution of Scandinavian boulders in Britain. *Geological Magazine* 63, 433–454.

Potts, P.J., Webb, P.C. and Watson, J.S. 1984: Energy-dispersive X-ray fluorescence analysis of silicate rocks for major and trace elements. *X-Ray Spectrometry* 13, 2–15.

Renfrew, C. 1973: *Before Civilisation—The Radiocarbon Revolution and Prehistoric Europe* (Harmondsworth, Penguin).

Renfrew, C. 1979: *Investigations in Orkney.* (London, Reports of the Research Commitee of the Society of Antiquaries of London 38)

Renfrew, C. 1983: Introduction: the megalith builders of western Europe. In Renfrew, C. (editor), *The Megalithic Monuments of Western Europe* (London, Thames and Hudson) 1–17.

Startin, W. and Bradley, R.J. 1981: Some notes on work organisation and society in prehistoric Wessex. In Ruggles, C. and Whittle, A.W.R. (editors), *Astronomy and Society during the Period 4000–1500 BC* (Oxford, British Archaeological Reports British Series 88) 289–296.

Stone, J.F.S. 1948: The Stonehenge cursus and its affinities. *Archaeological Journal* 104, 7–19.

Strahan, A., Cantrill, T.C., Dixon, E.E.L., Thomas, H.H. and Jones, O.T. 1914. *The Geology of the South Wales Coalfield, Part XI, The country around Haverfordwest* (London, His Majesty's Stationary Office).

Summerfield, M.A., and Goudie, A.S. 1980: The sarsens of southern England: their palaeoenvironmental interpretation with reference to other silcretes. In Jones, D. (editor), *The Shaping of Southern Britain* (London, Special Publication of the Institute of British Geographers), 71–100.

Synge, F.M. 1970: The Pleistocene period in Wales. In Lewis, C.A. (editor), *The Glaciations of Wales and Adjoining Regions* (London, Longman) 315–350.

Thomas, H.H. 1923: The source of the stones of Stonehenge. *Antiquaries Journal* 3, 239–260.

Thomas, H.H. and Cox, A.H. 1924: The volcanic series of Trefgarn, Roch, and Ambleston (Pembrokeshire). *Quarterly Journal of the Geological Society of London* 80, 520–548.

Thomas, N. 1976: *A Guide to Prehistoric England* (London, Book Club Associates).

Thomas, R.G. 1978: *The Stratigraphy, Palynology and Sedimentology of the Lower Old Red Sandstone Cosheston Group, South-West Dyfed, Wales,* (Bristol, University of Bristol PhD Thesis).

Thorpe, R.S., Leat, P.T., Bevins, R.E., and Hughes, D.J. 1989: Late-orogenic alkaline/subalkaline Silurian volcanism of the Skomer Volcanic Group in the Caledonides of south Wales. *Journal of the Geological Society of London* 146, 125–132.

Thorpe, R.S. and Williams-Thorpe, O. 1991: The myth of long-distance megalith transport. *Antiquity* 65, 64–73.

Thorpe, R.S., Williams-Thorpe, O., Jenkins, D.G. and Watson, J.S. in press. The geological sources and transport of the bluestones of Stonehenge, Wiltshire, U.K. *Proceedings of the Prehistoric Society.*

Proceedings of the British Academy, **77**, 163–184

Counting Broken Objects:
The Statistics of Ceramic Assemblages

C. R. ORTON & P. A. TYERS

Department of Prehistory, Institute of Archaeology, University College London,
31–34 Gordon Square, London WC1H 0PY.

Summary. To estimate and compare the proportions of different types of pottery in ceramic assemblages ('type' being defined according to need, e.g., functional type, chronological type), archaeologists need a measure of the amount of each type. The most suitable proposed measure is the 'eve' (estimated vessel equivalent), for which each measurable fragment is scored as a fraction of a complete vessel.

The 'Pie-slice' project, funded by SERC-SBAC and the British Academy, uses a new statistical transformation (the 'pseudo-count transformation'), which converts eves into 'pies' (pottery information equivalents), with the property that an assemblage of n pies has the same error structure as one of n complete objects. This enables assemblages to be compared by techniques for categorical data, mainly log-linear and correspondence analyses; reduction of the data matrix is usually needed. Case studies of a variety of problems are presented.

1. The need for quantification

1.1 Introduction

An important part of the archaeological study of pottery is the comparison of assemblages, groups of pottery that in some sense belong together. This can be done at many levels: for example, the pottery from a single context or a feature (e.g., a rubbish pit), from a phase of a site, or from a period in a town. An assemblage can be characterised by its composition, i.e., the proportions of different types of pottery of which it is made up; the definition

Read 13 February 1991. © The British Academy 1992.

of 'type' is flexible and can be chosen to meet particular needs (see below). Assemblages can be compared in terms of their compositions. Different levels of assemblage and different definitions of type can be used to answer different questions, the main sorts of which are chronological, spatial and social/functional.

To be able to characterise assemblages in this way, we need a measure of the amounts of the various types of pottery of which they are comprised. If an assemblage consisted of whole vessels there would be no problem—one could just count the pots. In practice whole vessels are relatively rare and assemblages consist of pottery in varying degrees of fragmentation and survival. Measuring the quantities of different types under these circumstances is the core problem. In section 2 we shall see how it has been approached in the past.

1.2 Chronological questions

It is often assumed that the usage of types of pottery follows a simple continuous and unimodal pattern over time—introduction, increasing usage, steady usage, decreasing usage, demise. If this is so, the relative proportions of types in assemblages which form a chronological sequence at a location will also follow a simple pattern (Figure 1). If the proportions are known but the sequence is not, it can be reconstructed by organising the compositions into this sort of pattern. This is the basis of the technique of seriation, which

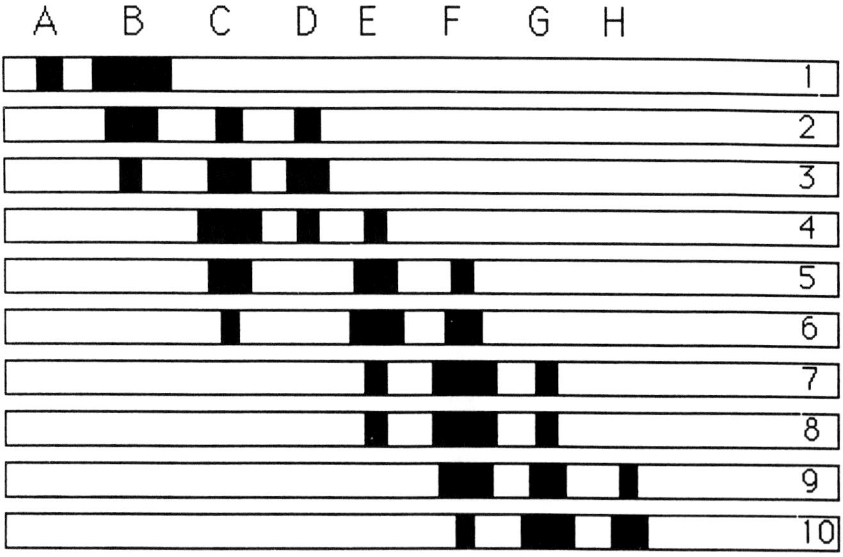

Figure 1. Hypothetical seriation of the proportions of types A-H in contexts 1–10.

is of great value in archaeological research, although its assumptions are sometimes challenged (see Marquardt 1978 for a review; the definitive work is likely to be Laxton, forthcoming).

1.3 Spatial questions

If a type of pottery is traded or distributed from a centre of production, the proportion of it that one would expect to find in assemblages decreases as we move away from the centre. The rate and shape of this fall-off can be interpreted in terms of the methods of distribution and marketing (Hodder and Orton 1976, 104–119). The problem can be studied from either end, (i) looking at the distribution of a particular type or ware across a region (e.g., Lyne and Jefferies 1979, Figures 42–53) or (ii) looking at all the sources of pottery found at a location (e.g., Green 1980, Figures 42–45).

1.4 Social/functional questions

On all but the smallest sites, different parts may have been used for different purposes, e.g., cooking and eating. This may be reflected in the usage of different types of pottery, and, if methods of rubbish disposal were localised, in the archaeological record (e.g., rubbish pits). This approach formed the basis of Millett's (1979a) study of pit-groups from the late Roman fort of Portchester. On a wider scale, social differences within a town might be reflected in differences between assemblages from different parts of the town. There has been surprisingly little work of this nature; a good example is Redman's (1979) work at Qsar es-Seghir.

1.5 Summary

In all these circumstances, which use different levels of assemblage and definitions of types, there is a need for a measure which can be used to determine the proportions of the types, and to compare them between assemblages. In the next section we shall look at various measures that have been proposed, and attempts that have been made to compare them.

2. Previous work

2.1 The initial phase

The first use in the field was seriation (Petrie 1899). Its application to quantified assemblages of pottery started in the USA nearly twenty years later (Spier 1916). Comparisons were made in terms of numbers of fragments of each type (the sherd count), because this was the level at which pottery was generally studied in the USA at that time. Techniques developed through to the 1960's (e.g., Ford 1962), but the use of sherd counts was not challenged.

Realisation that even apparently 'coarse' wares could be distributed over wide areas came in the 1930's (e.g., Shepard 1942), but it was not until the 1960's and '70s that quantified distributional studies became common (e.g., Peacock 1977). No great attention was paid to the question of measures; for example, even the often-quoted work of Fulford and Hodder (1974) relied on sherd counts.

2.2 Competing measures

Part of the revolution that occurred in pottery studies around 1960 (Orton *et al.* forthcoming) was the opening-up of the question of measures and the emergence of rivals to the ubiquitous sherd count. The first alternatives were number of vessels represented (Burgh 1959) and weight (Solheim 1960), followed by vessel-equivalents (the idea can be found in Bloice 1971 and Egloff 1973; the term was coined in Orton 1975—see below for definition), surface area (Glover 1972, 93–6; Hulthén 1974) and displacement volume (Hinton 1977). The last two are very similar to weight, and need no explanation; the term 'vessel-equivalent' may be less familiar. Starting from the idea that every sherd is a certain proportion of the whole pot of which it once formed part, we can (in theory) assign these proportions to sherds as 'scores' and add them up to find the total amount of a type. Since a whole pot would give a score of 1, we can say that a group of sherds with a total score of x is equivalent to x pots (x is usually not a whole number). In practice it is not usually possible to assign a score to every sherd, and one is restricted to sherds such as rim sherds whose size can be measured in terms of the proportion of some whole (e.g., a complete rim). Since we are sampling the measurable sherds from an assemblage, we refer to the estimated vessel equivalent (abbreviated to eve).

2.3 Comparisons

Once there was more than one measure, attempts were made to compare them. Glover (1972, 96), comparing sherd count, weight and surface area, concluded that "any one would be quite accurate as a measure of frequency". Hinton (1977) compared sherd count, rim sherd count, weight and displacement volume, concluding that weight was the fastest but sherd count probably the most accurate measure, but of what it is not clear. Millett (1979b) compared sherd count, weight, adjusted weight (an estimate of surface area) and minimum number of vessels; he concluded that they were all highly correlated but, for practical reasons, weight was probably the best.

The development of our view can be traced in a series of papers (Orton 1975; Orton 1982; Orton and Tyers 1990). These studies have ruled out sherd count and number of pots as biased, and favour eves (where practicable) with weight as a respectable but less useful measure.

3. The pie-slice project

3.1 History of the project

Our work on this topic (Orton 1975; 1982) had achieved some results, but had ended in frustration because of its inability to attach standard deviations to estimates of proportions of types, and hence to test the significance of observed differences between assemblages. The publication of the CODA technique (Aitchison 1986) seemed to offer a way out of the impasse, and a two-year project, the Statistical Analysis of Ceramic Assemblages, started in 1988 with the theoretical aims of:

i) being able to set confidence limits on the proportions of a ceramic assemblage that belong to different types,

ii) being able to compare, numerically and graphically, the compositions of two or more assemblages in terms of the proportion of each type present in each assemblage, and to assess the statistical significance of the differences between them, and

iii) the practical aim of applying the theory to assemblages from a wide range of sites, of different types and periods, to assist in their interpretation, and hence the interpretation of the sites themselves. It was expected that the work would lead to recommendations about the recording of ceramic assemblages, and that CODA would be heavily used. The fortuitous non-availability of the CODA package at the start of the project led to the development of a new approach, described below, which made CODA unnecessary for pottery assemblages.

3.2 Basic theory

The numbers of records of the jth type in an assemblage is denoted by m_j, $(j = 1, \ldots, T)$, and the total number of records by m.

The measure of the ith record of the assemblage is denoted by w_i, $(i = 1, \ldots, m)$.

The total measure of a type is denoted by W_j $(j = 1, \ldots, T)$, and the overall total by W (note that upper case is used for type and assemblage totals, and lower case for individual values).

The symbol $\sim j$ refers to all types except the jth, and Σ_j means summation over the jth type.

The unadjusted sum of squares $\Sigma_j w_i^2$ is denoted by S_j^2.

3.2.1 Estimates of proportions in a single assemblage

The proportion p_j is estimated by:

$$\hat{p}_j = W_j/W, \text{ for } j = 1, \ldots, T.$$

We define two new variables $x(j)$ and $y(j)$ for all records by:

$$x_i(j) = w_i$$

$$y_i(j) = w_i \text{ if the ith record relates to the jth type,}$$

$$= 0 \text{ otherwise.}$$

Then $\hat{p}_j = W_j/W = \Sigma y_i(j)/\Sigma x_i(j)$, a ratio estimate.

Cochran (1963, 30–1) gives a formula for the variance of a ratio estimate, leading to:

$$\text{var}(\hat{p}_j) \approx (m/(m - 1)W^4)\{W_{\sim j}^2 S_j^2 + W_j^2 S_{\sim j}^2\} \tag{1}$$

and:

$$\text{cov}(\hat{p}_j, \hat{p}_k) = -(m/(m - 1)W^4)\{WW_j S_k^2 + WW_k S_j^2 - W_j W_k S^2\} \tag{2}$$

3.2.2 Comparing proportions in two or more assemblages

Given any type j, we can compare $\text{var}(\hat{p}_j)$ with the variance of an estimate based on a binomial model, i.e., on an assemblage of complete vessels.

In the latter case, the formula is $\text{var}'(\hat{p}_j) = \hat{p}_j \hat{q}_j/n$, for a population of size n, where $\hat{q}_j = 1 - \hat{p}_j$.

So the variances would be the same if $\text{var}(\hat{p}_j) = \hat{p}_j \hat{q}_j/n$.

We can turn this round and define $n_j = \hat{p}_j \hat{q}_j/\text{var}(\hat{p}_j)$, so that n_j is the number of whole vessels that would give the same value of $\text{var}(\hat{p}_j)$ as our sample of m measurable records.

The full formula is:

$$n_j = ((m - 1)/m)W_j W_{\sim j} W^2/\{W_{\sim j}^2 S_j^2 + W_j^2 S_{\sim j}^2\} \tag{3}$$

The weakest condition so far found for n_j to be the same for all j is that $S_j^2/W_j = c$ for all j, which is satisfied if all types have the same mean and variance of w. In this case we pool our estimates of the mean and sum of squares of w, obtaining W/m and S^2 respectively, and replace W_j by $W(m_j/m)$, S_j^2 by $S^2(m_j/m)$. So:

$$n_j = ((m - 1)/m)(m_j/m)(m_{\sim j}/m)W^4/\{W^2(m_{\sim j}/m)^2 S^2(m_j/m)$$

$$+ W^2(m_j/m)^2 S^2(m_{\sim j}/m)\}$$

$$= ((m - 1)/m)W^2/\{(m_{\sim j}/m)S^2 + (m_j/m)S^2\}$$

$$= ((m - 1)/m)W^2/S^2 \tag{4}$$

So that if all the types have the same mean and variance of w, we can by pooling estimates obtain a common value $n = n_j$ for all j.

We now have the background theory we need to look at the comparison of several assemblages, say A of them.

We have vectors of measures $\{W_{r1}, \ldots, W_{rT}\}$,

of numbers of observations $\{m_{r1}, \ldots, m_{rT}\}$,

of sums of squares $\{S_{r1}^2, \ldots, S_{rT}^2\}$,

and estimates of proportions $\{\hat{p}_{r1}, \ldots, \hat{p}_{rT}\}$,

and variance-covariance matrices $\| \text{cov}(\hat{p}_{rj}, \hat{p}_{rk}) \|$,

for all $1 \leqslant r \leqslant A$.

We want to compare the vectors of estimated proportions, e.g., to test a hypothesis H_o : all assemblages are 'the same', i.e., can be thought of as samples from the same parent population.

We assume that each assemblage has a single n-value, which we call n_r, for $1 \leqslant r \leqslant A$.

We replace each W_{rj} by $n_r(W_{rj}/W_r)$, for $j = 1, \ldots, T$ and $r = 1, \ldots, A$.

Calling the new numbers $W'_{rj} = (n_r/W_r)W_{rj}$,

we have $W'_r = n_r$ for all assemblages r.

The estimates of proportions are unchanged:

$$\hat{p}'_{rj} = W'_{rj}/W'_r = W_{rj}/W_r = \hat{p}_{rj},$$

and so are their variances and covariances:

$$\begin{aligned} \text{var}(\hat{p}'_{rj}) &= (m/(m - 1))(S_r'^2/W_r'^2)(m_{rj}/m_r)(m_{r\sim j}/m_r) \\ &= (m/(m - 1))(S_r^2/W_r^2)(m_{rj}/m_r)(m_{r\sim j}/m_r) \\ &= \text{var}(\hat{p}_{rj}), \end{aligned}$$

since $S_r'^2 = (n_r/W_r)^2 S_r^2$ and $W_r'^2 = (n_r/W_r)^2 W_r^2$.

And:

$$\begin{aligned} \text{cov}(\hat{p}'_{rj}, \hat{p}'_{rk}) &= (m/(m - 1))(S_r'^2/W_r'^2)(m_{rj}/m_r)(m_{rk}/m_r) \\ &= (m/(m - 1))(S_r^2/W_r^2)(m_{rj}/m_r)(m_{rk}/m_r) \\ &= \text{cov}(\hat{p}_{rj}, \hat{p}_{rk}) \end{aligned}$$

for the same reason.

Recalling (4) and writing $m_{rj}/m_r \approx \hat{p}_{rj}$, etc., since the assemblages are homogeneous, we have:

$$\text{var}(\hat{p}_{rj}) \approx \hat{p}_{rj}\hat{q}_{rj}/n_r$$

and

$$\text{cov}(\hat{p}_{rj}, \hat{p}_{rk}) \approx \hat{p}_{rj}\hat{p}_{rk}/n_r \ .$$

But these are exactly the same as the variance and covariances we would obtain from a multinomial distribution with parameter p and sample size n.

This is a very important result. It means that, as a large-sample approximation, we can treat the transformed data as a series of samples from multinomial distributions. We can therefore treat the data collectively as a contingency table, and use any of the theory appropriate to contingency tables (e.g., log-linear models or correspondence analysis; Greenacre 1984).

For the first time, this approach enables to make proper statistical comparisons between the proportions of different types in different assemblages. We refer to the transformed values W'_{rj} as pseudo-counts. They are not integers, but can be treated for statistical purposes as if they were. We call the transformation expressed in equation (4) the 'pseudo-count transformation' (pct), the numbers n_j 'pseudo-counts' (because they behave like counts but are not integers), and the total n the 'pseudo-total'. When applied to pottery the pseudo-counts are called 'pies' (pottery information equivalents) because one pie contains as much information (in the statistical sense) as one whole pot.

3.2.3 Log-linear and quasi-log-linear analysis

Suppose we have a three-way (context-by-fabric-by-form) table of pseudo-counts **n**. To follow the standard notation (e.g., Fienberg 1977) we replace n by x, with subscripts i, j and k for three variables, usually context, fabric and form respectively. Context is treated as an explanatory variable, and fabric and form as response variables. We can construct nested models of increasing complexity and archaeological reality, from complete independence at one extreme to the saturated model at the other. The intermediate models correspond to different archaeological needs:-

   i) the common (but not universal) situation of different forms being produced in different fabrics,

   ii) a functional approach, in which the primary source of variation between contexts is thought to be function, represented by different proportions of the different forms present,

   iii) a spatial (inter-site) or chronological approach, in which the primary source of variation between contexts is thought to be the sources of the pottery, representing either geographical or temporal variation (or both).

Within each model, we can calculate the estimates $\hat{m}_{ijk}$ and carry out a goodness-of-fit test, using the likelihood ratio statistics $G^2(1)$, $G^2(2)$, $G^2(3)$, $G^2(4)$, where (Bishop *et al.* 1975, 125):

$$G^2 = 2\Sigma x \log(x/\hat{m}).$$

This approach enables us to find the simplest model that fits the data reasonably.

Unfortunately, there are many fabric-by-form combinations that cannot exist, and many fabric-by-context and form-by-context ones that do not exist in a particular dataset. The design of the data is incomplete, and the theory of quasi-log-linear models (Bishop *et al.* 1975, 177–228) must be used. This theory raises important and difficult questions about which zeros are structural and which are random, which also have crucial implications for the calculation of the number of degrees of freedom.

We have looked at three approaches to the problem of which zeros should be treated as structural:-

i) treat all zeros as random, i.e., use log-linear models [2.5]. This leads to high numbers of degrees of freedom, and a situation in which almost any model would fit the data [3.4] (references in square brackets are to sections of the archival report *Statistical Analysis of Ceramic Assemblages*; see Section 3.4).

ii) treat zeros as structural if they correspond to a zero in a marginal two-way table [2.6.5]. This approach ('conditioning on all the data') gives realistic degrees of freedom but obscures the points which may be of most interest archaeologically.

iii) treat zeros as structural if they correspond to a zero in a marginal two-way table which has already been shown to relate to a significant interaction ('conditioning on the model' [2.6.2]). This gives rise to fewer degrees of freedom than (i) but more than (ii); more importantly, it seems to correspond most closely to archaeological reality. It does however seem prone to trouble from sparse datasets (see below).

3.3 Problems

Two main problem areas which require a theoretical response have been encountered: (i) inhomogeneity and (ii) sparseness.

3.3.1 Inhomogeneity

Inhomogeneity occurs when not all types in an assemblage have the same distribution of w. There are two situations in which it is likely to arise: the first depends on site formation processes and the second on the nature of the types.

If the post-depositional history of pottery is seen as a series of 'events', at each of which further breakage and dispersal may occur, then w̄ decreases (weakly) at each event. Types which have had a longer post-depositional history are likely to have a smaller w̄, which in principle identifies them. This has long been known intuitively in archaeology and is known as residuality; for most comparative purposes it is useful to be able to isolate any residual types.

This argument rests on the assumption that all types break equally readily and at the same rate. In practice this is not the case, and we can identify types which are more resistant to breakage than the usual run of types. They are usually small and/or thick-walled or (if we are measuring rims) have a small rim diameter, e.g., flagons. We call them 'chunky' types. Their inclusion in an assemblage boosts both w̄ and S^2 unrealistically; we have therefore developed a technique for adjusting for chunkiness [2.4].

Inhomogeneity seems to be a manageable problem. The latter sort is identified by unusually high values of w̄ and can be allowed for statistically. The former is identified by unusually low values. We have devised an approach which should accommodate this effect (the 'hinged' contingency table) and intend to implement it in phase 2 of the project. Identifying either sort requires a multiple comparison method; unexpectedly, the most satisfactory was one of the earliest: Fisher's least significant difference (LSD) test (1935).

3.3.2 Sparseness

Even when using quasi-log-linear analysis, we encounter problems because of the many 'small' cells in the table. They are:

i) if there are many such cells, they may contribute greatly to the number of degrees of freedom, but little to the overall X^2 or G^2 statistic, thus masking any potential significance of other parts of the table,

ii) the presence of a very small expected value together with a positive observed value can give an abnormally high contribution to the X^2 or G^2 statistic.

The answer seems to be merge or delete rows and/or columns of the table to remove small cells. We adopted the criterion that all cells should have an expected value of at least 1.0 (see Craddock and Flood 1970), and devised a technique called 'simultaneous reduction of dimension' (srd) to achieve this aim (Orton and Tyers 1991). At present, use of this technique may cause problems in the interpretation of any subsequent analysis because it affects significance levels; this will be tackled in phase 2 of the project.

3.4 The present situation

In the interval between the two phases of the project (September 1990 to April 1991) we can stop and take stock. We have available:

i) a computer package written in C and running in 'command-line' style over Unix on 80386-based micros. It has three main elements—the pseudo-count transformation (pct), the simultaneous reduction of dimension (srd) and the quasi-log-linear analysis (qlla). It makes use of the correspondence analysis program (ca) in the iastats package (Duncan *et al.* 1988).

ii) computer-based catalogues of ceramics from Roman, medieval and post-medieval sites in Chelmsford*, Lambaesis (Algeria)*, London, Silchester basilica, Winchester, Worcester (urban sites), Usk (military site), Ewell (Surrey), Leicestershire*, Witham (Essex)* (rural sites) and Southwark* (kiln site). Funding for the computerisation of catalogues from the sites marked with a * was provided by the British Academy.

iii) an archival report on the project, including case-studies on sites in London, Silchester, Winchester, Usk and Ewell.

Dr. Tyers worked in France from January to April 1991, applying Pie-slice to assemblages of Roman pottery from various sites.

3.5 Future work

Three main theoretical tasks and one practical one face us in phase 2. The theoretical ones are:

i) extension of our current 'large-sample' theory to 'small-sample' problems. This is likely to require monte carlo methods and should yield information on the minimum size of a viable dataset.

ii) the treatment of inhomogeneous assemblages of the first sort defined in Section 3.3.1.

iii) most seriously, the interface between srd and qlla and ca needs attention. The use of srd to merge categories carries the risk of altering the real significance levels of tests carried out in subsequent qlla, making the differences between groups appear more significant than they actually are. There are also problems in combining archaeological and statistical criteria in decisions about merging categories. The answer to both is probably to make srd more flexible and to move away from an over-riding strictly hypothesis-testing approach.

The practical problem is to make this work accessible to ordinary archaeologists working on pottery, through the creation of a 'friendly front-end' running in a windowing environment such as Open Desktop.

4. Case studies

4.1 Introduction

The uses made of the datasets have been at four levels:

i) checking the operation of the programs,

ii) answering specific technical questions, e.g., on structural zeros,

iii) searching for the appropriate level of aggregation of fabrics, forms and assemblages for different questions,

iv) producing interpretable results for discussion with the originators of the datasets.

Artificial datasets have also been used to help with i) and ii). Questions at levels ii) and iii) are discussed elsewhere in this paper, as they arise. Here we concentrate on level iv) but are inhibited by the need to maintain confidentiality of unpublished data. We shall look at the results thematically rather than site-by-site.

4.2 Chronological patterns

So far, these have dominated our analyses, especially of the late pre-Roman and Roman periods. It is well known (see Madsen 1988, 24) that a chronological sequence should be represented by a 'horse-shoe' shaped curve (approximately a parabola) on a correspondence analysis plot. We have observed such patterns at Usk (AD 55–70), Lime Street, London (AD 70–160), and Silchester (*c*.15 BC–AD 60). Perhaps more interesting than the expected horse-shoe were the deviations from it:

i) at Lime Street, 'rag-bag' categories (e.g., 'fine imported wares') occupy locations well off the curve, towards the centre, because they are an amalgam of types of different dates,

ii) at Silchester, context-groups with apparently high proportions of residual material also lie off the inside of the curve, towards the 'early' end.

4.2.1 Lime Street [7.3]

Comparison of fabrics with phases gave an apparently horse-shoe-shaped curve (Figure 2), with fabric SHEL (shell-tempered ware) early in the sequence and BB1, BB2 (black-burnished wares) and MORT (mortaria) late in the sequence indicated by the ordering of the phases, but with most of the points bunched in the apex of the curve.

The removal of SHEL opens up the curve (Figure 3). Phase 1 (which has

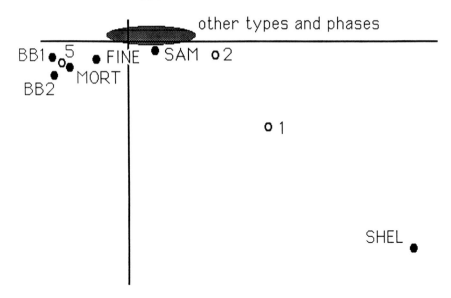

Figure 2. Correspondence analysis plot of fabric against phase, Lime Street site, City of London.

become very small by the removal of SHEL) and phase 6 (always very small and possibly residual) are out of sequence, but the major phases (3, 4 and 5) are in the 'right' order. The fabric FINE IMP now stands out from the curve; its removal would open out the curve.

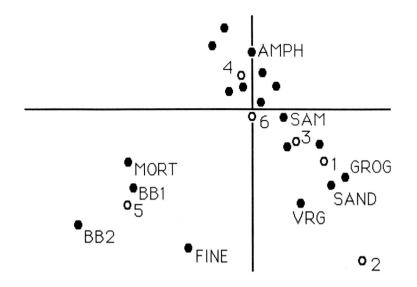

Figure 3. As figure 2, with fabric SHEL removed.

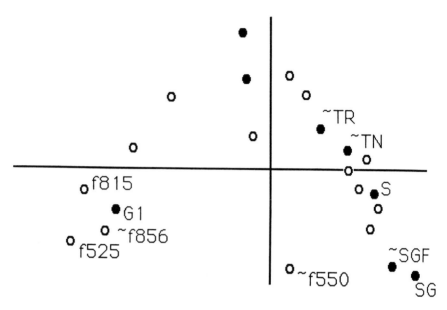

Figure 4. Correspondence analysis plot of fabric against feature-group, Silchester basilica site.

4.2.2 Silchester basilica [7.2]

In the period to which the data relate, both forms and fabrics changed rapidly, with many introductions of new types. In the ca plot (Figure 4) the features and fabrics are arranged in a horse-shoe-shaped curve suggesting a broadly chronological progression. The 'early' end of the curve would be fabric G1 (the 'Belgic' grog-tempered wares) and feature groups ~f856, f525 and f815. They include most of the phase 1 and phase 2 deposits. The 'later' part of the curve includes the sequence ~ TR, ~ TN, and SG which would be the expected order of introduction for the fine ware fabrics terra rubra, terra nigra and South Gaulish samian.

The group ~f550 lies towards the centre of the curve and has a slight positive residual on fabric G1—the 'early' grog-tempered ware. This may suggest a higher proportion of residual material in these contexts.

4.3 Spatial patterns

The opportunity to investigate spatial patterns between sites has not yet arisen, but we intend to compare Chelmsford and Witham (Essex), and possibly some of the Leicestershire sites, in phase 2 of the project. It might be possible to compare Ewell (Surrey) with a London site, but it would be difficult to find a site that matches chronologically. Within-site analyses are considered under functional/social patterns (see below).

4.4 Functional/social patterns

We had hoped to observe such patterns on the Silchester and Aldgate, London (17th-18th century) sites. At Silchester we have so far been unsuccessful, because any such pattern seems to be masked by chronological changes in the forms available.

At Aldgate [7.4] there are four main types of feature—cesspits, cellars, make-up layers and structural features (e.g., foundation trenches)—at least one of which could be expected to correlate with the pottery. Although the obvious association of chamber pots with cesspits was detected, and a further one (cups and dishes with some make-up layers) was suggested, the results on the whole were difficult to interpret. Contexts tended to be grouped with contexts from other features rather than with other contexts from the same feature. While this could arise if several pits or cellars were open simultaneously and receiving contemporary material, this interpretation seems to be optimistic. Examination of the published functional typology (Orton and Pearce 1984, 63) shows that in this example broad categories of form cannot be simply equated with function, since the function of (for example) a bowl depends on whether it is decorated or not—information that is not available in this analysis.

It was the medieval tenements at Brook Street, Winchester [7.5], that gave the clearest indications of this sort of patterning. A preliminary analysis of forms by 'final phases' (phases within buildings) showed a three-way opposition between cooking-pots, jugs and lamps, with bowls (including bowl/dish and bowl/jar) occupying a central, roughly neutral, position (Figure 5). The final phases that can be linked with these forms through the ca show an association of lamps with industrial activity (dyeing, metal-working), jugs with a stone-built house and cooking-pots with less substantial houses. The interpretation of these results is at an early stage and must be seen as provisional.

4.5 Discussion

It is clear that the statistical analyses are not a panacea, and make careful archaeological preparation and interpretation more, rather than less, necessary. The definitions of fabrics, forms and assemblages, and their grouping into larger units for specific purposes (see below) have to be carefully thought out. But provided this is done, there does seem to be scope for the detection of patterns which might otherwise have gone unnoticed.

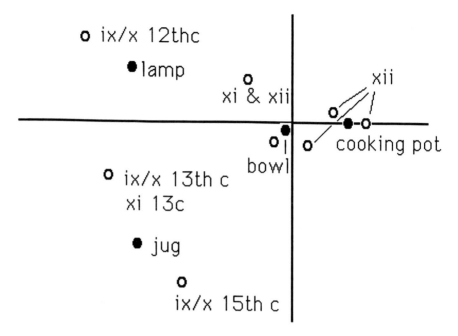

Figure 5. Correspondence analysis plot of form against final phase, Brook Street site, Winchester.

5. Implications for pottery studies

5.1 Recording methods

In Section 3.2, we saw that the weakest condition for the existence of a pseudo-total n was that:

$$S_j^2/W_j = c \text{ for all types j;}$$

this seems to mean in practice that all types should have the same mean and variance of the measure w. Of the four measures considered in Section 2.2, only vessel-equivalents and number of vessels represented meet this requirement; weight could do so if it were possible to scale all types to a common weight (thus becoming an alternative estimate of the vessel-equivalent—the standardised weight approach). Earlier work (Orton 1975; see Section 2.3) has shown that number of vessels represented has serious and unpredictable biases; the only suitable measure is the vessel-equivalent or its estimate, the eve.

There remains the question of the best way to estimate the vessel-equivalent. The most commonly-used is the rim-eve, but other approaches should always be considered. When the necessary information is available, the standardised weight (see above) is likely to give a very good estimate.

The amount of pottery comprising the individual record is very important. Strictly, if we are to use the pct and subsequent statistical theory, each record should contain the measure of all measurable sherds of the same pot in the same assemblage (the 'measurable sherd family'). If one family is divided between two or more records (the 'over-detailed record'), the theory is not applicable because the observations are not independent. If two or more families make up the same record (the 'conflated record') the theory may be used but the variances are inflated. In practice, we can tolerate a low level of the occurrence of either of these problems [4.2.2]. Nevertheless, when recording pottery archaeologists should strive to achieve the 'one measurable sherd family per record' rule.

5.2 Definitions of fabrics, forms and assemblages

Throughout this work, there has been a tension between the need to aggregate data to make datasets acceptable for statistical purposes, and the need to maintain a fine enough level of detail for useful archaeological interpretation. In general, it is likely that some grouping of both fabrics and forms, as defined by conventional archaeological methods, will be needed before statistical analysis can be undertaken. It is probably better, if it is possible, to form preliminary groupings on archaeological criteria before starting the statistical analysis.

In a chronological study it will usually be necessary to incorporate other sorts of evidence, especially stratigraphy and direct dating evidence, such as coins and C14 dates. The combining of different sorts of data in a chronological study is a topic in itself, and is beyond the scope of this project. Nevertheless, we offer some general guidelines, while aware that they may need to be over-ruled in some practical situations:

i) forms should where possible be grouped according to style or decoration, as these are the aspects most likely to reflect chronological change.

ii) it may make sense to group fabrics according to source and, if possible, phases within sources.

If, however, we are looking for spatial (inter-site) differences, we should concentrate on groups of fabrics based on source. Groupings of forms may not be possible unless forms distinctive of sources can be identified.

A search for functional or social differences demands a third approach. A grouping of fabrics according to technological aspects might be more appropriate, e.g., fine and coarse wares, or perhaps a finer division based on the degree of tempering. Forms should be grouped into functional types, e.g., cooking pots, drinking vessels.

This discussion shows that no one typology, of fabrics or of forms, will serve for all purposes. The recorder is faced with a dilemma—which to use for the basic recording of the pottery? The ultimate uses of the data will not be known at the time of recording, and it seems undesirable to strait-jacket the data by immediately-perceived needs. The answer is to record in as fine a level of detail as is possible within the resources available, and to indicate ways in which types may be grouped for different purposes. The same data can then be analysed in different ways according to the groupings employed.

Just as for fabrics and forms, there is scope for choosing different groupings of assemblages to meet different needs. If chronology is the main concern, grouping contexts into stratigraphic phases will make sense. For inter-site spatial analysis, aggregation to site-groups is an obvious choice, but has a pitfall if sites are not exactly contemporaneous. Different proportions of different fabrics on the sites may then represent chronological as well as spatial differences. Grouping by phase within site may then be a safer option. To look for functional differences, groupings should be based on the supposed 'function' of contexts, though there is a danger of circular argument here, and a finer level of detail may be safer. Social differences may be marked by differences between assemblages at the level of individual buildings or features (e.g., pits or associated groups of pits).

On any site, there is likely to be more than one such need. Pottery should therefore be recorded according to the finest level of stratigraphic detail (usually the context), with indications of which groupings of contexts would be appropriate for particular purposes. It may be desirable to sub-divide extensive layers spatially (e.g., by grid squares), but this should not be seen as an endorsement of 'digging by spits', which can wreck an attempt at ceramic analysis.

To merge assemblages is to run the risk of breaking the rule set out in Section 5.1, if the same vessels are present in two or more of the groups. However, the situations in which the extent of such 'cross-joining' is so great as to cause serious problems seem to be rare [4.4.1].

6. The broader picture

6.1 Application to other classes of find

In principle the theory could be applied to any class of find which occurs in quantity and usually in broken form—to so-called 'bulk finds' such as animal bones and building materials (brick, tile, etc.). Classes which are not usually broken can be studied as categorical data without the need for a transformation.

The question is most often raised in the context of animal bone studies. It is tempting to equate the whole animal with the whole pot and to look for 'animal equivalents' to correspond to eves in the way that the MNI (minimum number of individuals) statistic corresponds to the 'minimum number of vessels' statistic sometimes used as a lower bound for the number of vessels represented. The analogy, we believe, breaks down because the use of eves depends on the implicit assumption that different parts of the same broken pot are not selectively discarded—which is known not to apply to different parts of the same animal. However, an analogy might be possible at the level of the individual bone, which itself is often broken. One could then use the pct to set up a three-way table of bone name, species and context, and use qlla as before.

Building material, especially tile, seems to be a more promising candidate. Tiles are almost always found broken and can readily be "eve'd", either by standardised weight or counting corners. The standardised nature of the product means that there may be some difficulty in establishing sherd families. However, it seems a worthwhile approach to an otherwise rather intractable class of find.

6.2 Comparison of pottery with other classes of find

Use of the pct enables us to compare and combine pottery assemblages with other classes of finds for which counts are the appropriate level of data, e.g., coins or 'small finds', and to perform for example a joint correspondence analysis. It would be very interesting, for example, to try to integrate pottery into the work done on medieval small finds from Winchester (Biddle *et al.* 1990).

Acknowledgements

This work has been carried out as a two-year research project (October 1988 to September 1990) at University College London Institute of Archaeology, funded by the Science-based Archaeology Committee of the Science and Engineering Research Council (SERC-SBAC) grant GR/E 95873, with additional funding for data entry being provided by the British Academy. These grants enabled Dr P. A. Tyers to be employed for two years as Research Assistant and Mr M. Johnston for two months as Data-entry Assistant, the Principal Investigator being Mr C. R. Orton. A further 18 months' funding has been obtained from SERC-SBAC to cover the period April 1991 to September 1992, to enable the tasks outlined in Section 3.5 to be undertaken. Equipment (principally a Nimbus VX386 microcomputer) is provided by the Prehistory Department of the Institute of Archaeology, and upgraded from the SERC-SBAC grant.

We are very grateful to the following, who have supplied data and much valuable background information:

Aldgate and Lime Street—Department of Urban Archaeology, Museum of London;

Chelmsford, Essex—Mr C. Going, Chelmsford Archaeological Unit;

King William IV, Ewell, Surrey—Nonsuch Antiquarian Society;

Lambaesis, Algeria—Ministry of Culture, Algeria;

Leicestershire rural sites—Leicestershire Museums Service;

Mark Brown Wharf, Southwark—Department of Greater London Archaeology, Museum of London;

Silchester Basilica excavations—Professor M.G. Fulford and Dr J. Timby, Department of Archaeology, University of Reading;

Usk, Gwent—Prof. W.M. Manning, Department of Archaeology, University College Cardiff;

Winchester—Professor M. Biddle and Ms K. Barclay, Winchester Research Unit;

Witham, Essex—Mr C. Wallace, Essex County Council Archaeology Service;

Worcester—County Museum Archaeology Service, Hereford and Worcester Archaeology Service.

We are particularly grateful to Professors M. Biddle and M. Fulford for permission to publish the results relating to Winchester and Silchester respectively. The views and interpretations expressed here are, however, entirely our own.

We have benefited from many discussions with colleagues at the Institute of Archaeology and at Computer Applications in Archaeology Conferences, particularly Nick Fieller and Andy Scott.

References

Aitchison, J. 1986: *The Statistical Analysis of Compositional Data* (London, Chapman and Hall).

Biddle, M., Barclay, K. and Orton, C. 1990: The chronological and spatial distribution of the objects. In Biddle, M. (editor), *Object and Economy in Medieval Winchester* (Oxford, Clarendon Press) 42–73.

Bishop, Y.M.M., Fienburg, S.E. and Holland, P.W. 1975: *Discrete Multivariate Analysis* (Cambridge, Massachussetts Institute of Technology Press).

Bloice, B.J. 1971: Note. In Dawson, G.J. Montague Close Part 2. *London Archaeologist* 1, 250–1.

Burgh, R.F. 1959: Ceramic profiles in the Western Mound at Awotovi, Northeastern Arizona. *American Antiquity* 25, 184–202.

Cochran, W.G. 1963: *Sampling Techniques* (New York, Wiley).

Craddock, J.M. and Flood, C.R. 1970: The distribution of the chi-squared statistic in small contingency tables. *Applied Statistics* 19, 173–81.

Duncan, R.J., Hodson, F.R., Orton, C.R., Tyers, P.A. and Vekaria, A. 1988: *Data Analysis for*

Archaeologists: the Institute of Archaeology Programs (London, University College Institute of Archaeology).

Egloff, B.J. 1973: A method for counting ceramic rim sherds. *American Antiquity* 38, 351–3.

Fienberg, S.E. 1977: *The Analysis of Cross-classified Categorical Data* (Cambridge, Massachusetts Institute of Technology Press).

Fisher, R.A. 1935: *The Design of Experiments* (Edinburgh, Oliver and Boyd).

Ford, J.A. 1962: *A Quantitative Method for Deriving Cultural Chronology* (Washington, Pan American Technical Manual 1).

Fulford, M.G. and Hodder, I.R. 1974: A regression analysis of some late Romano-British fine pottery: a case study. *Oxoniensia* 39, 26–33.

Glover, I.C. 1972: *Excavations in Timor* (Canberra, Australian National University PhD Thesis).

Green, C. 1980: Roman Pottery. In Jones, D.M. *Excavations at Billingsgate Buildings 'Triangle' Lower Thames Street, 1974.* (London, London and Middlesex Archaeological Society Special Paper 4).

Greenacre, M.J. 1984: *Theory and Applications of Correspondence Analysis* (London, Academic Press).

Hinton, D.A. 1977: 'Rudely made earthen vessels' of the twelfth to fifteenth centuries AD. In Peacock, D.P.S. (editor), *Ceramics and Early Commerce* (London, Academic Press) 221–38.

Hodder, I.R. and Orton C.R. 1976: *Spatial Analysis in Archaeology* (Cambridge, Cambridge University Press).

Hulthén, B. 1974: On choice of element for determination of quantity of pottery. *Norwegian Archaeological Review* 7, 1–5.

Laxton, R.R. forthcoming: *Seriation—the Theory and Practice of Chronological Ordering in Archaeology* (Chichester, Wiley).

Lyne, M.A.B. and Jefferies, R.S. 1979: *The Alice Holt/Farnham Roman Pottery Industry* (London, Council for British Archaeology Research Report 30).

Madsen, T. 1988: Multivariate statistics and archaeology. In Madsen, T. (editor), *Multivariate Archaeology* (Aarhus, Jutland Archaeological Society Publications 21) 7–27.

Marquardt, W. 1978: Advances in archaeological seriation. In Schiffer, M.B. (editor), *Advances in Archaeological Method and Theory 1* (New York, Academic Press) 257–314.

Millett, M. 1979a: An approach to the functional interpretation of pottery. In Millett, M. (editor), *Pottery and the Archaeologist* (London, Institute of Archaeology Occasional Publication 4) 35–48.

Millett, M. 1979b: How much pottery? In Millett, M. (editor), *Pottery and the Archaeologist* (London, Institute of Archaeology Occasional Publication 4) 77–80.

Orton, C.R. 1975: Quantitative pottery studies: some progress, problems and prospects. *Science and Archaeology* 16, 30–5.

Orton, C.R. 1982: Computer simulation experiments to assess the performance of measures of quantity of pottery. *World Archaeology* 14, 1–20.

Orton, C.R. and Pearce, J.E. 1984: The Pottery. In Thompson, A., Grew, F. and Schofield, J. Excavations at Aldgate, 1974. *Post-medieval Archaeology* 18, 34–68.

Orton, C.R. and Tyers, P.A. 1990: Statistical analysis of ceramic assemblages. *Archeologia e Calcolatori* 1, 81–110.

Orton, C.R. and Tyers, P.A. 1991: A technique for reducing the size of sparse contingency tables. In Lockyear, K. and Rahtz, S.P.Q. (editors), *Computer Applications and Quantitative Methods In Archaeology 1990* (British Archaeological Reports International Series 565) (Oxford, Tempus Reparatum) 121–126.

Orton, C.R., Tyers, P.A. and Vince, A.G. forthcoming: *Pottery in Archaeology* (Cambridge, Cambridge University Press).

Peacock, D.P.S. (editor) 1977: *Pottery in Early Commerce* (London, Academic Press).

Petrie, W.M.F. 1899: Sequences in prehistoric remains. *Journal of the Royal Anthropological Institute* 29, 295–301.

Redman, C.L. 1979: Description and inference with the late medieval pottery from Qsar es-Seghir, Morocco. *Medieval Ceramics* 3, 63–79.

Shepard, A.O. 1942: *Rio Grande Glaze Paint Ware; a Study Illustrating the Place of Ceramic Technological Analysis in Archaeological Research* (Washington, Carnegie Institute).

Solheim, W.G. 1960: The use of sherd weights and counts in the handling of archaeological data. *Current Anthropology* 1, 325–9.

Spier, L. 1916: An outline for the chronology of Zuni ruins. *Anthropological Papers of the American Museum of Natural History* 18, 207–231.

Archaeological Evidence for Food

Proceedings of the British Academy, **77**, 187–208

The Survival of Food Residues:
New Methods of Analysis, Interpretation
and Application

R. P. EVERSHED, C. HERON,* S. CHARTERS & L. J. GOAD
*Department of Biochemistry, University of Liverpool, P.O. Box 147,
Liverpool L69 3BX, U.K.*

Summary. In order to gain a better understanding of the nature of organic matter of archaeological interest, chemists are faced with the task of characterising a wide range of natural products. Gas chromatography (GC) and combined GC/mass spectrometry (GC/MS) are the methods of choice for the analysis of complex lipid mixtures. Application of these techniques to the investigation of amorphous residues preserved in potsherds would appear to hold considerable promise for use in studies of diet and vessel function. Modern capillary GC columns achieve complex mixture separation of a wide range of compound classes, e.g., intact acyl lipids, free fatty carboxylic acids, sterols and hydrocarbons. Computerised data-handling techniques are essential for processing the large amount of gas chromatographic and mass spectral data which arises from potsherd analyses. A large number of potsherds are being analysed in an effort to investigate patterns of vessel usage. The characteristic compounds, or groups of compounds that are revealed correspond to 'markers' or 'indicators', and provide a 'fingerprint' that can be used chemotaxonomically, to deduce the nature of foodstuffs associated with ceramic vessels and classify vessel function. Interpretations are supported by the analysis of lipid extracts of contemporary foodstuffs, and by the results of degradation and cooking simulation experiments.

* Current address: Department of Archaeological Sciences, University of Bradford, Bradford BD7 1DP, UK.
Read 14 February 1991. © The British Academy 1992.

1. Introduction

Insights into the diets of early societies can be gained, indirectly, from cultural evidence (artefacts related to food procurement, preparation and consumption) and human skeletal remains (Gilbert and Mielke 1985). However, more direct evidence for dietary constituents derives from the identification of intact plant and animal remains, e.g., charred seeds and grain, pollen and animal bone (Dimbleby 1978; Parmalee 1985; Carbone and Keel 1985). This approach inevitably introduces a bias toward more durable materials, with the result that the question of 'missing foods' exist in many attempts to characterise dietary components (Hall 1987; Hillman 1989). Problems of this nature emphasise the need for a multidisciplinary approach to palaeonutritional and dietary studies.

One technique involves the examination of the vessels and implements used in the storage, preparation and consumption of food since the form of a ceramic vessel or artefact may have a functional relationship to a specific cultural practice (see Rice (1987) for an overview of vessel form and use-related properties). A perhaps obvious, and potentially more specific, approach to deducing diet, is to examine the amorphous remains of foodstuffs associated with artefacts. Organic residues adhering to the surface, of say a flint cutting tool, or absorbed into the porous fabric of an unglazed ceramic cooking vessel, should provide information regarding usage and diet.

Potsherds occur ubiquitously in the archaeological record, and thus offer particular promise for systematic study. The basis of our approach is founded on the phenomenon of transfer of organic matter between foodstuffs and the vessels, and other utensils, used in the preparation and consumption of the food. Our objective is to detect the food remnants, adhering onto, or absorbed into, the wall of a ceramic vessel, during its usage, and relate their chemical composition to a specific faunal or floral origin. This paper discusses our approach to the study of preserved organic matter associated with buried potsherds, with particular focus on the derivation of dietary information.

2. Analytical strategy

The interdisciplinary analytical strategy adopted in this work is summarised schematically in Figure 1. A close collaboration between analytical chemists, biochemists and archaeologists is fundamental in the delineation of problems to be addressed. Moreover, the archaeological expertise is essential in assisting in the sampling of individual potsherds for investigation and in providing conventional ceramic interpretations, contextual and environmental information.

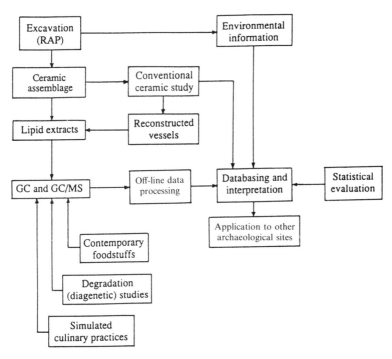

Figure 1. Analytical strategy adopted for the investigation of organic residues preserved in potsherds. RAP refers to the Raunds Area Project, which has provided the majority of the potsherds we have investigated to date.

Until now the analysis of organic matter associated with potsherds has been attributed little more than novelty value. A contributory factor to this situation has been the tendency for analyses to be performed upon single vessels or small groups of vessels of particular form or function. The approach we are developing involves carrying out analyses of large numbers of potsherds. In this way it will be possible to determine whether or not the organic residue found in a particular vessel is 'typical' or 'atypical' of its type, date or context. Thus, we will be able to judge the significance of the use of one vessel, or a series of vessels, against a background knowledge of general use (Heron *et al.* 1991a).

In our experience, the occurrence of visible surface residues is atypical. Hence, in order to provide a technique of potentially wide application to archaeology, we have concentrated on developing the investigation of organic matter absorbed into the pot wall. Clearly, this approach may be limited in the case of well-glazed pottery, but as much early pottery is unglazed or poorly glazed there is considerable scope for this analytical approach.

Few of the investigations of the preserved organic matter associated with potsherds, or intact vessels, have succeeded in confidently identifying food constituents (see examples given in Jones 1986). Failure to achieve positive identifications in early work arose from a lack of analytical techniques capable of detecting and characterising the low levels of organic matter preserved in many samples. Additionally, even in some more recent studies, there has been a tendency to over-simplify the analytical approach required to characterise the complex organic residues, especially in the light of pre- and post-depositional chemical changes that will have ensued (see section 5).

It is our contention that characterisation of the organic residues associated with buried potsherds must begin with the identification of the individual compounds present. Only in this way is it possible to recognise and differentiate between preserved compounds, and compounds whose structures have altered, either by cooking or post-depositional diagenetic processes. In essence we are addressing a problem of biochemical phylogeny or chemotaxonomy, for which precise structural information is a prerequisite (Nes and Nes 1980). The characterisation of organic residues relies on matching a specific compound or mixture of compounds to that of a contemporary plant or animal natural product likely to have been exploited in antiquity. Mills and White (1987) provide a useful review of the chemical composition of some appropriate natural products.

Although we are considering all classes of molecule comprising foodstuffs as potential chemical 'indicators' or 'markers' of diet, our investigations have focused initially on the lipid components. Lipids offer considerable potential for use in the classification of the organic residues in general, owing to the huge body of biochemical data that exists regarding their: (i) structure; (ii) distribution in natural materials; (iii) biosynthesis, and (iv) degradative pathways. In addition, lipids have hydrophobic properties, which will limit their translocation from potsherds, particularly by dissolution in waterlogged environments (*cf*. Evershed and Connolly 1988; Evershed 1990, 1991), unless severely structurally altered or degraded. Moreover, analyses of potsherds and adhering burial soil, recovered from Raunds, Northamptonshire, U.K., indicate that lipids migrating from the burial soil are not a serious source of interference (Heron *et al*. 1991b). The analysis of soil samples to serve as controls should be a routine procedure in any organic residue analysis programme. Contamination by microbial lipids does not appear to be serious; however, this subject is poorly understood and worthy of further investigation.

The following discussions are restricted solely to the techniques used in the investigation of lipids occurring in potsherds, and their application to the determination of diet and vessel usage. Presented here is an overview of the analytical protocol used in our laboratory for the investigation of lipids from

potsherds. Our approach to the interpretation of the compositional information derived from GC and GC/MS analyses is summarised. Central to
interpretation is a consideration of the decay processes known to occur in the
lipid constituents of foodstuffs. We have therefore taken this opportunity to
introduce some of the more commonly occurring degradative pathways of
lipids, with examples drawn from our recent work.

3. Experimental methods

3.1 Sample preparation

Methods for the analysis of lipids from biological materials are well
developed (see Kates (1989) for a compilation of general methods) and
readily applied to the examination of potsherds. Owing to the small amounts
(often < 1 mg/g) of lipid generally present in potsherds, refinement of the
standard analytical approach is required to avoid contamination of the
endogenous lipids. Many of the substances used in subsequent interpretations occur widely in nature and handling of the sherds should be avoided to
minimise contamination with lipids from the hands. A less obvious source of
contamination are laboratory reagents and glassware. All glassware must be
scrupulously clean and reusable glassware should be washed with powerful
oxidising agents (e.g., concentrated nitric acid) prior to use; washing with
organic detergents must be avoided. Disposable glassware, e.g., vials and
pipettes, should be used wherever possible, to avoid cross-contamination
between samples and all new glassware must be washed before use. All
reagents and solvents must be of high grade. Where doubts exist concerning
the purity of solvents they should be distilled before use.

Lipids are obtained by solvent extraction (chloroform/methanol, 2:1) of
powdered sherds (typically 2 g samples) or visible surface residues (sample
sizes vary according to availability). Ultrasonication to aid the extraction
process is preferred to other techniques, e.g., Soxhlet extraction, as smaller
sample sizes are readily accommodated. Moreover, the solvent volumes
should be kept small (ca. 10 ml) and extractions carried out at ambient
temperature, so minimising potential problems of contamination and degradation of extracted lipids.

3.2 High-temperature gas chromatography

Evaporation of the extracting solvent affords the total lipids. Gas chromatography has been employed previously to investigate lipid extracts derived
from potsherds. Until now analyses have been performed on low resolution
packed columns (e.g., Condamin et al. 1976). Capillary GC columns offer
spectacular improvements in resolution compared to packed columns; thus

greatly enhancing the compound identification and compositional information that can be derived from the small amounts of complex lipid mixtures
obtained from potsherds. In addition, the analysis of these extracts is greatly
simplified by the availability of high-temperature stable crosslinked polysiloxane stationary phases (Evershed *et al.* 1990a). Columns coated with
these phases allow the direct analysis of the wide range of lipid species
preserved in many potsherds, including low volatility species, such as triacylglycerols, without the need to perform chemical or enzymatic degrada-
tions used in earlier investigations. The only chemical treatment of the lipid
extract required prior to analysis, is trimethylsilylation of protic sites (e.g.,
hydroxyl moieties present in free fatty carboxylic acids, monoacylglycerols,
diacylglycerols, sterols, etc.) using *N,O-bis*(trimethylsilyl)trifluoroacetamide
(or other reagents) to enhance GC properties (e.g., Myher and Kuksis 1984).
For routine GC work an apolar dimethyl polysiloxane (OV-1 type) stationary phase is sufficient, while availability of capillary columns coated with
high-temperature stable polarisable (65% phenyl 35% methyl) polysiloxane
stationary phases, raises possibilities for the separation of high molecular
weight intact acyl lipid species according to the degree of unsaturation. This
facilitates the detailed assessment of the level of fat degradation in experimental and archaeological samples. Compound identifications by GC
involve retention time comparisons to compounds of known structure, and
an understanding of the chromatographic behaviour of homologous and
other closely related structures. Owing to the small amount of lipid present
unambiguous compound identifications must rely on combined GC/MS and
there will rarely be sufficient material available for other analytical techniques such as ^{1}H and ^{13}C nuclear magnetic resonance spectroscopy.

3.3 Gas chromatography/mass spectrometry (GC/MS)

Combined GC/MS is used routinely for the analysis of lipids extracted from
a wide variety of biological, environmental and geological materials. GC/MS
is regarded as a 'natural combination' as both techniques deal with volatile
or semi-volatile compounds, and attain optimum performance with sample
sizes in the nanogram (10^{-9} g) range. The high absolute sensitivity of GC/MS
means it is well-suited to the study of the small amounts of lipid derived from
potsherds. GC/MS work in our laboratory is performed on a double-focus-
ing magnetic sector mass spectrometer. Electron ionisation at 70 or 20 eV is
most commonly used to generate molecular (M^+) and fragment ions.
Negative ion chemical ionisation, using ammonia as reagent, can also be used
to rapidly assess the nature of fatty acid moieties in intact acyl lipids, e.g.,
triacylglycerols (Evershed *et al.* 1990b). By operating the mass spectrometer
at low resolution (typically m/Δm = 1000), mass measurement to nominal

mass is readily achieved. At this level of performance the mass spectra recorded can be used to identify the majority of lipid species encountered so far in this work.

4. Data analysis and interpretation

Analysis of the raw data derived from the GC/MS analysis of the lipid extracts of potsherds is performed according to well-established procedures. Briefly, the identification of peaks displayed in the total ion current (TIC) chromatogram relies on an assessment of the recorded mass spectra and GC elution orders. The mass spectra of the individual components of the lipid mixtures are interpreted either manually, on the basis of known fragmentations of organic compounds, or automatically, by computer searching of mass spectral databases.

For example, Figure 2 shows the GC profile obtained from the high-temperature GC analysis of a total lipid extract of a Late Saxon/Medieval potsherd from Raunds. The normalised chromatogram suggests a relatively simple lipid composition, the major components, identified from their EI mass spectra, being the free fatty carboxylic acids palmitic ($C_{16:0}$) and stearic ($C_{18:0}$) acid. However, closer examination of the expanded (x-axis) GC profile, obtained using computerised data handling facilities, reveals nearly 100 components in all, including other fatty carboxylic acids, monoacylglycerols, diacylglycerols, triacylglycerols, long-chain alkyl compounds and sterols. Other samples reveal a wide range of other compound types, such as wax esters, hydrocarbons, ketones and alcohols.

The various distributions of compounds that are observed represent the net result of a range of pre- and post-depositional and post-excavational processes. Hence, the organic extracts of potsherds can contain:

i) substances absorbed by the vessel during usage, and preserved in their native (undegraded) state;

ii) substances absorbed by the vessel during usage, which are structurally altered (degraded), initially through a particular culinary practice, or subsequently, during vessel use;

iii) substances absorbed by the vessel during use which are structurally altered, chemically or enzymatically, during burial (natural decay);

iv) substances arising through migration from the burial environment, or microbial and fungal activity, leading to lipid deposition within the potsherd, and,

v) substances transferred to potsherds due to post-excavational activities (contamination, e.g., plasticisers and lipid from hands).

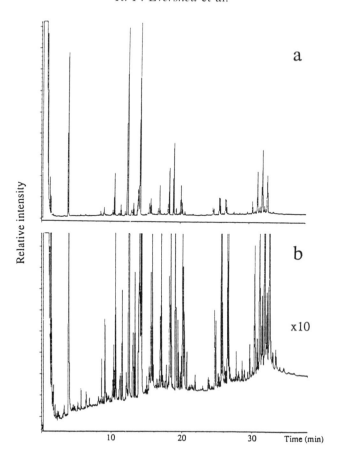

Figure 2. GC profiles obtained for the total lipid extract of a potsherd from a Late Saxon/Early Medieval cooking vessel showing (a) the chromatogram normalised to the major component (stearic acid) and (b) expansion (x10) of the x-axis to reveal nearly one hundred components in all. The peaks were identified from their electron ionisation mass spectra obtained by combined GC/MS. The compounds present comprise mainly acyl lipids, ranging from free fatty carboxylic acids (as their trimethylsilyl (TMS) ester derivatives) at short retention time (12.5 mins), to intact triacylglycerols eluting at longer retention times (30 mins). The peak identities of the major components are given in Figure 2 of Evershed *et al.* 1990b. The analysis was performed on a 12 m × 0.22 mm i.d. fused silica capillary column coated internally with BP-1 stationary phase (immobilised dimethyl polysiloxane, 0.1 μm film thickness). Following on-column injection at 50°C, the GC oven temperature was held at that temperature for 2 mins, programmed to 350°C at 10°C, then held at that temperature for 10 mins. The carrier gas was helium at a column head pressure of 25 psi. A flame ionisation detector was used at a temperature of 350°C.

In addition, the identification of food residues must take account of a range of non-culinary activities, such as the use of natural organic sealants (for example, resins and other organic extracts; *cf.* Rice 1987, 163) that might affect lipid composition and lead to misinterpretations.

5. Chemical changes in the lipid constituents of foodstuffs

A substantial body of information exists concerning the changes that occur in the lipid constituents of contemporary foodstuffs as a result of chemical and/or microbial decay. This information can assist in unravelling the complex mixtures often observed in potsherd extracts. The most commonly occurring of these decay processes are discussed briefly below, with examples drawn from our recent investigations; these discussions are also relevant to the interpretation of data derived from the analysis of other organic remains of archaeological interest.

5.1 Hydrolysis

The bulk of the extractable lipid in foodstuffs, corresponds to the fatty carboxylic acids present in acyl lipids, e.g., triacylglycerols and phospholipids. These acyl lipids will be susceptible, during cooking, storage and burial, to both chemical and enzymatic hydrolysis. The hydrolysis of triacylglycerols is presented schematically in Figure 3. We have succeeded in producing a slow hydrolysis of an animal fat in the laboratory to yield a distribution of acyl lipids comparable to that observed in many of the potsherd extracts. Figure 4a shows the distribution of acyl lipids derived from the partial hydrolysis of a contemporary animal (beef) fat. The distribution obtained through high-temperature GC analysis of the intact lipids clearly reflects the compositional changes anticipated from the degradative pathway presented in Figure 3. An analogous pattern of degradation would be expected for other animal fats and vegetable oils. Further experiments aimed at simulating triacylglycerol degradation in the archaeological context are currently in progress.

Distributions of acyl lipids comparable to those presented in Figure 4a have been observed in lipid extracts of potsherds (e.g., Figure 4b) dating back to the Bronze Age (Evershed, Heron, Charters and Goad, unpublished results). These profiles suggest usage of the original vessel in the processing of a fatty foodstuff. More specific assignment to a plant or animal origin would rest on sterol analysis. For example, GC/MS analysis of the lipid mixture shown in Figure 4b showed cholesterol to be the only sterol present. This observation is consistent with this acyl lipid mixture having arisen from an animal fat. Vegetable oils would be expected to yield phytosterols, possessing additional alkylation at the C-24 position of the sterol side-chain, e.g., campesterol, sitosterol and stigmasterol (note also the presence of a Δ^{22} double-bond). The structures of these commonly occurring animal and plant sterols are presented in Figure 5 together with their EI mass spectra.

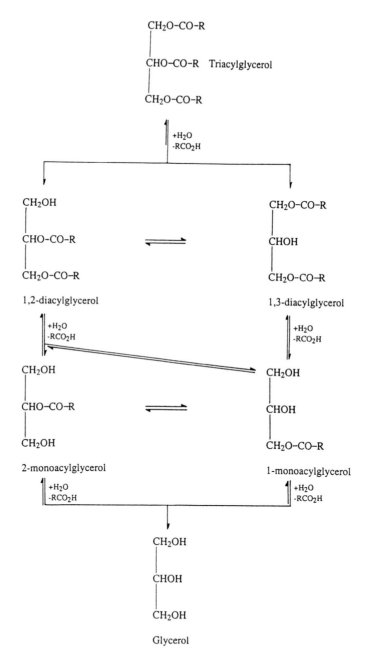

Figure 3. Hydrolysis of triacylglycerols.

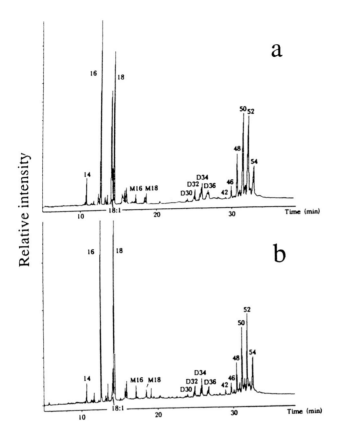

Figure 4. GC profiles of the acyl lipids derived from (a) beef subjected to slow hydrolysis (deionised water, room temperature, 12 months) and (b) the total lipid extract of a Late Saxon/Early Medieval cooking vessel. The experimental conditions are identical to those given in the caption to Figure 2.

5.2 Oxidation

As certain functional groups present in lipids are particularly sensitive to oxidation, this is amongst the most frequently observed degradative reaction of lipids in food materials (Chan 1987). The oxidation of unsaturated lipids occurs most readily with singlet oxygen produced in the atmosphere or directly in the food or vessel wall.

The most likely mechanisms of degradation involve the formation of endoperoxides, through direct attack across double-bonds, which subsequently rearrange into hydroperoxides (e.g., Figure 6). These hydroperoxides are reactive species that can: (i) react further with singlet oxygen to produce hydroxyepidioxy and dioxalane derivatives; (ii) combine to give peroxy dimers by recombination of peroxy radicals; (iii) disproportionate into hyd-

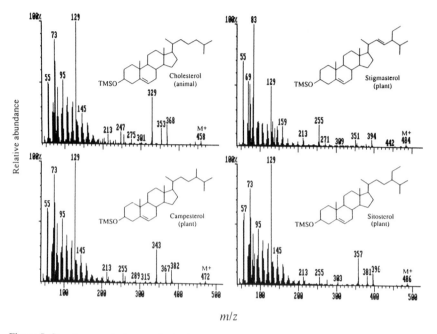

Figure 5. Structures and electron ionisation mass spectra of commonly occurring animal and plant sterols as their TMS ether derivatives. The mass spectra clearly reflect the minor structural differences in the sterol side chain.

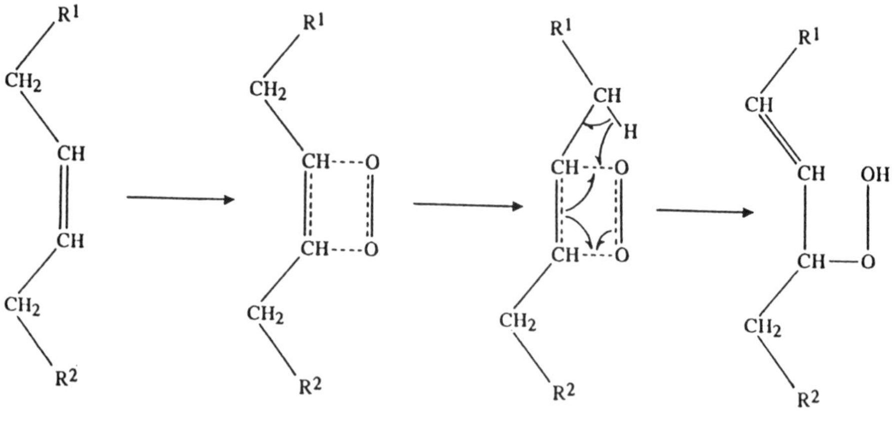

Figure 6. Mechanism of oxidation of isolated double-bonds by singlet oxygen.

roxylic and oxodienoic derivatives; (iv) produce epoxides by inter- and intramolecular reactions; (v) cleave to give low molecular weight aldehydes, alkenes, alcohols and alkanes, and (vi) form covalent bonds with other food components, e.g., proteins, to produce compounds which are insoluble in lipid-extracting solvents.

All the above oxidative reactions serve to deplete the unsaturated fatty acid components commonly observed in lipid extracts of contemporary biological materials. The outcome of these reactions is clearly demonstrated in our archaeological samples. For example, polyunsaturated fatty acids are so sensitive to oxidation that they are rarely observed in archaeological materials. Although linoleic acid ($C_{18:2}$) is widespread in animal and plant tissues we have yet to observe it, either as the free compound, or in intact acyl lipids, in any potsherd extract. However, oleic acid ($C_{18:1}$) is frequently observed, albeit in widely varying abundance; this variability presumably reflects the source foodstuff and/or the level of oxidative/reductive damage experienced by the lipid.

As alluded to above, sterols are amongst the most important of the minor components of fats and oils used diagnostically in classifying the lipid extracts of potsherds. In the pure form, sterols are relatively resistant to autoxidation, but are much more susceptible to oxidation in peroxidising fats and oils (Maerker 1987). By analogy with other lipids, the autoxidation of sterols is enhanced by contact with atmospheric oxygen at elevated temperatures. The pathway for the autoxidation of cholesterol is shown in Figure 7. The oxidation of cholesterol proceeds by hydrogen abstraction, predominantly at the C-7 position, and leads initially to the formation of allylic hydroperoxides. These unstable hydroperoxides decompose to yield various hydroxylic, oxo and epoxy derivatives. We have observed cholesterol autoxidation products in a number of lipid extracts. The chromatogram reproduced in Figure 8 shows the presence, albeit in low abundance, of cholesterol, and its 7-hydroxy and 7-one oxidation products in a mixture which is consistent with a highly degraded animal fat. This extract was derived from an Anglo-Saxon lamp sherd, which would presumably have been fuelled with animal tallow—an obvious by-product of meat processing. The detection of these oxidation products, together with degraded acyl lipids may indicate heating of the fat either during cooking (*cf.* Bascoul *et al.* 1986) or subsequently during the use of the lamp. Further investigations, particularly cooking simulation experiments using unglazed pottery vessels, will shed further light on the nature of sterol autoxidation products arising from a range of plant and animal foodstuffs.

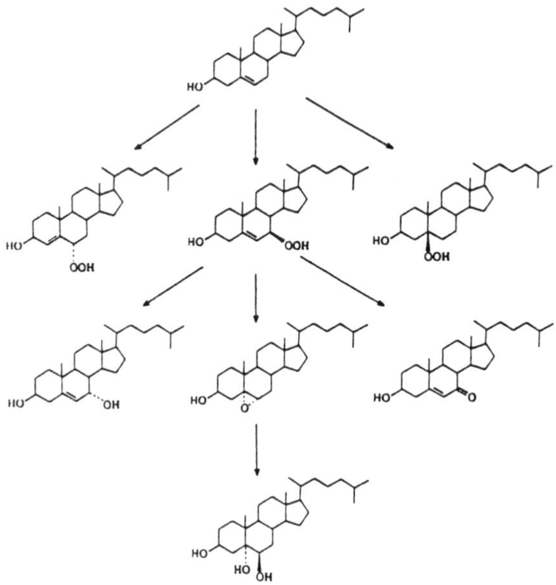

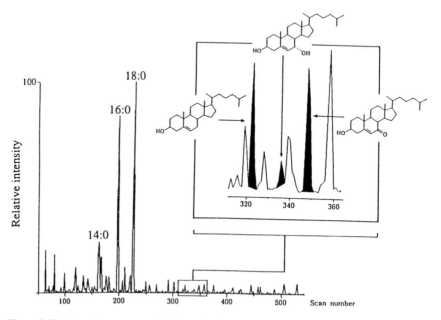

Figure 7. Oxidation products of cholesterol resulting from attack by singlet oxygen (compiled from Smith 1981).

Figure 8. Total ion chromatogram (TIC; equivalent to a GC profile but derived from combined GC/MS) of the total lipid extract of Late Saxon/Early Medieval lamp sherd showing the major free fatty acids (as TMS ester derivatives), and an expansion of the sterol elution region, to reveal cholesterol oxidation products.

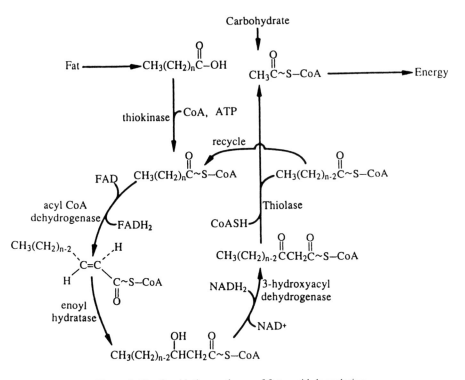

Figure 9. The β-oxidation pathway of fatty acid degradation.

5.3 Microbiological degradation

Buried organic matter, unless protected in some way, will be open to the full impact of decay by microorganisms active in the burial matrix. The population of microorganisms will be governed by the conditions prevailing in the burial environment, i.e., climate, degree of aeration, humidity and pH.

Enzymatic hydrolysis has already been discussed briefly in relation to the degradation of animal fats and vegetable oils. The microflora and microfauna that exist in soil contain enzymes that are capable of mediating a wide range of other structural changes in lipids. The most well known mechanism of fatty acid metabolism under aerobic conditions is β-oxidation (Figure 9). β-Oxidation is the stepwise degradation of fatty acids to yield acetyl-CoA (a building block of many essential natural substances) and metabolic energy. Microbial β-oxidation may also occur under anaerobic conditions (Gurr and James 1975), and evidence for this process in archaeological specimens has come from studies of adipocere formation (den Dooren de Jong 1961; see also below). This metabolic route will very rapidly deplete the acyl lipid content of the organic matter absorbed in potsherds. Straight-chain, branched, saturated and unsaturated fatty acids alike are potential substrates for the

β-oxidation pathway. Other oxidative pathways are also known which could also be involved in the degradation of lipids absorbed in potsherds during burial, e.g., lipoxygenases are widely distributed in microorganisms and capable of producing site-specific hydroperoxy derivatives of essential fatty acids (Gurr and James 1975).

Anaerobic environments are generally more conducive to the preservation of organic matter. In the case of food residues preserved in potsherds, anaerobic decay will only occur under certain burial conditions. Reduction is a well-recognised degradative process that can occur in lipids, mediated by microorganisms active in anaerobic environments. Structural alterations of this nature obviously rely on the availability of lipid species to the micro-organisms.

The microbial reduction (hydrogenation) of Δ^5-sterols to stanols under anaerobic conditions is a well-established process in sediments (Gaskell and Eglinton 1975; Mackenzie *et al.* 1982). 5α-Stanols have been detected by GC/MS in a number of lipid extracts of potsherds. However, their co-occurrence together with the corresponding Δ^5-sterols, indicates that microbial reduction of the sterols has not proceeded to completion. As this microbial reduction is generally a relatively rapid process, it would appear that not all the lipid is available as substrate to the microorganisms active in the burial matrix (in this instance the soil), or that cessation of microbial activity has occurred for some reason. Assuming no enzyme specificity exists microbial reduction should affect all the absorbed Δ^5-sterols equally, hence the sterol: stanol ratio should be constant at each carbon number, i.e. both cholesterol (C_{27}) and sitosterol (C_{29}) should be equally affected. If this is not the case then post-excavational contamination must be suspected, e.g., through handling of potsherds which would introduce cholesterol from skin lipids.

The double bonds in fatty acids will also be susceptible to biohydrogenation under anaerobic conditions. We have not yet fully assessed whether or not the acyl lipids absorbed in potsherds are readily reduced by microbes. However, there are indications from analyses of ancient adipocere, and studies of the anaerobic degradation of whole animal and plant fats in the laboratory, that reduction does occur (den Dooren de Jong 1961; Morgan *et al.* 1973; Thornton *et al.* 1970). Both these groups found that fatty materials decomposing anaerobically, under waterlogged conditions, are susceptible to hydrolysis, hydration, reduction and carbon-carbon bond scission reactions. In the case of triacylglycerols containing predominantly oleic acid, relatively rapid (two months incubation at 25°C) degradation occurs to yield predominantly palmitic acid. For palmitic acid to be formed from oleic acid, hydrogenation of the mid-chain double-bond, and shortening of the alkyl chain by two methylene groups, must be invoked. Chain shortening is thought to proceed via β-oxidation (den Dooren de Jong 1961), but this has not been

established unambiguously using radio- or stable isotope labelling techniques. The formation of 10-hydroxystearic acid (Evershed 1990) and scram-
bling of the double-bond position in monoenoic fatty acids (Evershed 1991)
present in human adipocere, suggests that the mechanism of fat degradation
in a waterlogged anaerobic environment is not straightforward. Fatty
materials absorbed in potsherds buried in waterlogged anaerobic contexts are
also presumed to be susceptible to degradation in this way.

6. Identification of food residues

Although considerable promise exists for the identification of food residues
from the analysis of preserved lipids, these interpretations by necessity must
proceed cautiously, taking full account of the decay processes that will have
occurred over archaeological time. For example, lipid profiles of the type
shown in Figure 4b occur with reasonable regularity, and provide a clear
indication of the vessel having a function associated with the preparation
and/or storage of a fatty food. More definite assignment to either a plant or
animal source can be made through the analysis of the trace sterol components. In this case, the finding of cholesterol as the major sterol indicated
the preserved fatty residue was of animal origin. Precise assignment of this
residue to a particular animal species is problematical, as a result of the
similarity of the acyl lipid composition of various species. Moreover,
degradation of the dominant unsaturated fatty acids will complicate interpretations. Species identifications based on the distribution of the saturated
fatty acid components should be made with caution, owing to the possibilities
for double-bond reduction and chain shortening of fatty acids seen under
anaerobic conditions (see above). In some cases, preserved acyl lipid distributions can be very diagnostic. For example dairy product residues are readily
recognisable by the presence of short-chain fatty acids, with less than twelve
carbon atoms, in the free fatty acid and intact acyl (mono-, di- and triacylglycerol) lipid fractions (Rottländer and Schlichtherle 1979; Evershed,
Heron, Charters and Goad unpublished data).

The abundant long-chain alkyl compounds found in plant epicuticular
waxes are of particular use in deriving dietary information relating to the
preparation and consumption of leafy vegetables. Compounds of this type
have been detected, sometimes in substantial quantities (> 3 mg/g of the
sherd), in a number of unglazed Late Saxon/Early Medieval vessels recovered
from the West Cotton site in Northamptonshire. The distribution of
compounds detected in these samples included nonacosane, nonacosan-15-
one and nonacosan-15-ol, provides strong evidence for *Brassica* vegetables,
most likely *B. oleracea* (cabbage), or possibly *B. rapa* (turnip leaves) being a

significant component of the diet of the community at West Cotton (Figure 10; Evershed *et al.* 1991). This new method of identifying preserved epicuticular leaf waxes should have wide application, since the exploitation of many leafy vegetables by early communities remains undetected by traditional palaeobotanical techniques (Hall 1987).

In the light of the potential of this approach we have recently been establishing a database of epicuticular leaf compositions for comparison with total lipid extracts from potsherds. By this means we have derived evidence for the consumption of leeks (*Allium porrum*). The epicuticular leaf wax of leek is composed predominantly of hentricontan-16-one, and the detection of

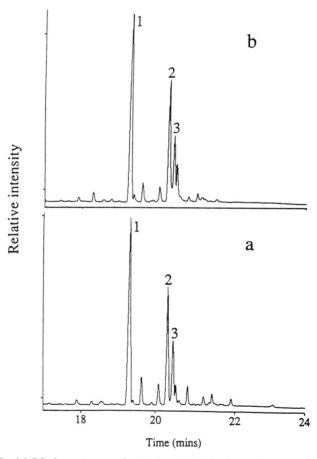

Figure 10. Partial GC chromatograms for (a) the total lipid extract of a potsherd from a Late Saxon/Early Medieval cooking vessel, and (b) the hexane soluble fraction of the epicuticular leaf wax of *Brassica oleracea* (cabbage). The numbers on the peaks correspond to the structures given in Figure 11. GC conditions were the same as those given in the caption to Figure 2.

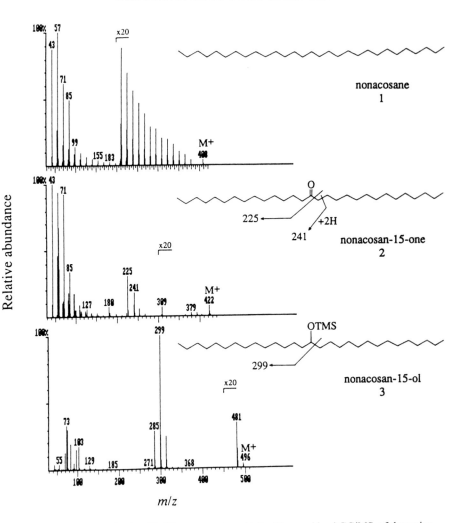

Figure 11. Electron ionisation (70 eV) mass spectra, obtained by combined GC/MS, of the major long-chain alkyl components of the partial GC chromatograms presented in Figure 10. Note that the nonacosan-15-ol was analysed as its TMS ether derivative. All other experimental details are the same as those given in the caption to Figure 2.

this compound in a significant number of potsherds is consistent with leeks being a dietary component at this site. Again, as is often the case, palaeo-botanical evidence for the utilisation of leeks at this site has, until now, been lacking. This finding is in complete agreement with documentary evidence for the widespread cultivation of leeks during the Medieval period (Hallam 1988). We would again add a note of caution here, in that the identification of dietary components on the basis of a single marker compound is an uncertain practise, in view of the large number of plant species that remain to be investigated.

7. Summary

A wide range of mechanisms exist for the decay of organic matter in archaeological contexts. However, by application of modern chromatographic and mass spectrometric methods we have demonstrated that sufficient organic matter remains preserved in potsherds for deductions to be made concerning the identity of a variety of constituents. Lipids appear to be relatively well-preserved and hold particular promise for use as chemotaxonomic markers of food remains. The data that has been obtained shows that extensive decay of the original organic matter occurs during burial, hence, the lipid distributions ('fingerprints') of potsherd extracts rarely match those of contemporary foodstuffs. For this reason we are performing laboratory simulations of decay of selected foodstuffs, in order to obtain suitable reference material to aide in interpretations. The distributions are also complicated by factors such as non-specific usage, consequently the lipid profiles will represent contributions from a variety of foodstuffs. The use of a range of ingredients in recipes will also yield complex lipid profiles reflecting such mixtures. In an effort to deconvolute data arising from these practices, we are carrying out simulation experiments with contemporary foodstuffs cooked in replica ceramic vessels. Special consideration is also being given to the possibility of post-firing treatments being employed by early potters to improve appearance or decrease permeability of unglazed vessels (Rice 1987). Modern ethnographic practices include: the application of resinous coatings, or the scalding of milk to seal the interior of new unglazed vessels. The implications of these practices to interpretations based on the analysis of preserved organic matter are obvious, and should be given due consideration when making deductions concerning diet and vessel function based on chemical analysis. Provided due consideration is given to these factors in the interpretation of the analytical data, there are clear indications that potential exists for the study of food preparation and consumption, and pottery function.

Acknowledgements

In presenting this paper we would like to thank Mark Prescott for invaluable assistance with GC/MS analyses and Ann Leyden for assistance in sample preparations and GC analyses. Varian Denham and Paul Blinkhorn are thanked for valuable discussions and ceramic interpretations. Thanks are also due to Mark Robinson and Gillian Campbell for environmental information. We are indebted to the Northamptonshire Archaeology Unit for co-operation in provision of samples from the Raunds Area Project. The financial support of the Science and Engineering Research Council Science-based Archaeology Committee (SERC-SBAC) and English Heritage Historic Buildings and Monuments Commission (HBMC) for England are gratefully acknowledged.

References

Bascoul, J., Domergue, N., Olle, M. and Crastes De Paulet, A. 1986: Autoxidation of cholesterol in tallows heated under deep frying conditions: evaluation of oxysterols by GLC and TLC-FID. *Lipids* 21, 383–387.

Carbone, V.A. and Keel, B.C. 1985: Preservation of plant and animal remains. In Gilbert, R.J. and Mielke, J.H. (editors), *The Analysis of Prehistoric Diets* (London, Academic Press) 2–19.

Condamin, J., Formenti, F., Metais, M.O., Michel, M. and Blond, P. 1976: The application of gas chromatography to the tracing of oil in ancient amphorae. *Archaeometry* 18, 195–201.

Chan, H.W-S. (editor) 1987: *Autoxidation of Unsaturated Lipids* (London, Academic Press).

den Dooren De Jong, L.E. 1961: On the formation of adipocere from fats. *Antonie van Leeuwenhoek Journal of Microbiology and Serology* 27, 337–361.

Dimbleby, G. 1978: *Plants and Archaeology* (London, John Baker).

Evershed, R.P. 1990: Lipids from samples of skin from seven Dutch bog bodies: preliminary report. *Archaeometry* 32, 139–153.

Evershed, R.P. 1991: Bog body lipid taphonomy. In Budd, P., Chapman, B. Jackson, C., Janaway, R. and Ottaway, B. (editors), *Archaeological Sciences 1989* (Oxford, Oxbow Monograph 9) 352–361.

Evershed, R.P. and Connolly, R.C. 1988: Lipid preservation in Lindow Man. *Naturwissenschaften* 75, 143–145.

Evershed, R.P., Heron, C. and Goad, L.J. 1990a: Analysis of organic residues of archaeological origin by high-temperature gas chromatography/mass spectrometry. *Analyst* 115, 1339–1342.

Evershed, R.P., Prescott, M.C. and Goad, L.J. 1990b: High-temperature gas chromatography/mass spectrometry of triacylglycerols with ammonia negative-ion chemical ionisation. *Rapid Communications in Mass Spectrometry* 4, 345–347.

Evershed, R.P., Heron, C. and Goad, L.J. 1991: Epicuticular wax components preserved in potsherds as chemical indicators of leafy vegetables in ancient diets. *Antiquity* 65, 540–544.

Gaskell, S.J. and Eglinton, G. 1975: Rapid hydrogenation of sterols in a contemporary lacustrine sediment. *Nature* 254, 209–211.

Gilbert, R.I. and Mielke, J.H. (editors) 1985: *The Analysis of Prehistoric Diets* (Orlando, Academic Press).

Gurr, M.I. and James, A.T. 1975: *Lipid Biochemistry* (London, Chapman and Hall).

Hall, A. 1987: In pursuit of the uneatable (some thoughts on the search for archaeological evidence of vegetables). *Archaeology in York: Interim* 12, 1–7.

Hallam, H.E. 1988: *The Agrarian History of England and Wales Vol. 2: 1042–1350* (Cambridge, Cambridge University Press).

Heron, C., Evershed, R.P., Goad, L.J. and Denham, V. 1991a: New approaches to the analyses of organic residues from archaeological ceramics. In Budd, P., Chapman, B. Jackson, C., Janaway, R. and Ottaway, B. (editors), *Archaeological Sciences 1989* (Oxford, Oxbow Monographs 9) 332–339.

Heron, C., Evershed, R.P. and Goad, L.J. 1991b: Effects of migration of soil lipids on organic residues associated with buried potsherds. *Journal of Archaeological Science* 18, 641–659.

Hillman, G.C. 1989: Late Palaeolithic plant foods from Wadi Kubbaniya in Upper Egypt: dietary diversity, infant weaning, and seasonality in a riverine environment. In Harris, D.R. and Hillman, G.C. (editors), *Foraging and Farming: the Evolution of Plant Exploitation* (London, Unwin Hyman) 207–239.

Jones, R.E. 1986: Identification of materials carried by ceramic vessels. In Jones, R.E. (editor), *Greek and Cypriot Pottery: A Review of Scientific Studies* (Athens, British School at Athens Fitch Laboratory Occasional Paper No.1) 839–847.

Kates, M. 1989: *Techniques of Lipidology* (Amsterdam, Elsevier).

Mackenzie, A.S., Brassell, S.C., Eglinton, G. and Maxwell, J.R. 1982: Chemical fossils: the geological fate of steroids. *Science* 217, 491–504.

Maerker, G. 1987: Cholesterol autoxidation—current status. *Journal of the American Oil Chemists Society* 64, 388–392.

Mills. J.S. and White, R. 1987: *The Organic Chemistry of Museum Objects* (London, Butterworths).

Morgan, E.D., Cornford, C., Pollock, D.R.J. and Isaacson, P. 1973: The transformation of fatty material buried in soil. *Science and Archaeology* 10, 9–10.

Myher, J.J. and Kuksis, A. 1984: Determination of plasma total lipid profiles by gas-liquid chromatography. *Journal of Biochemical and Biophysical Methods* 10, 13–23.

Nes, W.R. and Nes, W.D. 1980: *Lipids in Evolution* (New York, Plenum Press).

Parmalee, P.W. 1985: Identification and interpretation of archaeologically derived animal remains. In Gilbert, R.I. and Mielke, J.H. (editors), *The Analysis of Prehistoric Diets* (Orlando, Academic Press) 61–95.

Rice, P.M. 1987: *Pottery Analysis: A Sourcebook* (Chicago, University of Chicago Press).

Rottländer, R.C.A. and Schlichtherle, H. 1979: Food identification of samples from archaeological sites. *Archaeo-physika* 10, 260–267.

Smith, L.L. 1981: *Cholesterol Autoxidation* (New York, Plenum Press).

Thornton, M.D., Morgan, E.D. and Celoria, F. 1970: The composition of bog butter. *Science and Archaeology* 2–3, 20–25.

Proceedings of the British Academy, **77**, 209–219

Food Remains, Food Webs
and Ecosystems

M. K. JONES

*Department of Archaeology, University of Cambridge, Downing Street,
Cambridge CB2 3DZ, U.K.*

Summary. It is the aim of this paper to take stock of recent developments in the techniques of bio-archaeology towards the reconstruction of past food webs, and to highlight some areas in which their
dynamics could be usefully pursued. Reconstruction of these webs is
explored in the first two sections following the introduction, the first
dealing with new developments in recognition and identification of
the building blocks, and the second with exploring the linkages
between them. The third and fourth sections consider some possibly
characteristic features of human webs and the detection of stress and
change within them.

1. Introduction

This conference marks a threshold that has been passed in the understanding
and reconstruction of past food economies. Over the last decade, a number
of volumes have addressed the difficulties of binding together independent
and sometimes very detailed archaeological studies of particular foods into
a coherent, and at least semi-quantitative analysis of early economies (*cf.*
Sheridan and Bailey 1981, Jones M. 1983). A recurrent proposal within those
volumes was that various ecosystem models, such as have been gaining
increasing currency in early palaeolithic studies, (*cf.* Foley 1977, 1986) had
considerable potential for studies of Holocene sites that were yielding in some
cases enormous quantities of bio-archaeological data (Thomas 1983, 1989).
At the same time it remained clear that the quantification of those various
categories of data recovered was fraught with difficulties. We now see the
burden of providing this quantitative overview being lifted as the study of

Read 14 February 1991. © The British Academy 1992.

human teeth and bones, human faeces, and vessels used directly in the consumption of food, are showing the potential to provide this information by chemical and isotopic means (*cf.* the papers by Evershed *et al.* and van der Merwe in this volume).

As these latter approaches break new ground in providing the broader framework of food consumption, the way becomes more open for the techniques of bio-archaeology to enrich those patterns with extremely fine qualitative detail. The two developments that enhance progress in this area are first the new methodologies that have grown within bio-archaeology over the last decade, and second, the fast growth in interest in the form and structure of food webs in various parts of the natural world (Pimm 1982; Lawton and Warren 1988). We are now considerably closer to being able both to build past human food webs through direct evidence of what their components are and how they are energetically or nutritionally linked, and to explore the dynamics of those constructed webs and consider the consequences for the trajectories of past human ecosystems.

2. Identifying the building blocks

Identification of food remains has traditionally been based on the visual comparison between modern reference collections and macroscopic archaeological fragments of durable plant and animal tissues or various forms of cast or mineral replacement fossil. Where such fragments survive, they contain considerable morphological detail, but their survival is restricted in range. This is less problematic for animals used as food, as the majority have at least some skeletal element, than it is for plant foods, of which a very large number are composed of non-durable tissues (*cf.* Harris 1969). Thus the critical research in this area has been, and continues to be, in extending the range through identifying new tissues, and in improving separation techniques.

The plant tissues most amenable to conventional analysis have been seeds and fruits of neolithic and later periods. There have been major gaps in palaeolithic food plants of all types, and root, tuber, leaf and stem foods for all periods, but these gaps are gradually closing (*cf.* Harris and Hillman 1989). At the Institute of Archaeology University College London, a great deal of success has been achieved in identifying fragmented parenchymatous tissues, which are proving a promising route to the identification of bulky plant foods such as tubers (Hather 1988). Similarly, at the Environmental Archaeology Unit at York University a wide range of stem tissues such as *Allium* have been successfully identified, as well as a number of economic non-food plants, on the basis of epidermal fragments retaining their stomata

(Tomlinson 1985). The identification of fragmentary vegetative tissue in general will have major significance in coprolite studies, where their survival is sufficient for some quite detailed analyses (Hillman 1986).

At the same time as the range is being extended, so the precision of taxonomic identification within food species is being enhanced in two ways. First, the cellular structure may often be more tightly genetically defined than the gross morphology so often relied upon in visual comparison, and there is in some cases a very direct relationship between cell size and levels of ploidy. Thus scanning electron microscopy has proved of great value in distinguishing cereal species (Körber-Grohne 1981, Körber-Grohne and Piening 1980) though the technique is not without practical difficulties in terms of within-tissue variation (S. Colledge pers. comm.). A second method of identification with undoubted long-term potential is the incorporation of the range of chemical methods discussed by Evershed *et al.* and Hedges and Sykes (both in this volume) with the study of the food fragments themselves. Two notable and promising examples are the isolation of taxonomically specific lipids from ancient cereals (McLaren *et al.* 1991) and of DNA from both plant and animal foods (*cf.* Hedges and Sykes, this volume)

Thus the state of play on improved identification is generally involving a continuing move from the macroscopic to the cellular, sub-cellular and chemical levels of analyses. This move is relaxing the traditional restraints on both the range of organs and tissues that can be successfully identified, and the genetic range and precision that can be entertained. In the case of DNA analysis at least, this potentially takes us for the first time beyond the range of genotypes that are extant in our current collections of reference material.

3. Food web interactions

Palaeo-economic studies have quite naturally concentrated on those food web interactions directly connecting with humans, in other words the plant and animal foods consumed by the humans themselves, and analyses of the skeleton and faeces of the humans themselves. In order to reach a dynamic understanding of the food web as a whole, that approach needs to be extended to other members of the past food webs we study. It is in other words fruitful to ask the same questions about the nutritional status of the animals associated with humans as we ask about the humans themselves, and indeed related questions about the nutritional status of the plants on which they feed.

Much work has been initiated in this direction. For example, the analyses of human teeth and jaws to explore diet, nutrition and health are well advanced (Hillson 1989, Hillson and Jones 1989), and some of these analyses are now being considered in the context of domestic animals. One example is the study of hypoplasia, a term referring to certain developmental defects that appear around the tooth crown (Hillson 1986, 127). Current research is demonstrating how these defects, which correlate with a range of metabolic and nutritional deficiencies, can be closely linked to life histories of the individuals concerned, by association with the cyclical physiology of tooth growth (Hillson 1989, Hillson and Jones 1989). They have been widely examined in human and hominid populations, and the analyses are now being explored in the context of non-human teeth, for example pig teeth, which have already been shown to be amenable to this kind of analysis. Periodontal disease can also be examined in the context of diet, ecology, and health (Hillson 1986, 305) and this too applies to animals as well as to humans. A further example is tooth microware analysis, also applied to a range of human and hominid specimens to establish the categories of food into which the teeth came into contact (Hillson 1986, 186) is currently being developed at Sheffield for application to domesticated animals (I. Mainland pers. comm.).

Faecal analyses have also been extended to animals. An example is a study by Robinson and Rasmussen (1989) of the waterlogged neolithic lake village deposits at Weier, north east Switzerland. Animal dung deposits were used to demonstrate the use of cereal grains and "leafy hay" (stripped tree foliage) in animal fodder. Gay Wilson's work on animal dung from a Roman well also provides evidence for the use of grain as fodder (Wilson 1979).

Extending methodology from humans to animals also applies to identifying their food sources directly, and this returns us to a problem already discussed, namely that the animals we use as food have tended to be heavily dependent on soft plant tissues that do not survive well. Studies of the rich waterlogged deposits of urban sites have allowed the recognition of meadow hay, for example in the Roman phases of Carlisle and York, together with some of its associated fauna, including horse roundworm eggs (Hall and Kenward 1990, Goodwin and Huntley in McCarthy 1991). The elusiveness of any similar evidence in prehistory may be as much to do with the relative importance of leafy hay from woodland, as opposed to meadow hay. At Sheffield work is in progress identifying leafy hay from insects and other "marker" fossils, including associated insects, pollen and dendrochronological traces (P. Halstead pers. comm.).

The nutritional status of plants must of be approached in a quite different way. The direct analysis of elemental assimilation in actual plant tissues has considerable potential but is in its early stages. Current research at Durham for example is examining trace element profiles fixed within carbonised wheat grains (J. Langston pers. comm.). Rather better established is a community ecology approach to the nutrient and water status of those communities exploited for plant food, and by implication the plant foods themselves. Analyses of the autecology and synecology of arable weed species has implicated nitrogen deficiency as a major problem of later prehistoric crop production, alongside concurrent problems in the hydrological management of the agricultural landscape (Jones M. 1984, 1988a, 1988b). This analytical approach is being given further statistical rigour through the application of various forms of multivariate analysis (Jones G. 1991).

In summary, the major moves forward have been in the extension of existing methodologies for the study of human remains to other members of the human food web, and in addition, the use of community ecological approaches to the primary levels of the food web.

4. Characteristic aspects of human food webs

It is frequently the case, at least in the Holocene, that the components of human food webs are extensively connected, not just by transfers of energy and nutrients from the consumed to the consumer, but also by transfers of information in the reverse direction, to "workgates" at lower trophic levels, steering energy flows in chosen directions (cf. Ellen 1982, chapter 5). These workgates that abound in "managed" ecosystems perhaps provide the sharpest definitions we can articulate around such concepts as environmental management and agriculture.

The archaeological recognition of management, including agriculture, has moved more and more away from dependence on oversimplistic correlates of a "domestication event" to examining direct evidence for these workgates. This represents in part a legacy of the work of Eric Higgs and his colleagues who suggested we split up the concept of domestication into more tangible component units, and stimulated a taphonomic route to the rediscovery of the processes people applied to their food plants and animals (Higgs 1972, 1975).

Isolating these processes has itself become ever more closely focussed. At first depending on the physical alterations visible on bones and seeds, our methods now focus also on the physiological response of plants and animals during their lives to human action (Higgs 1972, 1975). Best established in this field is the skeletal response of domestic animals to the wide range of "lifestyles" to which we subject our animals. An obvious example is the use of animals for traction, and the influence on forelimb morphology (Armour-Chelu and Clutton-Brock 1985). Plant taphonomy has only more recently moved from studying the physical separation of components (Hillman 1984, Jones G. 1984, Jones M. 1985) to this kind of morphological detail. Current research at Cambridge is exploring the relationship between harvest time and fruitstone morphology, and at London, extensive work has been conducted on the structural and molecular effects of cooking and digestion, an example of which is the use of electron spin resonance to elucidate thermal histories of food plants (Hillman *et al.* 1985).

Moving from a more obvious characteristic feature of Holocene human food webs to a more speculative one, a recurrent theme of interest in theoretical ecology has been the degree of interconnectedness or "connectance" of food webs, expressed as the proportion of theoretically possible feeding links that have actually been established in the real food chain (De Angelis 1975, Gardner and Ashby 1970, May 1972, Rosenzweig 1971). Some of this work has overturned an intuitive presumption that high levels of connectance bind the system together and thus endow it with greater stability. Indeed the reverse would appear to be true and systems would instead be expected to stabilise at lower levels of connectance.

Now that a number of detailed bio-archaeological studies of particular Holocene human food webs are in existence, or at least well on the way to publication, we can begin to make some provisional observations on apparent levels of connectance. What seems to be emerging is not a simple linear pattern towards stable levels of connectance, but instead levels that fluctuate considerably in space and time, frequently reaching levels that seem high in comparison with non-human webs. We can see this divergence in connectance by contrasting some inland and coastal food webs in the later British Holocene, both of which have received considerable attention from bio-archaeologists.

This can be illustrated by reference to the Viking coastal midden site of Freswick, Caithness (Rackham *et al.* 1984), where up to a metre of midden deposits yielded evidence of such terrestrial domesticates as ox, sheep/goat, domestic fowl, cultivated oats and six-row barley, a few wild dry land plants and animals that may have been consumed, together with over 20 species of coastal and marine molluscs, crustaceans and fish. In addition, both peat and seaweed were collected, both of which may plausibly have entered the human food web.

We can contrast this sustained dietary breadth with the progressive narrowing that is evident in later prehistoric terrestrial communities in Britain. There is much evidence that inland neolithic communities retained a fairly broad web, drawing on domesticated plant and animals as well as wild animals, nuts and fruits, but that this web contracted progressively towards the end of prehistory, as diet was more and more restricted to grain crops and domestic animals, bound together by much sharing of plant foods and secondary products within this restricted species group (Grant 1981; Jones M. 1983, 1988a) before broadening out again in the historic period (*cf.* Greig 1991).

Little has as yet been done to examine how these very variable degrees of connectance interact with information transfer along the workgates of the food web, beyond the intuitive observation that highly connected webs are also highly "managed". In turn their relationship with various forms of "stability" and "resilience" has much to offer, if indeed those concepts are the appropriate ones to articulate in the case of highly changeable systems (cf. Allen and Starr 1982, McGlade and Allen 1986).

In summary, recent theoretical ecology provides bio-archaeology with a language with which to define with greater precision the particularly human aspects of food webs. The next modelling steps are in their infancy, but the methodology nevertheless exists to move in that direction. That move involves consideration of such features as connectance and workgate structures in the context of deflection and change.

5. Deflection and change within past food webs

While, as mentioned at the outset, direct quantification of populations from bio-archaeological data has always been a particularly problematic area, those data have proved and are proving extremely well suited to the recognition of ecological stress within past human food webs, largely because the "scars" of that stress affect the ecosystem in so many of its parts. This has ranged from structural stress within the soils supporting the food webs (Dimbleby 1962, Limbrey 1975), nutritional stress in both the plant communities at the base of the food web (Jones M. 1984), and the herbivores feeding upon them (Baker and Brothwell 1980), and extending towards the human remains themselves (e.g., papers in *Journal of Archaeological Science* 11, 1984).

We can also find more finely tuned records of food web deflection in quite subtle demographic shifts, as exemplified by Andrew Jones' work on fish, which has examined a range of modifications of fish populations in conjunction with human exploitation (Wheeler and Jones 1989). Around the city of York for example, the development of early mediaeval "pollution" would appear to be mirrored in shifts in the fish consumed by its inhabitants (Jones A. 1988).

The extended campaign of bio-archaeological research that English Heritage has sponsored on a series of urban sites has also provided a detailed record of another gradual deflection of the human food web. As a corollary of the dense occupation of relatively protected settlements, our large and medium sized competitors have been held at bay, and energy within our food webs is instead more and more deflected to the invertebrates and microorganisms that are able to flourish in an ecosystem which is densely packed spatially. York is a key example, where the proliferation of invertebrate competitors can first be seen in positions in the food web adjacent to humans, such as the high populations of grain beetles in the Roman town. During the course of the first millennium AD this proliferation applies more and more to the humans themselves, as is dramatically illustrated by the incidence of intestinal worms. While nematode eggs are likely to have been but the tip of an iceberg of less visible diseases and parasites, they provide an extremely useful marker that can to some extent be quantified through time (*cf.* Hall *et al.* 1983, Hall and Kenward 1990)

6. Future directions

It was argued at the outset that advances in molecular, chemical and radiometric analyses have set a new agenda for bio-archaeology. The direct examination of surviving fragments of past human food webs is gradually being liberated from those questions they were least suited to answer, and instead, through analyses with these newer techniques, can provide the qualitative framework for a much more structured examination of the particular place of humans in past food webs. Much of this work has yet to be conducted, but what I hope to have demonstrated is that the bio-archaeology of the last twenty years has produced a data-set, and a key series of pilot studies, that provide a secure foundation for such a project.

Acknowledgements

I am grateful to very many colleagues for discussing ideas for this paper with me, in particular: Geoff Bailey, Allan Hall, Paul Halstead, John Hather, Gordon Hillman, Simon Hillson, Andrew Jones, Rosemary Luff, and Terry O'Connor, many of whom allowed me to discuss unpublished work. Much of the bio-archaeological work cited was publicly funded, in particular by the Science and Engineering Research Council, English Heritage, and the Scottish Development Department.

References

Allen, T.F.H. and Starr, T.B. 1982: *Hierarchy: Perspectives for Ecological Complexity* (Chicago, Chicago University Press).
Armour-Chelu, M. and Clutton-Brock, J. 1985: Notes on the evidence for the use of cattle as draft animals at Etton. In Pryor, F. *et al.* Excavations at Etton, Maxey, Cambridgeshire 1982–1984, *Antiquaries Journal* 65, 297–302.
Baker, J.R. and Brothwell, D. 1980: *Animal Diseases in Archaeology* (London, Academic Press).

Brown, T.A. and Brown, K.A. (in press): Ancient DNA and the archaeologist. *Antiquity*.

De Angelis, D.L. 1975: Stability and connectance in food web models. *Ecology* 56, 238–243.

Dimbleby, G.W. 1962: *The Development of British Heathlands and their Soils*. (Oxford, Oxford Forestry Memoir 23).

Ellen, R. 1982: *Environment, Subsistence and System: the Ecology of Small Scale Formations* (Cambridge, Cambridge University Press).

Foley, R.A. 1977: Space and energy. In Clarke, D.L. (editor), *Spatial Archaeology* (London, Academic Press) 163–188.

Foley, R.A. 1986: *Another Unique Species: Patterns in Human Evolutionary Ecology* (London, Longman).

Gardner, M.R. and Ashby, W.R. 1970: Connectance of large dynamic (cybernetic) systems: critical values for stability. *Nature* 228, 274.

Grant, A. 1981: The significance of deer remains at occupation sites of the Iron Age to the Anglo-Saxon period. In Jones, M.K. and Dimbleby, G.W. (editors), *The Environment of Man: the Iron Age to the Anglo-Saxon Period* (Oxford, British Archaeological Reports British Series 87) 205–213.

Greig, J.R.A. 1991: The British Isles. In van Zeist, W., Wasylikowa, K. and Behre, K.E. (editors), *Progress in Old World Palaeoethnobotany* (Rotterdam, Balkema) 299–334.

Hall, A.R., Kenward, H.K., Williams, D. and Grieg, J.R.A. 1983: Environment and living conditions at two Anglo-Scandinavian sites. *Archaeology of York* 14/4.

Hall, A.R. and Kenward, H.K. 1990: Environmental evidence from the Colonia. *The Archaeology of York* 14/6.

Harris, D.R. 1969: Agricultural systems, ecosystems and the origins of agriculture. In Ucko, P.J. and Dimbleby, G.W. (editors), *The Domestication and Exploitation of Plants and Animals* (London, Duckworth) 3–15.

Harris, D.R. and Hillman, G.C. 1989: *Foraging and Farming: the Evolution of Plant Exploitation* (London, Unwin Hyman).

Hather, J.G. 1988: *The Morphological and Anatomical Interpretation and Identification of Charred Vegetative Plant Remains* (London, University of London PhD Thesis).

Higgs, E.S. (editor) 1972: *Papers in Economic Prehistory: Studies by Members of the British Academy Major Research Project in the Early History of Agriculture* (Cambridge, Cambridge University Press).

Higgs, E.S. (editor) 1975: *Palaeoeconomy: being the Second Volume of Papers in Economic Prehistory by Members of the British Academy Major Research Project in the Early History of Agriculture* (Cambridge, Cambridge University Press).

Hillman, G.C. 1984: Interpretation of archaeological plant remains: the application of models from Turkey. In van Zeist, W. and Casparie, W. (editors), *Plants and Ancient Man* (Rotterdam, Balkema) 1–41.

Hillman, G.C. 1986: Plant foods in ancient diet: the archaeological role of palaeofaeces in general and Lindow Man's gut contents in particular. In Stead, I.M., Bourke, J.B. and Brothwell D. (editors), *Lindow Man: the Body in the Bog* (London, British Museum) 99–115.

Hillman, G.C., Robins, G.V., Odowole, D., Sales, K.D., and McNeil, D.A.C. 1985: The use of electron spin resonance spectroscopy to determine thermal histories of cereal grain. *Journal of Archaeological Science* 12, 49–58.

Hillson, S.W. 1986: *Teeth* (Cambridge, Cambridge University Press).

Hillson, S.W. 1989: Teeth; some current developments in research. In Roberts, C.A., Lee, F. and Bintliff, J. (editors), *Burial Archaeology: Current Research, Methods and Developments* (Oxford, British Archaeological Reports British Series 211) 129–149.

Hillson, S.W. and Jones, B.K. 1989: Instruments for measuring surface profiles: an application in the study of ancient human tooth crown surfaces. *Journal of Archaeological Science* 16, 95–105.

Jones, A.K.G. 1988: Provisional notes on fish remains from archaeological deposits at York. In

Murphy P.J., and French C. (editors), *The Exploitation of Wetlands* (Oxford, British Archaeological Report British Series 186) 113–127.

Jones, G.E.M. 1984: Interpretation of archaeological plant remains. In van Zeist, W. and
Casparie, W. (editors), *Plants and Ancient Man* (Rotterdam, Balkema) 43–61.

Jones, G.E.M. 1991: Numerical analysis in archaeobotany. In van Zeist W., Wasylikowa K. and
Behre K-E., *Progress in Old World Palaeoethnobotany* (Rotterdam, Balkema).

Jones, M.K. 1983: *Integrating the Subsistence Economy* (Oxford, British Archaeological Report
International Series 181).

Jones, M.K. 1984: Regional patterns in crop production. In Cunliffe, B.W. and Miles, D.
(editors) *Aspects of the Iron Age in Central Southern Britain* (Oxford, Oxford University
Committee for Archaeology Monograph 2) 120–124.

Jones, M.K. 1985: Archaeobotany beyond subsistence reconstruction. In Barker, G. and
Gamble, C. (editors), *Beyond Domestication in Prehistoric Europe* (London, Academic Press)
107–128.

Jones, M.K. 1988a: The arable field: a botanical battleground. In Jones, M.K. (editor), *Archaeology and the Flora of the British Isles: Human Influence on the Evolution of Plant Communities*
(Oxford, Oxford University Committee for Archaeology Monograph 14) 86–92.

Jones, M.K. 1988b: The phytosociology of early arable weed communities, with special reference
to southern Britain. In *Festschrift: Udelgard Körber-Grohne. Der prähistorische Mensch und
sein Umwelt* (Stuttgart, Konrad Theiss Verlag) 43–51.

Körber-Grohne, U. 1981: Distinguishing prehistoric grains of *Triticum* and *Secale* on the basis
of their surface patterns using the scanning electron microscope. *Journal of Archaeological
Science* 8, 197–221.

Körber-Grohne, U. and Piening, U. 1980: Microstructure of the surfaces of carbonised and
non-carbonised grains of cereals as observed in scanning electron and light microscopes as
an additional aid in determining prehistoric findings. *Flora* 170, 189–228.

Lawton, J.H. and Warren, P.H. 1988: Static and dynamic explanations for patterns in food
webs. *Trends in Ecology and Evolution* 3, 242–4.

Limbrey, S. 1975: *Soil Science and Archaeology* (London, Academic Press).

May, R.M. 1972: Will a large complex system be stable? *Nature* 238, 413–414.

McCarthy, M.R. 1991: *The Roman Waterlogged Remains and Late Features at Castle Street
Carlisle: Excavations 1981/2. Fascicule 1* (Cumberland and Westmoreland Antiquarian and
Archaeological Society Research Series 5).

McLaren, F.S., Evans, J. and Hillman, G.C. 1991: Identification of charred seeds from epipa-
laeolithic sites of S.W. Asia. In Pernicka, E. and Wagner, G.A. (editors), *Archaeometry '90*
(Basel, Birkhäuser Verlag) 797–806.

McGlade, J. and Allen, P. 1986: Disequilibrium models of human ecosystems. *Science and
Archaeology* 28, 44–50.

Pimm, S.L. 1982: *Food Webs* (London, Chapman and Hall).

Rackham, D.J., Batey, C.E., Jones, A.K.G. and Morris, C.D. 1984: Freswick Links, Caithness:
report on environmental survey 1979. *Circaea* 2, 29–55.

Robinson, D. and Rasmussen, P. 1989: Botanical investigations at the Neolithic Lake Village
at Weier, North East Switzerland. In Milles, A., Williams, D. and Gardner, N. (editors), *The
Beginnings of Agriculture* (Oxford, British Archaeological Reports International Series 496)
149–163.

Rosenzweig, M.L. 1971: Paradox of enrichment: destabilization of exploitation ecosystems in
ecological time. *Science* 171, 385–387.

Sheridan, A. and Bailey, G.N. (editors) 1981: *Economic Archaeology: Towards an Integration of
Ecological and Social Approaches* (Oxford, British Archaeological Reports International
Series 96).

Thomas, K.D. 1983: Agricultural and subsistence systems of the third millennium B.C. in north-west Pakistan: a speculative outline. In Jones, M. (editor) *Integrating the Subsistence Economy* (Oxford, British Archaeological Report International Series 181) 279–314.

Thomas, K.D. 1989: Hierarchical approaches to the evolution of complex agricultural systems. In Milles, A., Williams, D. and Gardner, N. (editors), *The Beginnings of Agriculture* (Oxford, British Archaeological Reports International Series 496) 55–73.

Tomlinson, P. 1985: Use of vegetative remains in the identification of dyeplants from water-logged 9th-10th century AD deposits at York. *Journal of Archaeological Science* 12, 269–283.

Wheeler, A. and Jones, A.K.G. 1989: *Fishes* (Cambridge, Cambridge University Press).

Wilson, D.G. 1979: Horse dung from Roman Lancaster: a botanical report. *Archaeo-Physika* 8, 331–349.

New Site Survey Techniques

Proceedings of the British Academy, **77**, 223–232

Remote Sensing in Archaeological Research

I. SHENNAN & D. N. M. DONOGHUE
Environmental Research Centre, University of Durham, Durham DH1 3LE, UK.

Summary. The adoption of remote-sensing data and their analysis within archaeological research has been significantly less than in other environmental sciences. Although some applications are limited by the nominal ground resolution of the sensors, multi-spectral remote sensing data from satellite platforms, mainly Landsat TM and SPOT, and the NERC airborne campaigns have been used successfully for archaeological applications. The vast reduction in hardware and software costs and the large archive of data available combine to provide a potential major archaeological archive. Such data can then be used for a range of investigations, at varying spatial scales, and also provide the foundation for comprehensive, cost efficient monitoring programmes. There are further archaeological applications in non-northwest European environments. Recent developments of new sensors and image analysis software also offer new archaeological applications.

1. Introduction

Remote sensing techniques, the imaging of phenomena from a distance, have long been a research tool in archaeology. Aerial photography is probably the most widely used of such techniques, and at the scale of individual site investigations various forms of geophysical and seismic survey can be applied. The methods to be discussed in this paper involve multispectral imagery from scanners mounted on aircraft and satellites to identify archaeological features represented by soil and crop marks. These methods should not be viewed as a replacement for other techniques, but as adding to a range which in certain circumstances will enhance the information available

Read 14 February 1991. © The British Academy 1992.

Vegetation Reflectance Spectrum

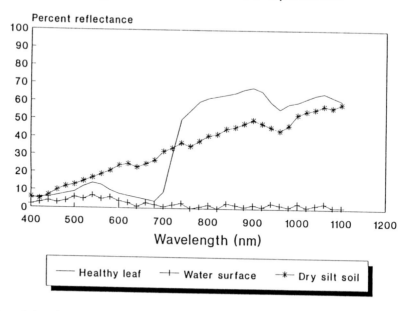

Figure 1. A typical reflectance spectrum for green vegetation, bare soil, and water in the range 400–1200 nanometres. The discrete bandwidths of the various sensors, Table 1, are used either individually or in combination to discriminate between such surfaces according to the reflectance characteristics.

for archaeological applications. In the wider context multispectral data can be integrated with any other form of spatially referenced information, particularly within a Geographic Information System, and many of the image enhancement methods applied to multispectral data can be used with suitably transformed, i.e., digitised, conventional air photography. Therefore multispectral remote sensing has the potential to become a fully integrated and routine technique in archaeological research. At present it is neither.

2. Background

Multispectral scanners, mounted on aircraft or satellites, measure the amount of light reflected from vegetated, ground and water surfaces in discrete parts of the electromagnetic spectrum (Figure 1 and Table 1). Different scanners employ different numbers of spectral channels and band-

Table 1. Summary of sensor specifications. Wavelength units are in nanometres.

Component of electromagnetic spectrum	Daedalus 1268 airborne scanner	Landsat 4 & 5 Thematic Mapper	SPOT Image MSS sensor	SPOT Image panchromatic sensor
visible	420–450			
visible	450–520	450–520		
visible	520–605	520–600	500–590	510–730
visible	605–625			
visible	630–690	630–690	610–680	
short wave IR	695–750			
short wave IR	760–900	760–900	790–890	
short wave IR	910–1050			
short wave IR	1550–1750	1550–1750		
short wave IR	2080–2350	2080–2350		
middle IR	8500–13000	10400–12500		
Sensor resolution	altitude dependent	30 m	20 m	10 m
No. of spectral channels	11	7	3	1

widths. The first major satellite borne sensor was the Landsat Multispectral Scanner, first carried on Landsat 1 in 1972, but with a nominal ground resolution too coarse to be considered for most archaeological applications. The Thematic Mapper (TM), carried first on Landsat 4 in 1982 and still operational on Landsat 5, has a ground resolution of 30 m and is capable of providing much valuable data for a wide range of environmental science applications. Within the United Kingdom these applications have developed alongside airborne and ground-based experiments, for example to evaluate the spatial resolution possible at which different types of feature can be identified.

In order to promote such remote sensing research one of the programmes sponsored by NERC was an airborne remote sensing campaign which has taken place annually since 1982. NERC funded the flying of a Daedalus 11 channel Airborne Thematic Mapper (ATM) together with black and white photography. Such scanners were first constructed in order to simulate satellite sensors such as Landsat TM and were initially experimental instruments. However they can now be used for general applications following radiometric and atmospheric correction (see Donoghue and Shennan 1988a). For mapping and overlay applications geometric correction is necessary, although this results in spectral degradation because of the re-sampling of data elements.

The Landsat TM has seven discrete spectral channels, three within the visible spectrum, and four infrared channels (Table 1). The eleven channels of the Daedalus scanner include seven which are very close to the specifications of Landsat TM. Since 1986 the SPOT Image satellites have been operational, with fewer channels than Landsat TM, but a finer ground resolution (Table 1). These three families of sensors are currently the major ones to be considered for archaeological applications. The discrete channels of the multispectral sensors are used in combination, for example as ratios or composites, to enhance features of interest identified as a result of the surface reflection and absorption characteristics (Figure 1).

3. Trial investigation

In 1985 a three year project was initiated to evaluate the capability of multispectral remote sensing data for detecting and mapping archaeological features manifest as crop and soil marks. The chosen test site was Morton Fen, located at the western margins of the Fenlands of eastern England.

The area consists of marine and freshwater sediments deposited at or near the coast over the last 6500 years. The fen is traversed by ancient drainage channels, now sediment-filled, equivalent to creeks on modern salt marshes and the spatial pattern of these former channels reflect the changing environmental conditions prevailing at the coastal margin due to man and to changing land-sea level relationships. Morton Fen has been investigated in detail on two occasions, between 1951–52, and between 1984-present. The former study involved a comprehensive regional survey of crop and soil marks and was published by Hallam in 1970. The latter study formed part of the Fenland Project (e.g., Lane 1988) which seeks to re-assess the archaeology and environmental history of the entire Fenland region surrounding the Wash estuary. During this study close links were forged with members of the Fenland Project who mapped Morton and surrounding fens and who provided advice on interpretation of the imagery and assistance with palaeoenvironmental reconstruction. We in turn provided new data on crop and soil marks as well as maps and dates of the sedimentary sequence.

The area was considered particularly suitable for remote sensing survey because its flat terrain simplifies spectral analysis yet it incorporates a wide variety of crop types and farming practices. In addition, land drainage and deep ploughing have caused changes in the surface soil due to peat oxidation and wind erosion. Consequently, there has been an overall reduction in altitude of the land surface and, with time, features once at depth are liable to be revealed at the surface. Thus, there is an urgent need for survey and monitoring of the wide areas so affected, lest archaeological information be lost.

Specific details of much of the project have been published elsewhere (e.g.,

Donoghue and Shennan 1988a, 1988b), and only the major conclusions are summarised here.

i) Digital multispectral data were processed and enhanced to reveal successfully a range of features of archaeological significance, though Landsat TM data (30 m ground resolution) yielded little useful archaeological information. In contrast, airborne data collected at nominal ground (pixel) resolutions of 2, 5, and 10 m highlighted a considerable amount of palaeoenvironmental and archaeological detail (Plate 3(a), see also Shennan and Donoghue 1988a, 1988b; SERC 1988). Degradation of the 10 m data has indicated that features are also revealed at 20 m nominal pixel resolution. These results suggested that the SPOT-1 panchromatic and multispectral data (10 m and 20 m ground resolution respectively) have the potential to provide information on archaeological and palaeoenvironmental features for large areas at a comparatively low cost, since a single scene can be purchased for *ca.* £1500 and covers an area 60 by 60 km. The potential appears confirmed by Plates 3(b) and 3(c), although the full image has yet to be analysed.

ii) Airborne multispectral data collected during the early growing season, May, revealed more information than all the available conventional air photography. This was primarily due to crop marks being more apparent at a waveband in the near infrared (760–900 nm) and soil marks particularly well defined in the wavelength range 630–690 nm. These results emphasised the additional benefits of sensing in several discrete rather than one single waveband. The ability to enhance data for discrete wavebands reduces the dependence on the time of year for revealing archaeological features.

iii) Quantitative analysis of the eleven wavebands of the airborne Daedalus scanner to select the three bands which will optimise image contrast (Sheffield 1985) pick out, following calibration, combinations of three wavebands out of bands 3, 4, 5, 6 and 7 (Table 1, and Donoghue and Shennan 1988b). In comparison, qualitative processing for detecting features shows that bands 5, 7, 10 and 11 proved to contain most information. Bands 3, 5 and 7 of the Daedalus scanner have similar bandwidths to multispectral channels on the SPOT MSS sensor. Bands 10 and 11 only have similarities with bandwidths on Landsat.

iv) Analysis of the airborne data demonstrated a necessity for their calibration, and for the development and implementation of various image enhancement and feature extraction algorithms. Establishing a physical basis for their interpretation and an operational methodology for information extraction served as the basis for this work. Where possible, procedures have been developed that can be applied to the analysis and interpretation of satellite data.

v) Archaeological features such as artificial and natural watercourses, ditches, salterns, peat-cuttings and settlements have been identified using methods such as contrast stretching, spatial filtering (directional high pass or Prewitt spatial box-filter) and numerical transforms (e.g., the Karhunen-Loeve transform). A number of these, and others, were programmed and installed on an IBM PC system (the main image processing was carried out on an I²S system).

vi) Multi-temporal coverage of the same site reveals extra information. For example a superficial crop mark revealed by seed germination patterns may not relate to the same feature that is revealed later in the year by a deeply rooting mature crop; overlaying (a technique common in Geographical Information Systems) eases such analyses.

vii) Considerable problems were encountered in relating the relative geometries of data from adjacent airborne flight lines. Similar difficulties arose in comparing and combining multi-temporal airborne data. These problems were attributed to the inherent instability of aircraft as data collection platforms, combined with the nature of the sensor used. Airborne linescan data commonly displays a varying geometry along and between flight lines. These variations are inconsistent, and unless detailed information on attitude changes for the platform are available, they cannot be fully compensated for. In contrast, satellite platforms are very stable thereby providing imagery with a consistent geometry which promotes both the comparison and combination of adjacent and overlapping data sets.

viii) Analysis of soil properties has led to a greater understanding of the physical processes that relate soil disturbance to spectral properties. Land drainage and farming methods in the Fenlands lead to changes in the surface due to peat oxidation, wind erosion and deep ploughing. Features once at depth become revealed as they begin to influence the rooting zone. A satellite-based monitoring system would be able to reveal these changes in a cost-effective manner and target smaller areas for specific study and possible conservation.

4. The current situation

Coles (1986) identified site preservation, display potential and cost effectiveness as particular problems facing current research in wetland archaeology. In the broader context site identification and management can be added. Survey using remote sensing data from aircraft or from high spatial resolution satellite data can provide detail of the context of sites and their landscapes, early detection of sites under threat and is rapid and repeatable. The techniques are particularly valuable in areas such as the English Fenland, the Humber estuary, north-west England and the Somerset levels and their hinterlands where previous survey work is fragmentary and the nature of the archaeology is difficult to convey to the public without the use of convincing maps and images of palaeoenvironments.

Though helpful to the Fenland Project it was apparent that the remote sensing programme could have been more useful if it had been coordinated with the Project. The two ran simultaneously rather by chance than due to pre-planning. If the remote sensing programme had been operational and available at the earliest stage of the Fenland Project the ability to survey rapidly a large area, *ca.* 4000 km^2, could have helped with the targeting of resources as well as providing significant environmental information.

The situation has changed significantly since 1985. At that time major limitations on the use of remote sensing were the costs of equipment, software and data. The processing during the trial investigation were performed using an image analysis system installed on a minicomputer. The total outlay excluding data, estimated commercial prices, would have been in the order of £70k to £100k. A number of the image processing methods which were found most useful during the trial investigation were incorporated into a system which could run on a personal computer with high resolution colour graphics display. Although there are limitations regarding data storage and the requirement for a facility to pre-process the satellite data delivered on computer tapes, it is now possible to analyse and display ATM, Landsat TM and SPOT data on a PC system with a capital outlay, including software but not data, of less than £5k. This puts such methods within the reach of most levels of archaeological research, national through to the county unit.

Commercial data costs are in the region of £1500 for a 60 × 60 km image, approximately £0.41 per square kilometre, for satellite imagery. In addition there are existing archives held by NERC which could be useful for any hindcasting approach and for establishing any monitoring programme. Similarly there are over 100 different sites flown between 1982 and 1990 (Figure 2) during the NERC ATM campaigns. These provide a very valuable data source, with multispectral data at a fine ground resolution, in some cases 2 m. This archive has not been systematically evaluated for archaeological users. It should also be possible to envisage specific future airborne campaigns structured to support major archaeological programmes.

While hardware and software costs have decreased by at least a factor of ten over the past five years there remain potential limitations on the wide adoption of remote sensing in archaeological research. Two that are easily recognised are perception and personnel. The trial investigation using Morton Fen was possible because of the foresight of SBAC to support another project originating essentially from outside the discipline of arch-

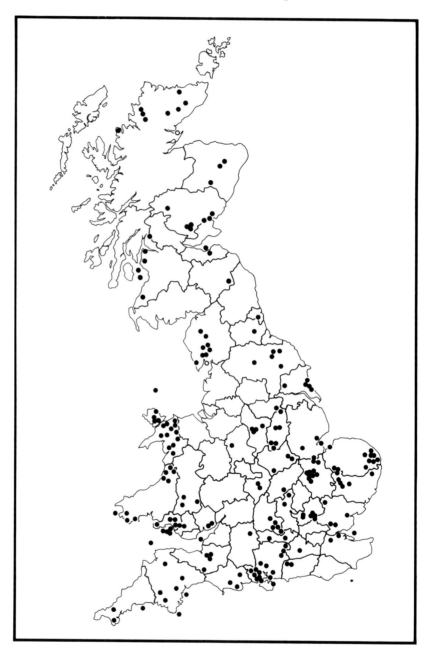

Figure 2. Location of sites flown during the NERC ATM campaigns 1982–89.

aeology. Only with similar open views will the methods become adopted. It is ironic that one comment which has subsequently been made about the project was that resources should not be committed to programming algorithms since they exist elsewhere. Yet it is precisely developments of such work which are now part of one of the commercially available software packages that allow processing to be carried out cheaply on a personal computer. The next stage is to view remote sensing as only one input into computer-based Geographic Information Systems, so that the results can be integrated with other archaeological data, both in a research and management role.

The second potential limitation is that of trained personnel. Remote sensing and image analysis is not a common part of archaeological training at present and it could take some years for this to take place. Furthermore, such skills are in short supply in the commercial sector, particularly environmental consultancy which is likely to be a growing field in the next decade. Given this situation the ability to attract and retain competent personnel may be a significant limitation.

5. Possible future developments

It would be optimistic to suggest that all of the following will occur, but the opportunity exists to employ satellite and airborne remotely sensed imagery in numerous archaeological applications. The NERC archive of satellite and ATM data should be routinely analysed; major archaeological projects should incorporate remotely sensed imagery at an early stage of project formulation in order to target ground resources; satellite data at 10 m and 20 m ground resolution could be used in initial surveys where an understanding of the large scale environmental context is lacking; annual monitoring programmes could become established within management strategies, since as soil changes occur due to drainage and agricultural activities existing information on both archaeological sites and environmental context may be destroyed while previously new information will be discovered. The ability to monitor large areas repeatedly using current technology is possible.

There are also continuing enhancements in sensor technology and image processing which have yet to be evaluated within an archaeological context. For example, archaeologically related crop marks are often associated with moisture or mineral stress of the vegetation canopy which may be observed as a systematic deviation in the reflectance curve from a that of healthy vegetation. Such features, which can be seen in laboratory measurements, require a spectral resolution of 10 nm or less in order to be resolved. Recent advances in instrument design have led to the use of imaging spectrometers with 10 nm spectral resolution in mineral exploration surveys. These data sets are likely to be of considerable value to archaeologists in the near future.

Another technique of major importance is the use of multispectral remote sensing at mid-infrared wavelengths for sediment mapping. In the mid-infrared many silicate, carbonate and sulphate minerals are characterised by their emittance variations in the 8000–12000 nm wavelength region. The strongest spectral features, known as the Reststrahlen band, are due to SiO_2 bending and stretching modes. The strengths and positions of absorptions at mid-infrared wavelengths give the potential for remote mapping quartz content in sedimentary facies. A preliminary investigation of this possibility is planned for the summer of 1991 using NASA's Thermal Infrared Multispectral Scanner (TIMS).

Acknowledgements

Much of this work was carried out with support from SERC Grant GRD22056, and NERC provided the resources for the ATM and SPOT data.

References

Coles, J.M. 1986: Precision, purpose and priorities in wetland archaeology. *Antiquaries Journal* 66, 227–247

Donoghue, D.N.M. and Shennan, I. 1988a: The application of multispectral remote sensing techniques to wetland archaeology. In Murphy, P. and French, C. (editors), *The Exploitation of Wetlands* (Oxford, British Archaeological Reports British Series 186) 47–59.

Donoghue, D.N.M. and Shennan, I. 1988b: The application of remote sensing to environmental archaeology. *Geoarchaeology* 3, 275- 285.

Hallam, S.J. 1970: Settlement around the Wash. In Phillips, C.W. (editor), *The Fenland in Roman Times: Studies of a Major Area of Peasant Colonisation with a Gazetteer Covering all Known Sites and Finds* (London, Royal Geographical Society Research Series 5) 22–113.

Lane, T. 1988: Pre-Roman origins for settlement on the Fens of south Lincolnshire. *Antiquity* 62, 314–321.

SERC 1988: *Science-based Archaeology Committee Report* 1985–88 (Swindon, Science and Engineering Research Council).

Sheffield, C. 1985: Selecting band combinations from multispectral data. *Photogrammetric Engineering and Remote Sensing* 51, 681–687.

PLATE 3

(c)

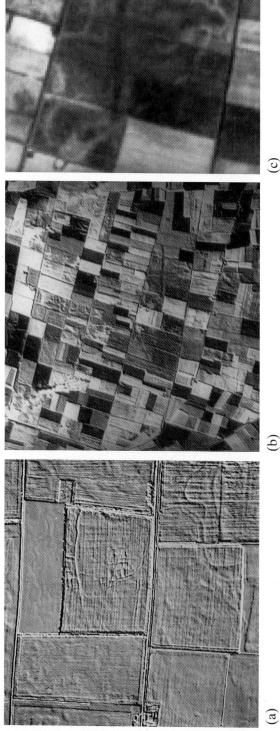

(b)

(a)

(a) Crop marks indicating a settlement site, and associated artificial and natural water courses. The data are from band 7 of the NERC ATM Daedalus scanner, Table 1, with a nominal ground resolution of 2m, and have undergone an edge enhancing procedure. (b) SPOT Image panchromatic image of Morton Fen, after edge enhancement. A series of features are visible, some of which are enlarged on Plate (c). The pixel resolution is 10m and the Plate shows an area ca. 10.2 km by 10.2 km. (c) SPOT Image panchromatic image of Morton Fen showing a medieval field boundary (T. Lane, pers. comm.), the dark horizontal line; a part of the 'Bourne–Morton Canal' (probable Romano–British age) running SW–NE on the right of the Plate; and various extinct, meandering tidal creeks.

PLATE 4

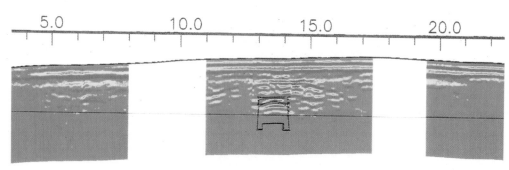

阿武山古墳地中レーダー　東西セクション
Ground probing rader surveying of *Abuyama* tumulus(E-W section)

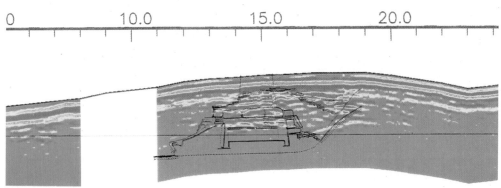

阿武山古墳地中レーダー　南北セクション
Ground probing rader surveying of *Abuyama* tumulus(N-S section)

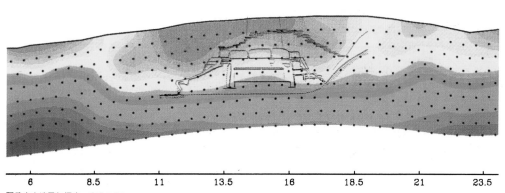

阿武山古墳電気探査　南北セクション
Resistivity surveying of *Abuyama* tumulus(N-S section)

Ground-probing radar sondages and resistivity pseudosection over a shallow tumulus. (a) radar E-W section. (b) radar N-S section. (c) twin-probe pseudosection, N-S. Subsequent excavation features are superimposed.

Proceedings of the British Academy, **77**, 233–244

New Developments in Geophysical Prospection

A. ASPINALL

*Department of Archaeological Sciences, University of Bradford,
Bradford BD7 1DP, UK.*

Summary. The application of remote sensing to the problems of field archaeology has developed from somewhat speculative research exercises in the late 1940's to, virtually, routine procedures demanded of major archaeological field investigation. It is now accepted practice for site developers to contract for geophysical survey prior to planning so as to assess the archaeological potential of the site. Thus the methodology has "arrived" and, because of its widespread routine application, the future of scientific research in the discipline can, on the face of it, be questioned. However, developers and archaeologists now demand more complete interpretation of their sites in advance of planning decisions. This paper discusses research developments in three, inter-related, directions —area survey, vertical section sondage, and data interpretation—in which very significant progress in prospection techniques is being made. Examples of recent developments in instrumentation and methodology are presented, together with illustrations of recent achievements in data presentation.

1. Introduction

New developments in the natural sciences have frequently found application in science-based archaeology and geophysical prospection continues to benefit in this way. Developers and archaeologists now demand more complete interpretation of their sites in advance of planning decisions. The vast catalogue of "routine" data already accumulated awaits enhanced interpretation and the planning of future survey strategies will increasingly rely on

Read 14 February 1991. © The British Academy 1992.

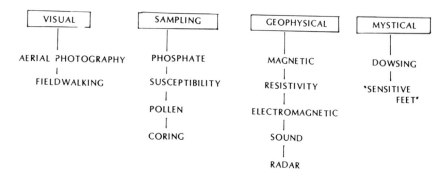

Figure 1. Archaeological prospection methods.

these improved procedures. It is, therefore, appropriate to discuss research developments along three directions:

 i) area survey,

 ii) vertical section sondage,

 iii) data interpretation.

These are, clearly, inter-related; current and future research activities may be identified under these headings and are discussed in the following sections.

2. Area survey

Assessment of the potential of sites through area reconnaissance continues to command the greatest attention amongst archaeologists. The techniques available may be considered, somewhat arbitrarily, as "true" remote sensing through airborne and satellite cover and as geophysical, land-based, prospection.

Developments in true remote sensing have been presented in the comprehensive paper by Shennan and Donoghue (this volume) and require no further comments here, other than an endorsement of the important role of these methods in rural site assessment. The present paper, however, will be concerned with advances in geophysical prospection.

It is convenient to list methods available for site location and identification as in Figure 1, where, for completeness, aerial photography has been included. The role of scientifically-controlled field-walking, using statistically valid sampling procedures, should not be minimised, particularly in terms of site identification and history. Coupled with other scientific sampling procedures listed, field-walking can produce site information of great archaeological significance. The description of dowsing as "mystical" will be

Figure 2. The twin-probe array in use with an RM4 earth resistivity system.

regarded by devotees as biased and unfair, which is certainly not intended. Indeed the technique should be viewed with an open mind, as having, as yet, no proven scientific basis, hence "mystical".

Geophysical prospection on a large scale is now an accepted procedure in field archaeology. *Earth resistance* and *magnetism* measurements carry by far the greatest work-load, with constantly improving field methodology and data-presentation. Computer-based data logging and on-site data processing are now routine, so that frequent up-dating of site strategy can be implemented. A schedule of two hectares per 12 hour day of survey is not uncommon using the techniques illustrated in Figures 2, 3 and 4. Because of this fast through-put of data, it now becomes economic to utilise the complementary nature of the anomalies detected by the two principal methods of survey. Thus a high resistivity response, coupled with a high magnetic signal is readily interpreted as an electrically impervious feature of igneous rock or human-fired structure such as a kiln. The ambiguous behaviour of resistivity measurements in the detection of ditches under different conditions of ground saturation may negate such conclusions, but this in itself offers scope for further investigative study (Clark 1990). A further research development offered by the speed of data retrieval lies in the interpretation of anomaly "shapes". Traditionally, readings of earth properties have been taken at discrete intervals, typically one metre. This sample interval gives inadequate evidence for study of the true variations of response obtained through continuous recording. However, by reducing the sampling interval to 0.25

Figure 3. Continuous earth resistance measurements with the RATEAU system and a mobile "square" array.

metre, a more realistic characteristic is obtained. Such close sampling is now entirely feasible (Figures 2, 3 and 4) in both resistivity and magnetometer surveys. In the former case multiprobe systems are in development (see section 3) which may provide interpretation of the depth and vertical characteristics of features. In magnetometry the comparison of practical and theoretical anomaly shapes provides similar information.

The simultaneous measurement of the electrically conductive and magnetic properties of the earth, using non-contact methods has been studied for the past three decades. The technique is described as an *electromagnetic method*, but, essentially, uses time-varying magnetic fields which induce secondary fields within the conductive and magnetic earth. Transmitting and receiving coils, appropriately spaced, continuously traverse without earth contact; phase and amplitude measurements of the secondary time varying fields may be interpreted in terms of magnetic and conductive properties (Scollar *et al.* 1990). Commercial systems are available to undertake such surveys, but they suffer the common limitation of linking adequate resolution with too shallow scanning depth. Alternative scanning systems may, however, be feasible. Skinner (1990) utilised a large transmitting coil which encompassed a selected area of a site and created a pulsed magnetic field which was, effectively, uniform to a useful penetration depth. The area within the loop was scanned using a smaller "search" coil to detect conducting

Figure 4. Rapid magnetic surveying with the FMl8 fluxgate gradiometer.

(metallic) or magnetically viscous bodies. Taken with corresponding magnetometer readings, the viscous anomalies can yield useful information on
the archaeological significance of such features. There remains, therefore, a
challenging area of study in the full interpretation of data, depending on
frequency of alternating field, depth of targets and, perhaps more interestingly, their magnetic properties.

   Although not strictly regarded as true remote sensing, the investigation of
archaeological potential through on-site soil sampling is attracting increasing
attention. The use of enhanced phosphate concentrations and magnetic
susceptibility of such samples is regarded as evidence for past occupation.
However, the adoption of a good code of practice in the choice of technique
for sampling, analysis and interpretation is long overdue as is the critical
assessment of other possible parameters, such as the trace element distribu-

tion under different environmental conditions. Recent work involving the analysis of vertical cores taken at strategic intervals in the vicinity of occupation sites (Dockrill and Gater 1991) has demonstrated the potential of the sampling approach.

3. Vertical section sondage

It is doubtful whether the concept of vertical sectioning without digging would find approval amongst some field archaeologists, but the total excavation of all recognised archaeological sites is clearly impracticable. There is, therefore, a demand for methods of vertical sondage, which will give a true representation of archaeological features. It is in this direction that the main thrust of research in geophysical prospection now appears to be aimed, with the application of traditional geological methods and the development of advanced electromagnetic systems.

When a buried object is "scanned" by the probe array of a typical earth resistivity system, the form of response obtained depends on a number of factors, including the interprobe separation, object dimensions and shape and the object depth. Thus the profile obtained is unique to these four parameters, but a single scan is not adequate to obtain other than an approximate estimate of object dimensions. However, repeated scans with different probe separations (Figure 5) result in a data assemblage from which an attempt may be made to resolve the four parameters. This technique creates a so-called *pseudo-section* (Edwards 1977) which, effectively, is a model vertical section through the earth along the line of survey, into which a perturbation, representative of the object, appears. Because of the, generally, sophisticated relationship between the resistivity response and the four variables, full identification of the object from the perturbation is not easy and becomes increasingly difficult if a complex of objects exists, perhaps in non-homogeneous earth; both conditions are common in archaeology. In geological practice, the field procedures for creating pseudo-sections have been slow and laborious. However, for archaeological applications, the largest inter-probe spacing needed is seldom greater than a few metres and, with the development of fast solid-state switching devices, it has now become feasible to lay out, in the field, multiprobe systems which are switched rapidly through the relevant inter-probe spacings, with automatic logging of data and, hence, fast pseudo-section production. Research can, therefore, focus on the effectiveness of different probe systems and on new data treatment techniques, which are appropriate for the complex responses obtained from archaeological features (Plate 4). An interesting development of the multiprobe concept has been in *tomography*. Traditionally this technique of selec-

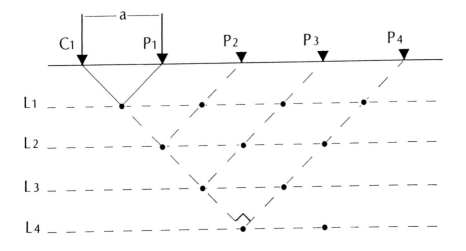

Figure 5. Pseudosection "pixels" using a multi-electrode, twin-probe array. 'Levels' (L) refer to 'pseudo-depths' with respect to interprobe spacing (CP).

tive imagery has been applied in X-radiography, but was extended to the study of softer body organs using *in situ* multi-electrode potential measurements. The latter approach has recently been applied to multiprobe systems in geophysical prospection by Noel and his colleagues (Noel and Walker 1991). However, the nature of the problem is considerably more complex than that of a controlled laboratory experiment involving "predictable" features and it may be assumed that data interpretation will encounter comparable problems to those inherent in pseudo-section theory.

The use of "echo-sounding" has excited interest from the earliest days of geophysical prospection of archaeology. *Sonic* and "shock" (*seismic*) techniques have been examined but, in general, have found limited use, primarily because of the low resolution obtained at the acoustic frequencies associated with geological applications. However, the possibility of studying buried interfaces utilising mechanical (elastic) property contrasts continues to offer promise in conditions where electrical and magnetic contrasts are low. Recent developments in high frequency transponders and in the selective use of refracted and reflected shear waves, based on geological experience, have led to practical systems for shallow surveys. At this stage, however, data throughput is slow and further study is required in the interpretation of sondages obtained from complex structures.

Undoubtedly the greatest potential for unambiguous sub-surface profiling lies at the high radio-frequency end of the electromagnetic spectrum, through *ground-penetrating radar*. The technique has recently generated great excitement amongst field archaeologists following a striking display of "realistic" vertical sections at an urban site in York. In fact the technique has been in use for about twenty years, primarily for civil engineering. Several commercial organisations are now offering services to archaeology in Britain and use of the technique, with varying degrees of success, has been reported world-wide. Perhaps the most significant investigations have been published by workers in Japan. Imai, Nishimura and their colleagues have carried out wide-ranging comparisons between radar and other techniques of prospection (Imai *et al.* 1987, 137; Nishimura and Kamai 1991, 757). In Plate 4 the resistivity pseudo-section of a shallow tumulus excavation is compared with the radar section, followed by confirmatory excavation.

Certainly, however, it would appear that the York survey was exceptional and that there is a requirement for considerably more research into the method before its potential is fulfilled. Two aspects of the technique will justify extended research programmes. Firstly the basic physical phenomena associated with ground propagation of radio-waves in the frequency range 100–1000 MHz must be clearly assessed for the specific boundary features, both man-made and natural, associated with archaeology. The contradictory requirements of high resolution and good ground penetration should be examined in terms of optimum frequency bands and antennae arrays for different ground conditions. Radar survey techniques currently in use are reminiscent of early days of more conventional geophysical surveys with a noticeable lack of mutual appreciation of the problems of surveyor and archaeologist. There is a clear need for a rational policy of site investigation based on such understanding and close collaboration between the two. The second, and related, point is that of adequate data processing and interpretation. By the nature of the technique, data processing has borrowed from the procedures of seismic survey. On-site presentation of data, through intensity-modulated scans of depth profiles is generally unsatisfactory, in terms of ready interpretation, except for the simplest of anomalies. Attempts to utilise the sophisticated software of the seismic geologist have had limited success. It is now necessary to develop software for the specific analysis of near-surface features based on the e.m. theory of near-distance scattering phenomena at interfaces of electrical permitivity contrast. This must be coupled to a realistic approach to the practical problems of surface topography, over which the profiling is undertaken.

4. Data interpretation

Whatever the method adopted for geophysical survey, the ultimate goal must be to provide the archaeologist with an unambiguous display, which is identifiable in its structural context. Individual methods of survey present their own problems of interpretation, which are symptomatic of the technique employed. Thus the geophysical "fingerprint" of a simple magnetic dipole beneath the earth's surface is recognised in terms of its pattern of a "positive", partly or wholly surrounded by a negative, anomaly, dependent on the magnetic latitude. Complex magnetic features may be modelled, based on such concepts and compared with "real" magnetic surveys using, for example, data inversion and cross-correlation methods to reveal specific structures (Tsokas *et al.* 1991).

The problems of data interpretation of ground-penetrating radar have been referred to above. More generally the apparent need to smooth or filter field data so as to obtain the optimum signal to "noise" response has led to increasing sophistication in methods adopted. The availability of microcomputer-based software and graphic displays has greatly facilitated these developments, so that rapid data handling is followed by a variety of display formats embodying the large range of grey scale and false colour levels available with modern graphics (Aspinall and Haigh, 1988). Typically, following an earth resistance survey of Kirkstall Abbey by the West Yorkshire Archaeological Unit, the data handling (Cheetham *et al.* 1991) included linear and non-linear grey-scale representations (Figures 6a, b, c), together with Fourier filter and edge enhancement procedures (Figure 6d). This last treatment emphasised feature edges in a spectacular way to create a new impression of the complexity of development of this site from the medieval to the Victorian period. There is, however, a real danger in applying image cleaning, of the type usually undertaken for "ordered" images where noise is truly random, to an archaeological site. Frequently, long-term occupation gives rise to a proliferation of, apparently, random long or short wavelength features such as post-holes, pits, levelled structures etc. A quite distorted view may be given, after filtering, compared with that seen by the archaeologist after stripping the site. Such ambiguities have given rise to serious misgivings amongst archaeologists, in the use of recent radar sondages, for example. Problems of this nature, however, are there to be solved. In the past decade, advances in geophysical area and sondage survey techniques and site presentation have utilised fast data acquisition and handling developments, very effectively. Doubtless this successful exploitation will continue to benefit the cause of field archaeology into the next century when the archaeologist's

A. Aspinall

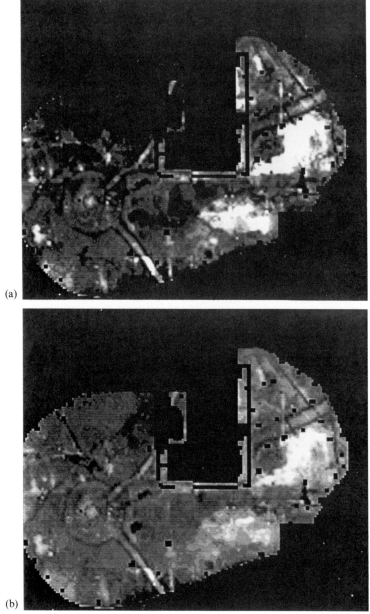

(a)

(b)

Figure 6. Kirkstall Abbey, W. Yorks: earth resistance grey-scale presentations. (a) linear: range black-white, 40–100 ohm. (b) non-linear to enhance contrast. (c) high pass Fourier filter. (d) high pass Fourier filter with edge enhancement. To the west (left) of the excavated guest house is a Victorian band-stand with radiating paths: to the south lies the kitchen area: to the east a Victorian garden scheme overlies earlier buildings. The production of 'artefact' edges is suspected in Figure 6.

(c)

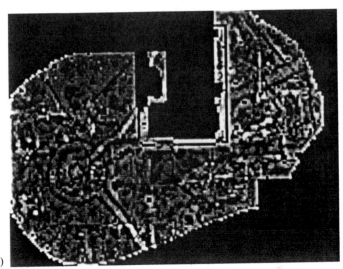

(d)

dream (or nightmare) of "peeling off" successive occupation layers on a site, without digging, may be an achievable goal.

Acknowledgements

I am indebted to the following colleagues who permitted my use of figures as follows:

J. Leckebusch, Figure 3
J.A. Pocock, Figure 5

Y. Nishimura, Plate 4

J.G.B. Haigh, Figure 6

Figures 2 and 4 are reproduced by courtesy of Geophysical Surveys, Bradford Ltd.

References

Aspinall, A. and Haigh, J.G.B. 1988: A review of techniques for the graphical display of geophysical data. In Rahtz, S.P.Q. (editor), *Computer and Quantitative Methods in Archaeology* (Oxford, British Archaeological Reports, International Series 446) 295–307.

Cheetham, P., Haigh, J.G.B. and Ipson, S. 1991: Archaeological perception of geophysical data. In Budd, P., Chapman, B. Jackson, C., Janaway, R. and Ottaway, B. (editors), *Archaeological Sciences 1989* (Oxford, Oxbow Monographs 9) 273–287.

Clark, A. 1990: *Seeing Beneath the Soil* (London, Batsford).

Dockrill, S.J. and Gater, J.R. 1991: Tofts Ness: exploitation and interpretation in a prehistoric landscape. In Spoerry, P.S. (editor). *Geoprospection in the Archaeological Landscape* (Oxford, Oxbow) in press.

Edwards, L.S. 1977: A modified pseudosection for resistivity and I.P. *Geophysics* 42, 1020–1036.

Imai, T., Sakayama, T. and Kaiomori, T. 1987: Use of ground-probing radar and resistivity surveys for archaeological investigations. *Geophysics* 52, 137–150.

Nishimura, Y. and Kamai, H. 1991: A study on the application of geophysical prospection. In Pernicka, E. and Wagner, G.A. (editors), *Archaeometry '90* (Basel, Birkhauser) 757–763.

Noel, M. and Walker, R. 1991: Development of a resistivity tomography system for imaging archaeological structures. In Pernicka, E. and Wagner, G.A. (editors), *Archaeometry '90* (Basel, Birkhauser) 767–776.

Scollar, I., Tabbagh, A., Hesse, A. and Herzog, I. 1990: *Archaeological Prospecting and Remote Sensing* (Cambridge, Cambridge University Press).

Skinner, J.R. 1990: *An Evaluation of Multi-channel P.I.M. in Archaeological Prospecting and Associated Laboratory Experiments.* (Bradford, University of Bradford PhD Thesis).

Tsokas, G.N., Papazachos, C.B., Loucoyannakis, M.Z. and Karousova, O. 1991: Geophysical data from archaeological sites: inversion filters based on the vertical-sided finite prism model. *Archaeometry* 33, 215–230.

SESSION V

The Study of Human Remains

Proceedings of the British Academy, **77**, 247–264

Light Stable Isotopes and the Reconstruction of Prehistoric Diets

N. J. VAN DER MERWE

Archaeometry Laboratories, Peabody Museum, Harvard University, Cambridge, MA 02138, USA.

Summary. Several stable isotope ratios have been measured in human skeletons to determine prehistoric diet. These include the isotopes of nitrogen, sulphur and strontium, which have been used to assess the importance of marine foods in human diets. The systematics of these isotopes in food chains are imperfectly understood, whereas that of carbon is quite well-known. Stable carbon isotope ratios (i.e., $^{13}C/^{12}C$ ratios, reported as $\delta^{13}C$ values) are of particular relevance to terrestrial foodwebs because of the characteristic isotope signatures of plants with different photosynthetic chemistry. The two dominant photosynthetic pathways produce C_3 plants (all trees and woody shrubs; temperate and shaded grasses) and C_4 plants (subtropical and tropical grasses, except those in shaded forests). The carbon isotope ratios of the two plant groups are distinctive and are passed along the food chain to herbivores and carnivores. This fact has been used to trace the spread of, for example, maize agriculture in the woodlands of North America and in the tropical forests of South America, as well as rice agriculture in China. Such applications have invariably made use of bone collagen as sample material, which has restricted their use to the last 10,000 years or so. The alternative is to use substituted carbonates in biological apatite, particularly in tooth enamel, after appropriate chemical cleaning to remove diagenetic carbonates. Although still controversial, this method is being used with success to study the diets of early hominids of more than two million years ago.

Read 14 February 1991. © The British Academy 1992.

1. Introduction

During the past fifteen years, measurements of light stable isotope ratios in bone have been convincingly shown to provide useful indicators of animal and human diets. From the first application in archaeology (Vogel and van der Merwe 1977), this procedure has been expanded to solve problems of prehistoric subsistence world-wide. In certain circumstances—particularly those surrounding the spread of maize agriculture in the Americas—isotopic analysis has become a routine research technique. This application is closely followed by situations where marine and terrestrial foods were involved in a prehistoric subsistence strategy. On a wider screen, isotopic tracing techniques have developed as powerful tools in the life and environmental sciences, from studies of the feeding habits of sardines to evaluations of atmospheric and climatic conditions of the distant past.

This paper is concerned with dietary tracing in archaeology by means of isotopic bone chemistry, specifically the stable isotope ratios of nitrogen and carbon (with emphasis on the latter). Early developments in this field have been reviewed in some detail (van der Merwe 1982; DeNiro 1987) and will not be repeated here. In recent years, as the number of researchers in this field has grown and the applications have multiplied, several seminars and conference panels have produced compilations of work in progress. Of particular significance have been the Advanced Seminars on Dietary Bone Chemistry, which first met in 1986 in Santa Fe, and produced a volume of edited papers (Price 1989). The seminar met again in 1988 at the University of Cape Town; the proceedings, edited by Andrew Sillen and George Armelagos, have appeared as a special issue of the *Journal of Archaeological Science* (volume 18 part 3) and again in Bad Hamburg, Germany, in 1991 (proceedings in preparation).

My involvement with isotopic dietary tracing took place at the University of Cape Town from the mid-1970's on, and more recently at Harvard. In the course of unravelling prehistoric diets in Africa, the Americas, and the Middle East, I have collaborated with many archaeologists and other isotope specialists. Some of them will be mentioned in this article, but this is not a review of the major contributions to this varied field of research. It is, instead, a selected and personal view of some of the highlights I have seen.

2. Bone and light stable isotopes

2.1 Composition of bone

Bone consists of two phases: organic and mineral. The organic phase consists primarily of collagen fibres, which provide a matrix for bone growth. The mineral phase is biological apatite, consisting mostly of calcium phosphate, but with a variety of ions (e.g., fluorine, strontium, carbonate) substituted in the apatite crystals as impurities (Lee-Thorp 1989). Since bone is constructed from the food an animal eats, it encodes information about the diet. Exactly which components of the diet contribute to the organic and mineral phases of bone is a subject of considerable debate and active research. The simplest model holds that dietary proteins build collagen, while carbohydrates and fats build apatite (Krueger and Sullivan 1984). Since humans cannot synthesise certain amino acids (so-called essential amino acids), it is clear that at least these building blocks of collagen must be obtained from dietary proteins. Even here, though, it can be shown that only the carbon skeletons of essential amino acids (excepting threonine and lysine, which are incorporated unchanged) pass directly from food to collagen, while nitrogen is obtained from a pool of glutamic acid in the body which derives from all the nitrogen in the diet (Hare *et al.* 1991). The non-essential amino acids in collagen may be taken directly from dietary proteins or synthesised from the energy portion of the diet. The carbon in apatite-carbonate comes from blood carbonate, which is most likely to derive from the energy portion of the diet. These relationships have not been conclusively demonstrated, which affects the interpretation of carbon and nitrogen isotope signals in bone.

Research on these topics is under way at several centres, but until the models are refined it will be difficult to obtain unequivocal quantitative interpretations of the contribution of major food groups to the building of bone. Qualitative interpretation of the relative importance of certain foods is, of course, possible and is widely applied in archaeology.

2.2 Measurement of isotope ratios

Isotopic dietary tracing is possible because of the uneven distribution in nature of ^{13}C and ^{15}N (the heavy stable isotopes of these elements). Certain categories of food have distinctive ratios of $^{13}C/^{12}C$ and $^{15}N/^{14}N$. These ratios are passed along the foodchain and are recorded in the bone of the consumers. Measurement of these isotopic signals in archaeological bone makes it possible to reconstruct particular elements of the diet. In the case of nitrogen and carbon, isotopic ratios are usually measured in bone collagen after the mineral phase has been dissolved away. The collagen is combusted to form nitrogen and carbon dioxide, which are cryogenically purified. The isotopic ratios of these gases are compared with the known ratio of a standard in a ratio mass spectrometer. The difference between the two ratios is given in parts per mil ($^{0}/_{00}$) in the delta notation, e.g.;

$$\delta^{13}C = \frac{^{13}C/^{12}C \text{ sample} - {}^{13}C/^{12}C \text{ standard}}{^{13}C/^{12}C \text{ standard}} \times 1000$$

For carbon isotope ratios, the standard is a marine carbonate called PDB with a value of zero. Most $\delta^{13}C$ values in nature are negative compared to PDB. For nitrogen the standard is air, and most $\delta^{15}N$ values are positive.

2.3 Nitrogen isotopes

$^{15}N/^{14}N$ ratios are strongly fractionated by metabolic processes; i.e., the ratios are altered. Each trophic level may increase the $\delta^{15}N$ value. A typical terrestrial biotic community in, say, England will have air with a $\delta^{15}N$ value of zero (the standard). Plants which can fix nitrogen in their tissues directly from the air (legumes) will have values near zero. Other plants may have values around $(+)3\,^0/_{00}$, herbivores $4-7\,^0/_{00}$, and carnivores $7-9\,^0/_{00}$. In the ocean, the foodchain is much longer, and the spread of values can range from zero (for air-fixing blue-green algae) at one extreme to values as high as $15-20\,^0/_{00}$ for swordfish and seals (Schoeninger et al. 1983). If an Arctic hunter could stand to live on polar bear meat, he would be so high on the foodchain that his $\delta^{15}N$ value would be above $20\,^0/_{00}$. This information can be used to determine the relative amount of seafood in prehistoric diets, provided that the archaeologist has a fair idea of where in the foodchain the people got their food. Seals and killer whales will yield results quite different from oysters.

Marine/terrestrial contrasts only work for nitrogen isotopes in areas with good rainfall. In dry regions, animals have $\delta^{15}N$ values above $10\,^0/_{00}$, and the top of the foodchain may approach $20\,^0/_{00}$ (Heaton et al. 1986; Ambrose and DeNiro 1986; Sealy et al. 1987). The relationship between annual rainfall and $\delta^{15}N$ values in herbivore bone appears to be inversely linear, with the value going above $10\,^0/_{00}$ as the rainfall drops below 400 mm/year. These values come from empirical field studies, and the phenomenon has not yet been completely explained (Ambrose 1991). High $\delta^{15}N$ values in drought-stressed animals result from the excretion of urea that is depleted in ^{15}N (Ambrose and DeNiro 1986) and also of similarly depleted ammonia. Part of this depletion may be due to urea recycling and intestinal microbial action in the animal (Sealy et al. 1987), which is necessary to extract scarce protein from arid region plants. The animal's metabolism effectively moves it several trophic levels up the foodchain. As a result of these high $\delta^{15}N$ values, it is not possible to tell marine and terrestrial foods apart in dry coastal regions by means of nitrogen isotope analysis. Conversely, however, aridity in the past can be established under certain circumstances.

Our understanding of the distribution of ^{15}N in nature is still in the developmental stages. Recent measurements of nitrogen isotopes in elephant bone from different African habitats (van der Merwe et al. 1990) show that tropical forest animals have relatively high $\delta^{15}N$ values (around $8\,^0/_{00}$), thus refuting the simple relationship with rainfall that had seemed to be established earlier. Archaeological interpretations cannot, as yet, be argued from first principles (as is the case for carbon), but need to be arrived at empirically by measuring the nitrogen isotopes in the natural environment of each case study.

2.4 Carbon isotopes

Dietary tracing in archaeology has been particularly successful with carbon isotopes. This method has been extensively used to trace the spread of maize agriculture in the Americas (some examples are described here), the prehistoric use of African cereals in Europe (Murray and Schoeninger 1988), the the start of rice agriculture in China (Cai and Qiu 1984), and the like. It has also been utilised to study the exploitation of marine foods by coastal people of British Columbia (Chisholm et al. 1982), Japan (Minegawa and Akazawa, in press), Australia (Hobson and Collier 1984), mesolithic Europe (Tauber 1981), and of South Africa (Sealy and van der Merwe 1985).

Stable carbon isotope ratios are fractionated by various natural processes, the most important in this context being different systems of photosynthesis (reviewed in van der Merwe 1982). Plants with C_3 photosynthesis (all trees and woody shrubs, grasses from temperate and shaded forest environments) have foliage with average $\delta^{13}C$ values of $-26.5\,^0/_{00}$. C_4 plants (grasses from the subtropics) have average $\delta^{13}C$ values of $-12.5\,^0/_{00}$. These values have been arrived at from cumulative assessments by many researchers in different parts of the world, and are particularly well demonstrated by the C_3 and C_4 grasses of South Africa (Vogel et al. 1978; Figure 1). The stability of such values depends on an average $\delta^{13}C$ value of about $-7\,^0/_{00}$ for atmospheric carbon dioxide, the source carbon for photosynthesis; it varies with the concentration of carbon dioxide in the atmosphere. Fossil fuel burning is slowly altering this value to about $-8\,^0/_{00}$, for example, while rotting leaf litter in the Amazonian forests produces air near the ground with values as low as $-15\,^0/_{00}$ (van der Merwe and Medina 1989).

When animals eat plants, enrichment in ^{13}C of about $+5\,^0/_{00}$ occurs during the formation of collagen (Figure 2). In savannahs with C_3 trees and shrubs and C_4 grasses, browsers (C_3 plant-eaters) have average collagen values of $-21.5\,^0/_{00}$, while pure grazers average $-7.5\,^0/_{00}$. Mixed feeders fall somewhere in between. For the mineral phase of bone, the enrichment is more extreme (Sullivan and Krueger 1981; Krueger and Sullivan 1984; Lee-Thorp 1989; Lee-Thorp and van der Merwe 1987), at about $+12\,^0/_{00}$, which results in browser apatite of about $-14.5\,^0/_{00}$ and grazer apatite of about $-0.5\,^0/_{00}$. The collagen of carnivores is enriched by a further $2\,^0/_{00}$ or so, but their apatite has about the same value as that of their herbivore prey. Lions in C_4 grassland, for example, have collagen values of about $-5.5\,^0/_{00}$,

N. J. van der Merwe

351 SOUTH AFRICAN GRASS SPECIES
(after Vogel, Fuls & Ellis 1978)

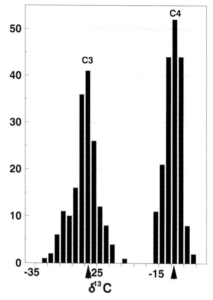

Figure 1. δ^{13}C values of 351 South African grasses illustrate the clear separation between C$_3$ and C$_4$ plants. (After Vogel *et al.* 1978).

while their apatite values average about $-0.5\,^0/_{00}$, like those of the grazing animals they feed on.

The carbon cycle in the oceans is more complicated than that on land (Sealy 1986). The source carbon includes atmospheric carbon dioxide, dissolved bicarbonates, and large deposits of marine carbonates that are continuously dissolved. The first trophic level is represented by various planktonic forms, which exhibit carbon isotope values that vary with water temperature. The second trophic level includes grazing and filter-feeding molluscs and zooplankton; on them are based a complicated foodweb with many trophic levels and a wide range of carbon isotope ratios. Human consumers of seafood may exploit this foodweb at many levels or only a few, depending on preference and technology, with concordant effects on their isotopic ratios. Two marine systems I have studied in detail are those of the Benguela current (western Cape coast, South Africa) described later and the Humboldt current of Ecuador (van der Merwe *et al.* in prep.). Both systems are cold temperate, with cold upwelling from the deep, and are very similar in carbon isotope composition. Foods available to humans vary from mollusc meat near $-18\,^0/_{00}$ to predatory ocean fish and seals with meat near $-12\,^0/_{00}$. In a diet consisting primarily of seafood, energy is provided mostly

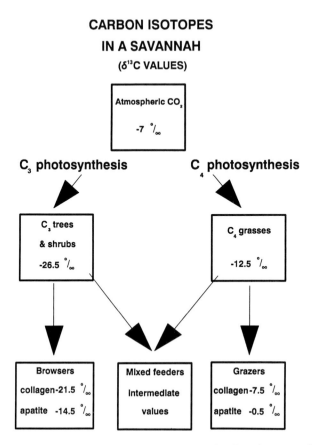

CARBON ISOTOPES

IN A SAVANNAH

(δ^{13}C VALUES)

Atmospheric CO_2

-7 $^{\circ}/_{\circ\circ}$

C_3 photosynthesis C_4 photosynthesis

C_3 trees & shrubs

-26.5 $^{\circ}/_{\circ\circ}$

C_4 grasses

-12.5 $^{\circ}/_{\circ\circ}$

Browsers

collagen -21.5 $^{\circ}/_{\circ\circ}$

apatite -14.5 $^{\circ}/_{\circ\circ}$

Mixed feeders

Intermediate

values

Grazers

collagen -7.5 $^{\circ}/_{\circ\circ}$

apatite -0.5 $^{\circ}/_{\circ\circ}$

Figure 2. Flow diagram of δ^{13}C values in a savannah foodweb, where the trees and shrubs are C_3 and the grasses are C_4 plants.

by fats, which are depleted by $5^{\circ}/_{\circ\circ}$ or more relative to the meat protein in the same animal (Lee-Thorp *et al.* 1989; Figure 3). The result is that the δ^{13}C values of collagen and apatite in human consumers with high seafood diets are very close together, instead of being spaced by about $8^{\circ}/_{\circ\circ}$ as in herbivores. Close spacing of collagen and apatite δ^{13}C values is a general indication of diets high in meats and fats. Omnivores, with carbohydrates and fats in their diets to provide energy, have spacing somewhere between that of herbivores and carnivores.

The carbon isotope values described here have been arrived at through field studies. Experiments with mice and chickens show enrichments of only 1 or $2^{\circ}/_{\circ\circ}$ between laboratory food and consumer collagen (DeNiro and Epstein 1978; Bender *et al.* 1981). In field studies, plant food δ^{13}C values are those of whole foliage, which include a range of food components and

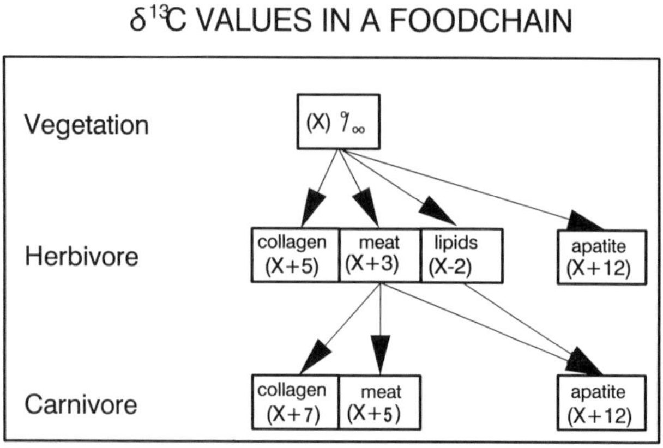

δ¹³C VALUES IN A FOODCHAIN

Figure 3. Flow diagram of $\delta^{13}C$ values on three trophic levels, showing the different storage tissues in animals. (After Lee-Thorp 1989).

cellulose. These differences do not imply that models based on field studies are wrong, but they do underscore the need for more refined models based on laboratory studies which use controlled combinations of different food components. Feeding studies with laboratory rats, designed to answer some of these questions, are currently being conducted by Lambert (Northwestern University), Buikstra (Chicago) and Ambrose (Illinois). A specialised feeding study with pigs (Hare *et al.* 1991) has shown how different amino acids in food translate into consumer tissue. We may expect to learn a great deal about human and animal metabolism from these and similar studies.

3. Prehistoric diets and carbon isotopes

This section includes descriptions of case studies which illustrate the use of carbon isotope ratios to decode prehistoric diets.

3.1 Maize in the American woodlands

The carbon isotope record of human skeletons from the North American Woodlands, particularly the Lower Illinois Valley, provided one of the earliest and most dramatic demonstrations of this dietary tracing technique (van der Merwe and Vogel 1978). In the 1970's and earlier, the consensus of archaeological interpretations held that maize agriculture had been introduced to this region by about AD 400 or earlier. With hindsight, this interpretation can be seen to have been based on little or no direct evidence for the presence of maize, but it provided a plausible subsistence base for the villages that were present and for the large constructions produced by

HUMAN COLLAGEN IN WOODLAND N. AMERICA
(van der Merwe & Vogel 1978)

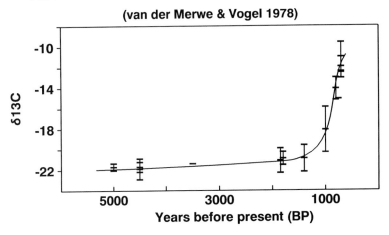

Figure 4. Changes in the δ^{13}C values of human skeletal collagen herald the adoption of maize agriculture in the North American Woodlands after 800 AD.

Hopewell peoples. A study of the dietary pathologies evident in the human skeletons led Jane Buikstra to conclude that the health problems associated with high maize diets did not appear until after AD 800, thus contradicting a generation's worth of archaeological beliefs (reviewed in Buikstra and Milner 1991).

The woodlands provide an ideal situation for determining the importance of a C_4 plant like maize with carbon isotopes, since this biome has essentially no indigenous C_4 plants. Skeletal δ^{13}C values for this region (Figure 4) proved to average about $-21.5\,^0/_{00}$ throughout the Archaic, Early Woodland and Middle Woodland periods, a value identical to that of C_3 herbivores. After AD 800, the carbon isotope ratios changed rapidly to reach $-10\,^0/_{00}$ after AD 1000. The latter value indicates that 75 per cent of the carbon in bone collagen was derived from C_4 plants, as can still be observed among maize-dependent peoples who live in C_3 biomes in other parts of the world. This period of rapid carbon isotope change in the Illinois valley was accompanied by large population increases and a change in settlement patterns, as people moved from villages in the valley bottoms to the uplands and concentrated in larger settlements. These results amply confirmed Buikstra's observations on the dietary status of human skeletons.

In retrospect, two items are noteworthy regarding the diets of Woodland peoples. In the 1980's, archaeologists documented a pre-maize period of horticulture based on indigenous C_3 plants for eastern North America (Smith 1989). This serves to resolve the apparent contradiction between archaeological observations about the complexity of Early and Middle Woodland cultures and the demonstrated absence of maize agriculture. Secondly, a careful study of the carbon isotope values for these periods show that maize may have been present in small quantities, below a level that can be conclusively documented with isotopic measurements. This would mean that the acceptance of maize as a staple was resisted for nearly half a millennium after it was first encountered. This resistance to changes in dietary staples (and their concomitant changes in lifestyle) has been observed ethnographically in many parts of the world; it should be expected as the norm rather than the exception in prehistoric studies of diet.

3.2 Maize in Amazonia

Maize is not an important crop among contemporary forest peoples of Amazonia, who depend on a traditional system of cassava swidden cultivation for calories and forest animals and river fish for protein. In the 1970's, most archaeologists assumed that this tropical forest system had provided the subsistence base for all food-producing peoples in Amazonia before European contact. The dense concentrations of people and incipient kingdoms observed by early European explorers in the floodplains of the lower Orinoco and Amazon were interpreted as intensified examples on fertile soil of the same subsistence base. Anna Roosevelt (1980) and others argued that intensive cassava cultivation could not have supported such large populations, since the modest availability of forest animals and fish during the rainy season limited the protein supply. They argued that another protein source such as maize and beans would have been necessary, and that these crops could have been grown in the floodplains during the short dry season, whereas cassava could not survive the seasonal waterlogging of the soil.

Roosevelt's excavations at Parmana on the lower Orinoco showed that significant cultural changes had taken place in this region between about 800 BC and AD 400. The number of villages and amount of refuse increased significantly, indicating population increases. The artefacts associated with food production changed from flint chips (set in resin on boards to grate cassava) and large ceramic griddles (for drying cassava pulp) to grindstones (for the processing of cereal grains). These changes, she argued, showed that maize agriculture had been adopted in the floodplains by AD 400, and had set the population on a path which resulted in the large concentrations of people seen in early historic times.

The gallery forests of the lower Orinoco valley have no C_4 plants, although the savannahs further from the river do. The forests and swidden fields also have pineapples, which have CAM photosynthesis (crassulacean acid metabolism) and can mimic the carbon isotope values of C_4 plants under certain circumstances. For Roosevelt's argument about a change in protein

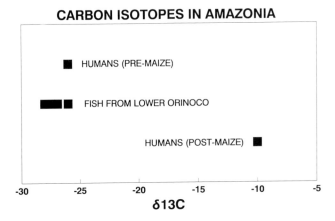

Figure 5. $\delta^{13}C$ values for skeletal collagen of humans and fish in the lower Orinoco show a shift in protein source from fish to maize between 800 BC and AD 400.

source to be sustained, the most telling support from carbon isotope measurements would be a change in human collagen values from pure C_3 to readings with a significant C_4 component. The results proved to be $-26\,^0/_{00}$ for skeletons of about 800 BC and $-10\,^0/_{00}$ for those of about AD 400 (Figure 5). These measurements amply proved her case and showed that the later group was fully dependent on maize as a staple crop.

A quick comparison of the Illinois and Orinoco examples spotlights the unusual value of $-26\,^0/_{00}$ for pre-maize humans in the latter case. In order to explain this value convincingly, it proved necessary to study in detail the carbon isotope ratios in Amazonian foodwebs. For this study (van der Merwe and Medina 1989, 1991) we collected river fish, forest animals, forest and swidden plants, and forest air along the upper Rio Negro in the Amazon basin. The results show (Figure 6) that the entire foodweb of this region has more negative $\delta^{13}C$ values than those encountered in open habitats (e.g., Figure 2). This is especially the case for fish, with collagen values as negative as $-29\,^0/_{00}$ in both the Rio Negro (Figure 6) and the Orinoco (Figure 5); the forest animals have collagen values between -22 and $-25\,^0/_{00}$. The pre-maize humans of the Orinoco appear to have acquired most of their protein from fish.

The depletion of ^{13}C in Amazonian foodwebs is the result of carbon recycling in the dense forests, where abundant leaves from the canopy ($-30\,^0/_{00}$) mix with those of less abundant undergrowth ($-36\,^0/_{00}$) to produce a thick layer of leaf litter ($-31\,^0/_{00}$) on the ground. The rotting leaf litter and the mat of air roots under it release large amounts of carbon dioxide to produce an air mixture under the canopy which is depleted in ^{13}C; this air is recycled by photosynthesis in the forest. Since the forest foodweb is ultimately

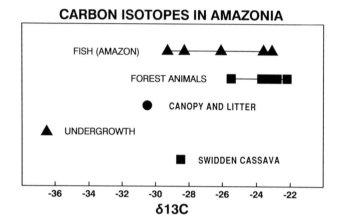

Figure 6. Extremely negative $\delta^{13}C$ values in Amazonian foodwebs are the result of recycled carbon from rotting leaf litter in the forests, as illustrated by this case from the upper Rio Negro.

based on forest plants, the depletion is transmitted through it. This argument does not account entirely for the very negative values in river fish, which are, on average, also more negative in the lower Orinoco than in the upper Rio Negro. This may be due to the contribution of water plants to the river foodweb. Such plants photosynthesise carbon dioxide from air dissolved in the surface waters. This air is derived from forest leaf litter, and the river dissolves more as it flows: in the lower reaches, the water is supersaturated with air isotopically more negative than the forest air (Martinelli *et al.* 1991).

3.3 Terrestrial and marine foods in South Africa

Reconstructions of the subsistence strategies of Holocene hunter-gatherers of the southwest Cape Province in South Africa has been the subject of a running debate and interactive research between archaeologists and isotope specialists at the University of Cape Town for several years. This is probably the most intensively studied area anywhere as far as the seasonality of archaeological food remains and their isotopic expression in human collagen is concerned. The debate has served to refine archaeological models for human subsistence in the area, and has raised many questions about human metabolism and the building of collagen from different food groups.

The southwest Cape Province is an arid coastal plain (annual rainfall below 400 mm) defined by a mountain range some 100 km inland from the shore. This is a winter rainfall area, with the result that the plant cover is essentially of the C_3 type (Figure 7). During the winter food is abundant at the coast: drowned seal pups wash ashore from island rookeries and shellfish are less likely to be contaminated by the toxic red tides that occur mostly in

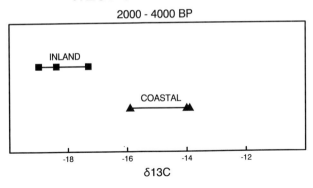

Figure 7. The $\delta^{13}C$ values for human skeletal collagen of hunter-gatherers of the southwestern Cape Province in South Africa between 4000 and 2000 years ago show differences between coastal and inland peoples. (After Sealy 1989).

summer months. During the summer, food is more abundant in the interior, consisting especially of the carbohydrate-rich corms of flowering geophytes and a variety of small antelope, tortoises, and hyrax (rock rabbits). Archaeological remains from cave sites at the coast and in the mountains reflect such seasonal abundances. These data have led John Parkington and co-workers to develop a model of seasonal movement between the coast and the interior for Holocene hunter-gatherer subsistence (Parkington 1976, 1977, 1984).

Isotopic data for human skeletons from the coast and the interior contradict such a model. The debate has settled on the period between 4000 and 2000 years ago, during which the archaeological data for seasonal movement are most persuasive. The carbon isotope ratios for coastal skeletons of this period range between -14 and $-16\,^{0}/_{00}$, while inland skeletons range between -17 and $-19\,^{0}/_{00}$ (Sealy and van der Merwe 1985; 1986; Figure 7). Marine foods (fish, shellfish and seal meat) range in $\delta^{13}C$ values between about -12 and $-18\,^{0}/_{00}$, with an average of $-15.5\,^{0}/_{00}$, while terrestrial foods (meat and plants) average about $-25\,^{0}/_{00}$ (Figure 8). We interpret these results to mean that the skeletons of the coast and the interior were from groups of people who did not have the same subsistence strategies—the inland people acquired some of their food at the coast, but the coastal people acquired more. It would appear that the region accommodated more than one lifestyle.

Parkington has questioned the interpretation of the carbon isotope data at various times as the debate has unfolded, particularly as regards the relative contributions of marine protein and plant carbohydrates to collagen carbon (e.g., Parkington 1991). Many of these questions have been incor-

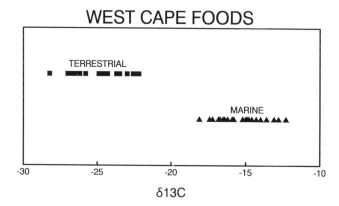

Figure 8. Marine foods (shellfish, fish, seals, birds) and terrestrial foods (plants and animals) of the southwestern Cape Province in South Africa have distinctly different $\delta^{13}C$ values. (After Sealy 1989).

porated in the isotopic research agenda. In her doctoral thesis, Sealy (1989) expanded the chemical evidence relating to dietary tracing in the southwest Cape by using nitrogen isotope, strontium isotope, and strontium/calcium ratios. Nitrogen isotope ratios of marine and terrestrial animals in this region proved to overlap substantially, due to aridity, while strontium/calcium ratios were shown to distinguish meat eaters from plant eaters only if one knows exactly which animals a particular carnivore preys on. For omnivores like humans the system is much too complex to determine the amount of meat in the diet by means of strontium/calcium ratios. Strontium isotope ratios, however—which differ substantially between the ocean and coastal marine sediments on the one hand and the rocks of the interior on the other —contribute isotopic signatures to human bone apatite which confirm the dichotomy between coastal and inland skeletons.

By now, the starting point of this debate has receded into the distance, even as it has served to drive archaeological and isotopic interpretations toward greater refinement. It continues to do so.

4. Further isotope studies

Isotopic studies of prehistoric diets are expanding into many parts of the world, as far as both practitioners and applications are concerned. Projects at the top of my own list include archaeological studies in Belize and Ecuador. The Belize case is a collaboration with Norman Hammond (Boston University), excavator of the site of Cuello. The preliminary isotope data from this site indicate that the pre-classic Maya had a substantial maize component in their diet, but were not as dependent on it as, for example, people of the post-classic period. They appear to have fattened some of their dogs on maize for eating, while leaving others to scavenge—these may have been different breeds of dogs. Contrary to some earlier speculation on our part, however, they did not feed maize to the deer in the vicinity to make them easier to kill. In Ecuador, Scott Raymond (University of Calgary), Julia Lee-Thorp (Cape Town) and I are trying to resolve the controversy over whether the people of the Valdivia culture of about 4000 BC – one of the earliest Formative culture in the Americas – depended primarily on maize or marine foods for subsistence. In this case the answer appears to be "neither", and we may have to start considering tubers more seriously.

These are examples of straightforward applications of our current knowledge of isotopes in bone, but what of future developments? My own curiosity pulls me in four directions: metabolic pathways, source tracing, isotope signatures in apatite, and past environments:

i) In order to make isotopic dietary tracing truly quantitative we need laboratory feeding experiments with isotopically labelled foods and isotopic measurements at the level of amino acids. Crucially, we need a chromatograph/mass spectrometer that can do rapid isotopic analysis of specific amino acids.

ii) We have demonstrated that a combination of isotope ratios (carbon, nitrogen, strontium) can serve to pinpoint the habitat in which an elephant tusk originated (van der Merwe et al. 1990) and are now doing the same for rhino horn. These techniques can be expanded to other biological materials, and have some obvious applications in archaeology.

iii) Apatite carries a dietary carbon isotope signal (Sullivan and Kreuger 1981) which can be isolated from fossil tooth enamel when collagen has disappeared. Sufficient work has now been done (Kreuger 1991; Lee-Thorp and van der Merwe 1987, 1991) to show that the biogenic signal can be isolated from diagenetic carbonates, following early objections (Schoeninger and DeNiro 1982). This technique has been used to determine the diets of C_3- and C_4-eating baboon species 1.8 million years old (Lee-Thorp 1989; Lee-Thorp et al. 1989). We are now using it to compare the diets of early hominid species, for which the C_4 dietary component apparently came from grazing animals and thus acts as an indirect measure of meat in their diets.

iv) Carbon isotopes in tooth enamel of mammal-like reptiles of 200 million years ago show that the mass extinctions of the Late Permian were coincident with substantial changes in the carbon isotope composition (and therefore carbon content) of the atmosphere (Thackeray et al. 1990). This technique provides one way of studying past climates and primary productivity of our planet.

There seems to be plenty to do.

Acknowledgements

I thank the many collaborators who worked on the problems described in this article. John Lanham and David Killick produced the drawings.

References

Ambrose, S.H. 1991: Effect of diet climate and physiology on nitrogen isotope abundances in terrestrial foodwebs. *Journal of Archaeological Science* 18, 293–318.
Ambrose, S.H. and DeNiro, M.J. 1986: The isotopic ecology of East African mammals. *Oecologia* 69, 395–406.
Bender, M.M., Baerreis, D.A. and Steventon, R.A. 1981: Further light on carbon isotopes and Hopewell agriculture. *American Antiquity* 46, 346–353.
Buikstra, J.E. and Milner, G.R. 1991: Isotopic and archaeological interpretations of diet in the central Mississippi Valley. *Journal of Archaeological Science* 18, 319–330.
Cai, Lian-zhen and Qiu Shih-hua 1984: Carbon 13 evidence for ancient diet in China. *Kaogu* 10, 949–955. (English translation by Susan Weld, unpublished.)
Chisholm, B.S., Nelson, D.E. and Schwarcz, H.P. 1982: Stable isotope ratios as a measure of marine versus terrestrial protein in ancient diets. *Science* 216, 1131–1132.
DeNiro, M.J. 1987: Stable isotopy and archaeology. *American Scientist* 75, 182–191.
DeNiro, M.J. and Epstein, S. 1978: Influence of diet on the distribution of carbon isotopes in animals. *Geochimica et Cosmochimica Acta* 42, 495–506.
Hare, P.E., Fogel, M.L., Stafford, T.W., Jr., Mitchell, A.D. and Hoering, T.C. 1991: The isotopic composition of carbon and nitrogen in individual amino acids isolated from modern and fossil proteins. *Journal of Archaeological Science* 18, 277–292.
Heaton, T.E., Vogel, J.C., La Chevallerie, V. and Collett, G. 1986: Climatic influence on the isotopic composition of bone nitrogen. *Nature* 322, 823–824.
Hobson, K.A. and Collier, S. 1984: Marine and terrestrial protein in Australian aboriginal diets. *Current Anthropology* 25, 238–240.
Kreuger, H.W. 1991: Exchange of carbon with biological apatite. *Journal of Archaeological Science* 18, 255–361.
Krueger, H.W. and Sullivan, C.H. 1984: Models for carbon isotope fractionation between diet and bone. In Turnland, J.R. and Johnson, P.E. (editors), *Stable Isotopes and Nutrition* (American Chemical Society Symposium Series No. 258) 205–220.
Lee-Thorp, J.A. 1989: *Stable Carbon Isotopes in Deep Time: the Diets of Fossil Fauna and Hominids* (Cape Town, University of Cape Town PhD Thesis).
Lee-Thorp, J.A. and van der Merwe, N.J. 1987: Carbon isotope analysis of fossil bone apatite. *South African Journal of Science* 83, 71–74.
Lee-Thorp, J.A. and van der Merwe, N.J. 1991: Aspects of the chemistry of modern and fossil biological apatites. *Journal of Archaeological Science* 18, 343–354.
Lee-Thorp, J.A., van der Merwe, N.J., and Brain, C.K. 1989: Isotopic evidence for dietary differences between two extinct baboon species from Swartkrans. *Journal of Human Evolution* 18, 183–190.

Martinelli, L.A., Devol, A.H., Victorian, R.L. and Richey, J.E. 1991: Stable carbon isotope variation in C_3 and C_4 plants along the Amazon river. *Nature* 353, 57–59.

Minagawa, M. and Akazawa, T. in press: Dietary patterns of Japanese Jomon hunter-fisher-gatherers: Stable nitrogen and carbon isotope analyses of human bones. In Aikens, C.M. and Rhee S.N. (editors), *Pacific Northeast Asia in Prehistory* (Washington, University of Washington Press).

Murray, M.L. and Schoeninger, M.J. 1988: Diet, status, and complex social structure in Iron Age Central Europe: Some contributions of bone chemistry. In Gibson, D.B. and Geselow-itz, M.N. (editors), *Tribe and Polity in Late Prehistoric Europe: Demography, Production, and Exchange in the Evolution of Complex Social Systems* (New York, Plenum Press) 155–176.

Parkington, J.E. 1976: Coastal settlement between the mouths of the Berg and Olifants Rivers, Cape Province. *South African Archaeological Bulletin* 31, 127–140.

Parkington, J.E. 1977: Soaqua: Hunter-fisher-gatherers of the Olifants River valley, western Cape. *South African Archaeological Bulletin* 32, 150–157.

Parkington, J.E. 1984: Changing views of the Later Stone Age of South Africa. In Wendorf, F. and Close, A.E. (editors), *Advances in World Archaeology* (New York, Academic Press) 90–142.

Parkington, J.E. 1991: Approaches to dietary reconstruction in the Western Cape: are you what you have eaten? *Journal of Archaeological Science* 18, 331–342.

Price, T.D. (editor) 1989: *The Chemistry of Prehistoric Human Bone* (Cambridge, Cambridge University Press).

Roosevelt, A.C. 1980: *Parmana* (London, Academic Press).

Schoeninger, M.J. and DeNiro, M.J. 1982: Carbon isotope ratios of apatite from fossil bone cannot be used to construct diets of animals. *Nature* 297, 557–558.

Schoeninger, M.J., DeNiro, M.J. and Tauber, H. 1983: $^{15}N/^{14}N$ ratios of bone collagen reflect marine and terrestrial components of prehistoric human diet. *Science* 220, 1381–1383.

Sealy, J.C. 1986: *Stable Carbon Isotopes and Prehistoric Diets in Southwestern Cape, South Africa* (Oxford, British Archaeological Reports International Series 293).

Sealy, J.C. 1989: *Reconstruction of Later Stone Age Diets in the Southwestern Cape, South Africa: Evaluation and Application of Five Isotopic and Trace Element Techniques* (Cape Town, University of Cape Town PhD Thesis).

Sealy, J.C. and van der Merwe, N.J. 1985: Isotopic assessment of Holocene human diets in the Southwestern Cape, South Africa. *Nature* 315, 138–140.

Sealy, J.C. and van der Merwe, N.J. 1986: Isotope assessment and seasonal-mobility hypothesis in the southwestern Cape of South Africa. *Current Anthropology* 27, 135–150.

Sealy, J.C., van der Merwe, N.J., Lee-Thorp, J.A. and Lanham, J.L. 1987: Nitrogen isotopic ecology in southern Africa: Implications for environmental and dietary tracing. *Geochimica et Cosmochimica Acta* 51, 2707–2717.

Smith, B.D. 1989: Origins of agriculture in eastern North America. *Science* 246, 1566–1571.

Sullivan, C.H. and Krueger, H.W. 1981: Carbon isotopes analysis of separate chemical phases in modern and fossil bone. *Nature* 292, 333–335.

Tauber, H. 1981: $\delta^{13}C$ evidence for dietary habits of prehistoric man in Denmark. *Nature* 292, 332–333.

Thackeray, J.F., van der Merwe, N.J., Lee-Thorp, J.A., Sillen, J.A., Lanham, J.L., Smith, R., Keyser, A. and Monteiro, P.M.S. 1990: Changes in carbon isotope ratios in the late Permian recorded in therapsid tooth apatite. *Nature* 347, 751–753.

van der Merwe, N.J. 1982: Carbon isotopes, photosynthesis, and archaeology. *American Scientist* 70, 596–606.

van der Merwe, N.J. and Medina, E. 1989: Photosynthesis and $^{13}C/^{12}C$ ratios in Amazonian rain forests. *Geochimica et Cosmochimica Acta* 53, 1091–1094.

van der Merwe, N.J. and Medina, E. 1991: The canopy effect, carbon isotopes and foodwebs in Amazonia. *Journal of Archaeological Science* 18, 249–259.

van der Merwe, N.J. and Vogel, J.C. 1978: ^{13}C content of human collagen as a measure of prehistoric diet in Woodland North America. *Nature* 276, 815–816.

van der Merwe, N.J., Lee-Thorp, J.A., Thackeray, J.F., Hall-Martin, A., Krueger, F.J., Coetzee, H., Bell, R.H.V. and Lindeque, M. 1990: Source area determination of elephant ivory by isotopic analysis. *Nature* 346, 744–746.

Vogel, J.C. and van der Merwe, N.J. 1977: Isotopic evidence for early maize cultivation in New York State. *American Antiquity* 42, 238–242.

Vogel, J.C., Fuls, A., and Ellis, R.P. 1978: The geographical distribution of Kranz grasses in South Africa. *South African Journal of Science* 74, 209–215.

Proceedings of the British Academy, **77**, 265

Carbon and Nitrogen Isotopes and the Amino Acid Biogeochemistry of Fossil Bone and Teeth

P. E. HARE

Carnegie Institute of Washington, Geophysical Laboratory, 1530 P Street, N.W., Washington DC 20005, USA.

Summary. Individual amino acids isolated from proteins in bone and teeth contain characteristic carbon and nitrogen isotope ratios reflecting the diet and metabolism of the living animal. The essential amino acid, threonine, is particularly useful because it does not participate in the reversible nitrogen exchange of normal amino acid metabolism. A comparison of the nitrogen isotopes in threonine with those of the non-essential amino acids reflects the trophic level of the organism.

Radiocarbon dating of certain amino acid residues can reveal the archaeological age of the bone, even when the total organic extract gives an erroneous radiocarbon date. Racemisation of amino acids occurs during the diagenesis of the proteins in bone and teeth. Amino acid racemisation in adequately preserved bone and teeth as well as other calcified tissues can be used to estimate fossil ages far beyond the range of radiocarbon dating.

Readers are referred to:

Hare, P.E., Fogel, M.L., Stafford, T.W., Jr., Mitchell, A.D. and Hoering, T.C. 1991: The isotopic composition of carbon and nitrogen in individual amino acids isolated from modern and fossil protein. *Journal of Archaeological Science* 18, 277–292.

Read 14 February 1991. © The British Academy 1992.

Proceedings of the British Academy, **77**, 267–283

Biomolecular Archaeology: Past, Present and Future

R. E. M. HEDGES[1] & B. C. SYKES[2]

[1]*Research Laboratory for Archaeology, 6 Keble Road, Oxford OX1 3QJ, UK*
[2]*Institute of Molecular Medicine, John Radcliffe Hospital, Oxford OX3 9DU, UK*

Summary. The information potentially available from biomolecules is vast, and often related to the most central concerns of archaeology. It is, however, entirely limited by the survival of such complex molecules and, further, by the sensitivity of the methods for their recovery and analysis. Recent advances in immunology, in protein chemistry and especially in the amplification of DNA sequences are beginning to show that antigens, proteins and nucleic acid sequences can be sufficiently well preserved in archaeological remains for useful results to be obtained. The history of such work shows the importance of establishing approaches that are reliable, specific, and not confused by contamination or diagenesis. Materials such as dried seeds, bone, and mummified skin, as well as artefacts bearing organic traces, have been studied, but a great deal remains to be learnt about the mode of preservation, the degree of biomolecular diagenesis, and the effect of the burial environment. One of the most important results from biomolecular studies is of the genetic constitution of an organism; recent work from several laboratories on the survival of DNA is described, with an account of the archaeological information which can now be contemplated.

Introduction

This review aims to give a unified perspective for a number of different approaches within archaeological science to the biochemical study of ancient

Read 14 February 1991. © The British Academy 1992.

remains. Our justification for a wide, rather than more detailed, view is that these approaches are undergoing rapid change, setting exciting promises for the future, and need a broad foundation for their significance to be appreciated.

Biomolecular archaeology can be described as using molecular techniques to obtain biological information about archaeological subjects. It is developing from the interaction of a number of distinct subjects; we here take four separate strands as a foundation. These are, in order of increasing focus:-

i) Which archaeological issues can molecular biology best address?

ii) Which molecules are most worthwhile to study?

iii) How are differences in survival to be taken into account?

iv) Which techniques are appropriate?

Each of these issues influences the others. In this review we consider them in the order given. The treatment must of necessity be brief. In practice, the field is strongly 'technique-led', and this confers a rather unpredictable character to its development.

1. Addressing the archaeological issues

Biological information can refer to an organism's *genetic structure*, or to its *environment*.

Taking the latter first, environmental information can be direct, for example, arising from the estimation of hormones, or of compounds involved in plant defences, or the biochemical effects of unusual or restricted diet. Or it may be indirect, inferred from other (often genetic) information. Examples here might be a malarial environment from a high incidence of the genetically determined condition of sickle-cell anaemia; inference of certain diseases from analysis of antigenically determined immunoglobulins; or, rather generally, the deduction of high population densities and their consequences.

Genetic information itself is rather more definite. It is convenient to distinguish three aspects:-

1.1 Taxonomy (identification)

There is obvious but very useful work to be done in identifying archaeological remains, especially of plants; in analysing relationships between species, e.g., of plants under domestication, or small rodents such as voles; and in the identification of sex of humans and animals. Less obvious possibilities for the future include the identification of diseases, especially viral, microbial and parasitic.

1.2 Phenotypic description

The expression of genetic information (the phenotype) seldom allows individual traits to be associated with the composition of a single gene. Such a situation is most commonly studied for genetic diseases, about which a great deal is now known. Their relevance to archaeology is, however, diminished by the rarity of (serious) genetic disease. One example of a minor defect is that of colour blindness. In the course of time medical and biological research will make the deduction of the phenotype from genetic analysis increasingly possible. Such a deduction could include physical characteristics (e.g., type of hair, colour of eyes), susceptibility to particular diseases, and metabolic characteristics (e.g., the ability for adult humans to digest lactose by secreting lactase; this genetic trait is controlled at a single locus and is associated with the occurrence of a dairy economy).

At present, then, there is little opportunity for deducing the phenotype from information of the genetic composition (although the identification of sex is of course one example). But this aspect can be expected to develop prodigiously over the next decade.

1.3 The genotype and polymorphisms

The timescale of evolution is such that archaeological genetics are mainly concerned with variation within a species, rather than speciation itself. But no mention of speciation should pass up the opportunity to consider the possibility of obtaining information on the genotype of Neanderthal humans. Results so far on archaeological material are encouraging for such speculation. Also, the effect of the severe selection pressure in human plant and animal breeding programmes should enable such cultural events as the neolithic transition to be reflected in major changes in the genotypes of whole populations.

However, as a rule the description of populations in terms of gene *frequencies* is likely to be most relevant. This implies a sufficient sample size to define the particular polymorphic structure. (This issue will be returned to later). A population can be delimited in all sorts of ways:—family groups, geographically isolated communities, cultural (e.g., linguistic) units—and polymorphic variation at the appropriate level must be studied. Three very broad levels are currently useful. These are; *'hypervariable regions'*—where so many alleles are to be found for a series of unlinked loci that only individuals closely related by descent share the same set of alleles (this is essentially the same as genetic "fingerprinting"); *'clinal variation'*—where small differences in the frequencies of alleles at many loci (10—30) can be precisely determined and mapped; and *'population markers'*—where extreme differences have been found to exist in the frequency of a particular allele in a given population relative to that for neighbouring populations. The two extremes are likely to be most useful in archaeological application. In addition, the analysis of gene frequencies enables the diversity or heterozygosity of a population to be estimated, from which it is possible to infer past effects of the size of the population (hence the recognition of 'bottlenecks').

2. The molecules most suitable to study

The main considerations here are occurrence, stability, and the inherent information content. It is convenient to consider two classes, the linear molecules (comprising proteins and nucleic acids), and non-linear molecules (the rest).

2.1 Non-linear molecular species

Many of these are small, specialised molecules, such as sterols, or polyphenols, which are well-known in natural product chemistry. The class includes more complex types, such as glycoproteins, or polysaccharides (which include the A,B,O blood group antigens). Also, many proteins, although linear in primary structure, are recognised by their secondary or tertiary structure.

Such molecules have not been extensively studied so far, because their chemistry is complicated by diagenetic processes, their information content is often low, and it is very hard to relate what is analysed in the laboratory to what was originally in the organism. But as understanding of diagenesis grows, and laboratory techniques improve, this area, particularly for the lower molecular weights, may well prove to be very worthwhile.

2.2 Linear molecules

Although not all molecules may be worth analysing, (for example collagen, probably the most abundant protein in archaeology, shows very little variation between individuals or species), linear molecules have enormous potential information content. What is more important is that it is much easier to validate the information in such a molecule through sequencing its components (amino acids or bases). Diagenetic change, though serious, can be corrected. Occurrence and stability can vary greatly.

3. What material survives

Understanding the survival of molecular species is crucial to the whole enterprise. The ability to recover information configured in macromolecules is diminished by the following processes:-

i) Loss of molecular abundance. The decrease of any surviving organic material with time is inevitable. Much of it is leached away through inter-action with groundwater movement.

ii) Decomposition of molecular integrity. Even if the majority of atoms remain, chemical changes within the molecules are liable to disrupt the configuration.

iii) Addition of external material. That is, contamination from the environment. This may be as a mixture, or more seriously, contamination may combine chemically with the chosen molecule (such as the cross linking between polyphenols and protein).

Survival is dependent on the particular environment, the type of tissue, and the molecular species. Occasionally survival is spectacular, and environ-ments may be ranked in terms of the survival of their material.

3.1 Environment

As examples:

i) A fossil Miocene *Magnolia* leaf, has been shown to contain recoverable DNA from the Clarkia deposits (Golenberg et al. 1990).

ii) The Windover site (Doran et al. 1986; Lawlor et al. 1991) in Florida, U.S.A. contains nearly 100 well preserved skulls containing soft tissue from 8000 BP. (The skeletal material is buried in neutral waterlogged peat).

iii) Frozen mummies from Peru, mammoths from the U.S.S.R. (Guthrie 1990) and more recent human burials from Greenland (Hart Hansen et al. 1991) have been studied.

iv) The deliberately mummified material from Egypt (Pääbo 1985).

v) Bog bodies (e.g., Lindow Man; Stead et al. 1986).

vi) Well-preserved bone; e.g., from the "Mary Rose" shipwreck of AD 1545.

vii) Bone and teeth from N.W. Europe—commonly found with several percent of total organic material remaining.

viii) Bone from hotter climates, where frequently there is less than 1 % of original protein remaining.

Obvious generalisations suggest that low temperature, low oxidation, low water activity (i.e., minimal wetting/drying cycles or water flow regimes), and above all, suppressed microbiological activity, are conditions for improved survival. At present our understanding of survival is more anecdotal than systematic, however.

Time, itself, has not been explicitly invoked as a determinant of survival. Certainly we would expect 'older' material containing biomolecular information to come from a far narrower range of environments. Very little organic study has been made on bone older than the Last Glacial Maximum, and it is too soon to predict with any confidence the maximum age for which hominid remains, for example, will be susceptible to biomolecular study.

3.2 Tissues

Early work concentrated on preserved soft tissue, partly because the abundance of DNA and protein is in general higher, but mainly because conditions which preserved the tissue as a whole might be expected to be conducive to preserving macromolecular integrity also. Although preserved soft tissue is not common, enough examples abound to enable plenty of investigations to be made. However, there is no doubt that the possibility of extracting information from commonly preserved tissues such as bone, tooth, and perhaps carbonised seed and pollen, dramatically increases the value of the whole approach.

Survival in a given tissue will be affected by microbiological action, by the local chemistry, and to an extent mechanically. Although microbiological action is ubiquitous, it is likely to diminish in time for bone, as limited resources are consumed, and it is interesting that a recent study (Thuesen and Engberg 1990) identified *Acetomycetes* contamination in preserved soft tissue but not in the associated bone. Bone has another point of interest, which is the affinity between hydroxyapatite and both protein and DNA. Hydroxyapatite columns have been used in the purification of DNA (Bernardi 1969), and may help to retain DNA and stabilise it from chemical degradation. (It appears that such is the case in preserving osteocalcin in situations where nearly all the collagen is lost). Bone can also act to buffer the pH of the local aqueous environment.

At this stage virtually nothing can be said about possible survival in pollen or carbonised seed (where the temperature of carbonisation is obviously crucial). Although not a tissue, the survival of proteins in 'residues' on stone tools (Loy 1983) has been claimed. The evidence for this is persistent, and certainly warrants fuller investigation than it has so far received. Of course the number of samples is not so very large, and replication of results is thereby made difficult.

3.3 Molecular species

It is well known that lipids survive in a wide range of Quaternary environments (Cranwell 1981), although they also undergo much molecular modification during burial. Polyphenols too are known to be stable, often cross-linking to form macromolecular aggregates, and contributing to the stability of humic and fulvic acids. A major problem with blood group determination (ABO system) is that the difference between the A and B antigens (oligosaccharides) is chemically very slight, and conversion may easily occur through chemical or biological action during burial.

Probably proteins and DNA need some form of 'protection', if only to reduce the rate of dissolution by groundwater movement. As mentioned above, different proteins appear to survive differentially, depending upon their immediate chemical environment (such as hydroxyapatite). The survival of RNA, generally considered to be less stable chemically than DNA, has not been systematically investigated. However, predicting the survival of specific molecules cannot be relied upon—few would have expected collagen to be so much more completely lost from bone than many of the plasma proteins; or for DNA to survive in a Miocene fossil under almost any conditions—and therefore any molecule for which reliable analytical techniques exist might reasonably be investigated.

A further aspect of molecular survival is the information it might give concerning the environment. For example, amino acid residues in protein that are easily oxidized (serine; methionine; cysteine) may find use as an environmental indicator, which in turn might predict the survival of other species.

4. Techniques

The low abundance, degradation and liability to contamination of the molecular species being analysed demand that techniques be extremely sensitive, highly specific, and can operate with poorly characterised or impure material.

4.1 "Conventional" chemical methods

These include standard separation methods, principally high pressure liquid chromatography and gel electrophoresis. Such methods are adapted to handle nanogram-picogram quantities of material. Major problems arise if one is dealing with material degraded to the point that it presents a continuum distribution, since no meaningful separation can then be effected. In principle polypeptides can be sequenced (e.g., by automatic sequencers using Edman degradation methods). so long as they have been completely purified first. Mass spectrometric methods are very sensitive and can operate with mixtures, and large molecules (e.g., polypeptides) can also now be analysed. While chemical methods are necessary in any case to bring about a concentration of the molecule under study, they are most useful in the study of smaller molecules (lipids; polyphenols; oligosaccharides) which degrade to a more discrete mixture than do protein and nucleic acids.

4.2 Immunochemical methods

The remarkable sensitivity and specificity of the antibody-antigen reaction enables, in principle, proteins and similar antigens to be detected if the relevant antiserum can be obtained. Early work suffered from both false positives and false negatives in detection because neither the specificity of the antiserum nor the integrity of the antigen could be adequately guaranteed. Technical improvements in sensitivity include particularly enzyme-linked inhibition assays (ELISA) (see, for example, Smith and Wilson 1990), and improvements in specificity have been brought about with the use of monoclonal antibodies (for an example, see Cattaneo *et al.* 1990). It is likely that the more specific the method, the smaller the detectable fraction of surviving biomolecule. This is because diagenesis is likely to reduce greatly the chance of a molecule retaining its epitopes intact. Therefore, in many archaeological applications, it seems that some form of compromise between specificity and sensitivity will be necessary if the changes in molecular configuration are to be studied.

4.3 DNA methods

The chemistry of DNA is frequently able to exploit its unique linear stranded complementary structure. Two approaches in particular that manage this are hybridisation and the polymerase chain reaction.

In hybridisation, the affinity between a DNA probe of known composition and the test DNA can be sensitively estimated (at the level of nanograms) in a manner analogous to immunochemical reaction. Here the probe binds to a complementary DNA if it is sufficiently homologous (about 90%).

In the "polymerase chain reaction" (PCR) an enzymic system is used to "amplify" (increase the number of) a template DNA sequence by repeated replication. After 30–40 repeats an amplification of over a million can be achieved. The template DNA sequence is typically 100—1000 bases long, and is defined by the choice of "primers" which are oligonucleotides of about 20 bases in length, complimentary to the beginning and end of the template sequence. Since the PCR can function in the presence of overwhelming quantities of (degraded and foreign) DNA, it is able to be both specific and extremely sensitive in that the chosen sequence (template) can be amplified against the background of all the impurities to a level where further analysis (such as sequencing) is possible. The PCR method is relatively new, and still undergoing rapid development. Technically, there are many difficulties in its application (for example, the amplification of contamination, non-specific amplification, inhibition of the enzymic system by unknown impurities), but the combination of sensitivity and specificity has enabled it to become the major technique in understanding ancient DNA (Pääbo *et al.* 1989).

5. Results

The results summarised here make no attempt to be comprehensive, but to point out some of the outstanding recent work. We believe that at least most of the published work on archaeological DNA sequences has been included.

5.1 Molecules other than proteins and nucleic acids

The analysis and identification of lipids is considered in this volume (Evershed *et al.* this volume; though with reference to a particular environment), and such compounds form the subject of a great deal of investigation in sediments (Cranwell 1981; Brassell 1985). Little work has been done so far on specific identification of lignins and polyphenols, at least in terms of their biological significance. However, the field is very broad, and much work has been published covering various aspects from the diagenesis of amber, the identification of resins on stone tools, to the ageing of varnishes in painting.

5.2 Proteins

We mainly consider proteins shown to survive in bone. Other materials have been studied, for example shell (Curry *et al.* in press) and "residues" on stone tools (Loy 1983), as well as preserved soft tissue, but bone is both the most studied and the most liable to provide biologically significant information.

The survival of collagen (90% of bone protein) is well known but is not very genetically informative. However, in environments where collagen is almost entirely lost, it appears that other non-collagenous proteins may have survived very much better. In particular osteocalcin has been extracted in large enough quantities for radiocarbon dating (Ajie *et al.* 1990). The immunological titre appears to be about 1 % of the extractable protein. Most of the other proteins recorded in bone in recent publications are plasma proteins. They include haemoglobin (identified by ELISA) (Smith and Wilson 1990), albumin (using monoclonal antibodies) (Cattaneo *et al.* 1990) and the immunoglobulins (using electrophoresis and immunoblotting)

(Tuross 1988). To our knowledge, no-one has yet detected a protein polymorphism, but the steady development of technique and the fact that several groups now have good evidence for the survival of non-collagenous proteins in bone over more than 2000 years is very promising.

5.3 Nucleic acids

Firstly, it is not yet clear to what extent *RNA* may survive. Being chemically much less stable, it is unlikely to be as worthwhile to study as DNA.

DNA has been studied in preserved soft tissue, in bone, and in dried and partially carbonised seeds. There is now reasonably good evidence that DNA survives consistently enough in bone (Hagelberg *et al.* 1989; Horai *et al.* 1989; Hanni *et al.* 1990; Thuesen and Engberg 1990; Williams *et al.* 1990) that its study in this tissue should be taken very seriously indeed, since bone is the most ubiquitous of archaeologically important tissues.

Most tissues appear to yield of the order of micrograms of DNA extracted from about a gram. If this is analysed for molecular weight by gel electrophoresis, it is shown to have a range of low molecular weight components (< 1000 bp in length), as well as high molecular weight material. All of this DNA may be non-indigenous, and in any case only a very small fraction appears to be chemically intact. Failure to detect DNA at this stage may not preclude failure to detect specific DNA later on. Pääbo in particular has analysed the chemical integrity of this extracted DNA (Pääbo 1989) and shown it to have extensive damage (for example, very few purine bases remained, and of the DNA that could be analysed, at least 5% of all sites were damaged). At this stage of investigation it seems likely that there is a correlation between apparent DNA preservation and apparent protein preservation—this would after all be expected—but in general still too little is known about conditions and correlates favouring DNA survival.

Some success has been achieved through hybridisation experiments. In these, purportedly human DNA has been hybridised with human DNA probes, mainly using mtDNA probes, but also repeat copy probes such as Alu (Thuesen and Engberg 1990; Williams *et al.* 1990). These show that perhaps one part in 10^5 of the extracted DNA is in sufficient condition to hybridise. It is still too early to be clear how reliable and specific the hybridisation approach can be; it has the advantage of being relatively straightforward and is less subject to contamination problems than is the PCR approach. The information achieved from hybridisation is essentially to learn of the specificity of a particular probe, so that species, or sex, rather than a distinct sequence, would be the main result. However, the technique is likely to remain useful as an overall screening method.

To be sure that indigenous DNA is present it is necessary to recover sufficient material to demonstrate that it has the 'correct' sequence. This may not be a sufficient criterion, since contaminant DNA may also have the correct sequence—it depends upon what sequence is being compared, and the nature of contamination. The most difficult case, although inevitably the one most chosen so far, is the analysis of human DNA, since contamination by other human DNA is quite feasible. To generate enough DNA for sequencing, some form of cloning or amplification is necessary, and this is now best achieved using the PCR. The number of published reports of DNA detected by PCR amplification from archaeological material is still very limited, and only a small fraction of such work has gone on to sequence the product. Virtually all the successful PCR so far has been on mtDNA, presumably because of its high copy number relative to nuclear DNA. Most of the DNA sequences that have been amplified are shorter than 200 bp, although evidence is beginning to accumulate that DNA from bone may be amplifiable in longer lengths (up to 400 bp). As already mentioned, the use of PCR carries with it a number of difficulties, which are described below.

5.4 Difficulties

5.4.1 Contamination

Contamination of the sample by genomic DNA, before the PCR reaction is carried out, undoubtedly can occur. How serious this is (in the sense of how frequent and how unavoidable) is not yet clear. The most likely contamination is by human DNA, and this has been observed when analysing non-human material. Too few such studies have been made for conclusions to be drawn at this stage. It is possible that modern contamination would amplify much better in longer lengths than ancient DNA, so that its presence might be generally detectable with enough work. Contamination by laboratory-derived DNA sequences is also a very real danger, but this can usually be detected by the careful use of controls. However, it is imperative that laboratories working in this field do take adequate precautions and publish controls, so that there is no room for doubt.

5.4.2 Non-specific amplification and 'jumping' PCR

Some experimental conditions may make the reaction less specific; this will be obvious if the product has a different molecular weight from the template; in any case, it is generally thought wise to sequence or hybridize the product in case of any doubt. A related complication is the ability for the reaction to 'jump' from one replicated strand to the next when DNA strands contain damage (Pääbo et al. 1990). This makes it possible for amplification to take place even when less than one intact template sequence is present. The resultant amplified product will be a mixture, from which a consensus can be obtained by sequencing. The ability to 'jump' is in general very useful, since a higher degree of damage can be sustained whilst still obtaining sequence information. However, it may not be the best way to reach consensus information from damaged sequences, and in any case where several alleles may be present (as in the amplification of diploid genes), it is possible for the PCR to bring about what amounts to recombination between them, and this may limit the information available from such genes.

5.4.3 Inhibition

Several groups have demonstrated that preparations made from extracted ancient DNA will inhibit the PCR. Treatment with a protein (e.g., bovine serum albumin) to precipitate possible contaminants (haem has been suggested) has been shown to help. However, there can be many ways in which the unknown degraded material present in archaeological preparations may disrupt the course of the PCR.

5.4.4 Sequencing

Most PCR products will require sequencing, and so far the method, although standard and well-proven, appears to be rather more difficult on amplified ancient DNA. In any case, sequencing is relatively time-consuming, and should be avoided if other forms of evidence are appropriate. However, if general polymorphic information is sought, it may be difficult to avoid the extra effort.

5.5 Summary of results

From most surviving tissues, and especially bone, enough DNA appears to survive for at least a few thousand years that it is possible to obtain sequence information at least of mitochondrial DNA. There remains a great deal to learn about the best way to operate the PCR, and to learn about the conditions for DNA survival, and the degree of damage to the remaining DNA, so that many more possibilities are likely to emerge with time; for example, the amplification and sequencing of single copy genes from animals. In our view, the most important finding at present is that many bones (very roughly between 10 and 50%) can be analysed for mtDNA. Nothing in the experimental work reported so far gives any indication as to how far back DNA might usefully survive. No doubt suitable material will become a decreasing fraction of the total surviving corpus of bone, itself a decreasing quantity with time. There is at least reasonable hope that Neanderthals and animals of their time may eventually be subjects for study.

6. Applications and future prospects

Applications to archaeology so far have been almost negligible, mainly because very little significant information can be obtained by a one-off analysis. Perhaps the most important pointer to future work is the analysis of the mtDNA control region sequence from a brain from Windover (Pääbo *et al.* 1988) which turns out to be unique (so far) for North American modern Indians, but similar to sequences common in East Asia. This result immediately points out the necessity to interpret any sequence data set in context, and of course there is as yet no very appropriate context for archaeological material.

In our view, the best way forward both builds from relatively modest archaeological projects which can supply their own context, and also emulates those successful studies of modern human populations which can act as analogues to archaeological populations. In both cases the requisite sample size of necessity should be small (< 100). The analysis of 100 samples by PCR followed by sequencing is by no means out of the question, and will no doubt become easier as the technology is developed, but the availability of samples, especially for pre-Neolithic times, will always be limited.

Two modern studies must stand as examples. The first (Cann *et al.* 1987; Horai and Hayasaka 1990) concerns the restriction fragment analysis (i.e., at less resolution than sequencing) of mtDNA from (initially) 150 humans world-wide. This has provided persuasive evidence for a bottleneck in the population of mitochondrial lineages estimated at 100,000—200,000 years ago, with the further suggestion that a founder population moved out of Africa at that time. Clearly this picture would be enormously enhanced if similar analyses on well-sampled individuals could be made for successive time-slices in the past (even if only as far back as 20,000 years).

Secondly, a recent study on 15 individuals from the !Kung of South Africa, with 68 control individuals from neighbouring regions (Vigilant *et al.* 1989) was able to recover interesting and relevant information on the diversity within and between populations. (In this case, two 400 base pair sequences were analysed in the mtDNA control region.) Two conclusions, especially relevant for archaeology, stand out. One is that the effective breeding size could be estimated as 5000—a figure, not unexpectedly, consistent with the known value—and secondly, that the average amount of migration (females only, since only mtDNA is observed) is not more than 13 metres per year. Again, it is quite possible to imagine a similar study being made on archaeological populations (although here the definition of population requires some careful consideration), leading to measures for the same parameters.

6.1 Archaeological projects

Firstly it is useful to distinguish between those on isolated or a very few individuals, and those made on populations.

On *individuals*, the first uses would be to act as controls, where the 'correct' answers are already known. For example, the assignment of species, and of sex. (Sex can, in principle be assigned through amplification of high copy number sequences found only on the Y chromosome. Several groups informally report achieving this, but none appears to be able to do so consistently at present.) Having established this, the same techniques can be used for sexing unknown individuals (human and animal), and to the identification of species. If DNA survives for long enough, palaeofauna can be studied, so that evolutionary relationships and ecological change can be followed.

For *populations* the analysis of burial assemblages is an obvious choice. In Oxford we are starting work on Anglo-Saxon cemeteries (such as Berinsfield and Lechlade in Oxfordshire), for which there is evidence (Härke 1990) that the possession of weapons is correlated with non-metrical epigenetic traits in the skeletons. It should be possible to relate mtDNA lineages with such cultural, epigenetic and possibly spatial information. Such work can be easily extended to cover the possible differentiation between Romano-British and Anglo-Saxon lineages, and also subsequent invasions (Viking and Norman). It should be noted that the first generation of invading warriors would not contribute their mtDNA lineages to the local community until invading females arrived and became established. A similar study might be made on burial assemblages in neolithic chambered tombs.

In these cases it is assumed that only mtDNA sequences are accessible to study. A reasonably optimistic view is that with time other highly polymorphic genes will be identifiable, and greatly contribute to our knowledge of the genetics of ancient populations. However, at this stage such work lies too far into the future to be clearly seen.

Acknowledgements

Our own work in this field is being supported by a Research Grant from S.E.R.C. We should also like to acknowledge here the contribution by our colleagues Martin Richards and Kate Smalley.

References

Ajie, H.O., Kaplan, I.R., Slota, P.J. and Taylor, R.E. 1990: AMS radiocarbon dating of bone osteocalcin. *Nuclear Instruments and Methods* B52, 433–438.

Bernardi, G. 1969: Chromatography of nucleic acids on hydroxyapatite. *Biochimica et Biophysika Acta* 174, 423–434.

Brassell, S.C. 1985: Molecular changes in sediment lipids as indicators of systematic early diagenesis. *Philosophical Transactions of the Royal Society of London* A315, 57–75.

Cann, R.L., Stoneking, M. and Wilson, A.C. 1987: Mitochondrial DNA and human evolution. *Nature* 325, 31–36.

Cattaneo, C., Gelsthorpe, K., Phillips, P. and Sokol, R.J. 1990: Blood in ancient human bone. *Nature* 347, 339.

Cranwell, P.A. 1981: Diagenesis of free and bound lipids in terrestrial detritus deposited in a lacustrine environment. *Organic Geochemistry* 3, 79–89.

Curry, G.B., Cusack, M., Endo, K., Walton, D and Quinn, R. in press: Intracrystalline molecules from brachiopods. In *Proceedings of the 6th International Conference on Biomineralisation, Odawara, Japan* (Tokyo, Springer-Verlag).

Doran, G.H., Dickel, D.N., Ballinger, W.E., Agee, O.F., Laipis, P.J. and Hauswirth, W.W. 1986: Anatomical cellular and molecular analysis of 8000 yr-old human brain tissue from the Windover archaeological site. *Nature* 323, 803–806.

Golenberg, E.M., Giannasi, D.E., Clegg, M.T., Smiley, C.J., Durbin, M., Henderson, G. and Zurawarski, G. 1990: Chloroplast DNA sequence from a Miocene Magnolia species. *Nature* 344, 656–657.

Guthrie, R.D. 1990: *Frozen Fauna of the Mammoth Steppe: the Story of Blue Babe* (Chicago, University of Chicago Press).

Hagelberg, E., Sykes, B. and Hedges, R. 1989: Ancient bone DNA amplified. *Nature* 342, 485.

Hanni, C., Laudet, V., Sakka, M., Begue, A. and Stehelin, D. 1990: Amplification de fragments d'ADN mitochondrial a partir de dents et d'os humains anciens. *Comptes Rendues d'Acadamie de Science de Paris* 310, 365–370,

Härke, H. 1990: "Warrior Graves'? The background of the Anglo-Saxon weapon burial rite. *Past and Present* 126, 22–43.

Hart Hansen, J.P., Meldgaard, J. and Nordqvist, J. 1991: *The Greenland Mummies* (London, British Museum publications).

Horai, S., Hayasaki, K., Murayama, K., Wate, N., Kioke, H. and Nakai, N. 1989: DNA amplification from ancient human skeletal remains and their sequence analysis. *Proceedings of the Japanese Academy* 65, 229–233.

Horai, S. and Hayasaka, K. 1990: Intraspecific nucleotide sequence differences in the major noncoding region of human mitochondrial DNA. *American Journal of Human Genetics* 46, 828–842.

Lawlor, D.A., Dickel, C.D., Hauswirth, W.W. and Parham, P. 1991: Ancient HLA genes from 7,500-year-old archaeological remains. *Nature* 349, 785–788.

Loy, T.H. 1983: Prehistoric blood residues: detection on tool surfaces and identification of species of origin. *Science* 220, 1269–1270.

Pääbo, S. 1985: Preservation of DNA in ancient Egyptian mummies. *Journal of Archaeological Science* 12, 411–417.

Pääbo, S., Gifford, J.A. and Wilson, A.C. 1988: Mitochondrial DNA sequences from a 7000-year old brain. *Nucleic Acids Research* 16, 9775–9787.

Pääbo, S. 1989: Ancient DNA: extraction, characterisation, molecular cloning and enzymatic amplification. *Proceedings of the National Academy of Sciences of the USA* 86, 1939–1943.

Pääbo, S, Higuchi, R.G. and Wilson, A.C. 1989: Ancient DNA and the Polymerase Chain Reaction. *Journal of Biological Chemistry* 264, 9709–9712.

Pääbo, S., Irwin, D.M. and Wilson, A.C. 1990: DNA damage promotes jumping between templates during enzymatic amplification. *Journal of Biological Chemistry* 265, 4718–4721.

Smith, P.R. and Wilson, M.T. 1990: Detection of haemoglobin in human skeletal remains by ELISA. *Journal of Archaeological Science* 17, 255–268.

Stead, I.M., Bourke, J.B. and Brothwell, D. (editors) 1986: *Lindow Man: the Body in the Bog.* (London, British Museum Publications).

Thuesen, I. and Engberg, J. 1990: Recovery and analysis of human genetic material from mummified tissue and bone. *Journal of Archaeological Science* 17, 679–689.

Tuross, N. 1988. Recovery of bone and serum proteins from human skeletal tissue: IgG, osteomectin and albumin. In Ortner, D.J. and Aufderheide, A.C. (editors), *Symposium on Human Palaeopathology: Current Syntheses and Future Options* (Washington, Smithsonian Institution).

Vigilant, L., Pennington, R., Harpending, H., Kocher, T.D. and Wilson, A.C. 1989. Mitochondrial DNA sequences in single haris from a southern African population. *Proceedings of the National Academy of Sciences of the USA* 86, 9350–9354.

Williams, S.R., Longmire, J.L. and Beck, L.A. 1990: Human DNA recovery from ancient bone. *Journal of Physical Anthropology* 81, 318.

APPENDIX: Some relevant characteristics of DNA

For those unfamiliar with the molecular biology of DNA we include the following relevant facts:-

i) Most DNA resides in the nucleus of each cell of an organism, usually as a complex with protein. The nucleus of somatic cells in animals contains two copies of the entire DNA sequence, divided between 23 chromosomes, one copy deriving from each parent. Male humans have a Y chromosome inherited from their fathers (males have one X, and females have 2 X chromosomes, inherited from either parent). The total sequence of nuclear DNA amounts to approximately 3×10^9 bp or about 0.03 ng per cell. Animals also contain a small amount of DNA in their mitochondria. Each mitochondrion contains about ten copies of a DNA sequence of about 16,000 bp, and is maternally inherited. There are several hundred mitochondria in most cells, and therefore far more mtDNA sequence copies than nuclear DNA sequence copies.

ii) Some expressed systems are highly polymorphic, notably the MHC gene complex on chromosome 6, where the variation within a population is there to provide an extensive repertoire of immune responses to infection. There are sufficient MHC alleles to be useful as genetic markers for individuals and could be used, for example, to explore kinship relationships in burial groups.

iii) Genetic variation is even higher in DNA sequences that are not expressed in the phenotype since new mutations are not eliminated by selection. Most powerful as genetic markers are the blocks of DNA where alleles differ in the number and arrangement of tandemly repeated oligonucleotide blocks. These variable number of tandem repeats (VNTR) systems are the basis for genetic fingerprinting and would be immensely valuable in precisely defining individual relationships.

iv) Less valuable but more accessible are the variable regions of mito-chondrial DNA (mtDNA). They are less valuable in defining kinships because mtDNA is inherited only through the maternal line so, for instance, brothers, sisters and their maternal aunts and uncles would all be indistingu-ishable. However, the maternal inheritance and the lack of genetic recom-bination does allow construction of mitochondrial lineages which will survive intact from ancient to modern times thereby allowing populations to be traced over considerable periods. It is more accessible because there are at least a hundred copies of mtDNA per cell compared to only two for nuclear genes, so when DNA survival is low there is a greater chance of recovery.

v) A feature of DNA sequences of particular relevance to ancient DNA studies is the copy number, which determines the likely concentration of a specific DNA sequence. Although most nuclear genes are single copy, many families of sequences exist which are copied throughout the genome, often to very high copy numbers (e.g., 10^4). A well known example is the Alu family. mtDNA has already been mentioned, with multiple copies by virtue of the large number of mitochondria per cell.

vi) A sequence of only about 20 bp has a chance of 4^{20} (about 1 in 10^{12}) of occurring at random, and so is virtually unique. Most ancient DNA amplifications are of about 100–400 bp in length, and it would be difficult to reconstruct long sequences in this way. Most genes are 100–10,000 in length, and molecular biology techniques are well adapted for such lengths. The length of VNTRs, which must be completely amplified for polymorphic information, are usually too long for present methods, unless the repeating segment is very short.

Proceedings of the British Academy, **77**, 285–293

The Identity and Future of Archaeological Science

A. C. RENFREW

Department of Archaeology, Downing Street, Cambridge CB2 3DZ, UK.

1. Introduction

It is now more than twenty years since the first symposium jointly organised by the Royal Society and the British Academy, under the title 'The Impact of the Natural Sciences on Archaeology'. The proceedings were promptly published (Allibone 1970a, 1970b) and give a clear picture of some of the outstanding preconceptions of the time. They constitute an interesting record for comparison with our present enterprise. The comparison is, I believe, a revealing one which can illuminate several aspects of the present state of our discipline.

In 1969 seventeen papers were presented of which eight were on the subject of dating. Five of these dealt with radiocarbon dating, the first of them by Willard Libby himself, whose pioneer work in that field (Libby 1949) must surely constitute the single most significant contribution in the field of archaeological science. There was one paper on statistics (more specifically on seriation, itself a technique directed toward dating), three on archaeological prospecting, and five on various aspects of the analysis of artefact materials.

If we compare that with the present programme, several obvious directions emerge. First, the life sciences, along with environmental archaeology, have now taken their place firmly alongside the physical sciences. Secondly, the sense of almost astonished novelty has gone: there is no longer a sense that natural sciences and archaeology are such separate spheres that their interaction is a matter of impact! The title of the present enterprise, 'New Developments in Archaeological Science', reflects the genuine effectiveness of

Read 14 February 1991. © The British Academy 1992.

the integration which I believe has now taken place. There has been at the meeting none of that separation, that feeling of a chasm dividing two disparate fields, which has sometimes characterised such gatherings.

Now it must be admitted that another feature of the present programme of speakers is that it contains not a single paper presented by an archaeologist. All the paper speakers may be classed either as scientists or as members of that new breed, archaeological scientists. But this was certainly not a deliberate decision by the Organising Committee, and I think it springs from the desire to describe new techniques rather than new applications. A more conscious wish was that questions of chronology should not be allowed to dominate this meeting as they have often done in the past. For that reason the Poster Session was devoted entirely to dating methods, and only dendrochronology was made the subject of a paper in the main session. But electron spin resonance and optical luminescence (a technique new to me) among others figure prominently among the posters.

The evolution of early hominids was another topic excluded from the present meeting since there will be another joint symposium of the Royal Society and the British Academy on that topic next year. But of course questions relating to the dating of fossil human remains were discussed by Dr. Hare in his treatment of amino-acid racemisation. And Professor van der Merwe gave us fascinating new insights into the diet and nutrition of Australopithecus.

On such an occasion it is of interest to gauge the composition of the participants. It seemed appropriate therefore to ask those present to raise a hand in order to identify their self-classification into one of the following categories:

i) archaeologist (about 40),

ii) archaeological scientist (about 60),

iii) scientist (about 40),

iv) other (about 25).

The figures suggest above all the extent to which the concept of 'archaeological science' has developed in recent years: it may be claimed that a new discipline has emerged.

In celebrating this new category of 'archaeological scientist' it is appropriate to look back to the origins of our discipline. The first period we may regard as ending in 1939 with the onset of the Second World War. It goes back as far as 1720, when Edmund Halley (a Fellow of the Royal Society) examined the stones of Stonehenge—although in the eighteenth century dolerite (whether spotted or otherwise) had not yet found its place in the terminology of petrology. From that time on, the sciences were occasionally applied to archaeology, especially in the appendices of excavation reports, for instance, those of Heinrich Schliemann. But archaeological science in the modern sense was a later development, seen for instance in the sustained researches in archaeometallurgy conducted by Richard Pittioni in the 1930's. And, of course, it was in the 1920's and 1930's that aerial photography, the first really productive technique of remote sensing, came into its own.

After the Second World War, the scientific enterprise in this country, initiated earlier by Sir Mortimer Wheeler at the Institute of Archaeology in London, was redeveloped. One of the most thorough early treatments was F.E. Zeuner's *Dating the Past* (Zeuner 1946). The foundation in Oxford of the Research Laboratory for Archaeology and the sustained efforts there of E.T. Hall and of Martin Aitken was one of the developments which has had the most positive influence on the growth of the subject. *Archaeometry*, the journal of the Laboratory, was first published in 1958, and a few years later the first Archaeometry Conference took place. In Cambridge, at about the same time, the ecological approach promoted by Grahame Clark and furthered by Eric Higgs and his students, ensured that the environmental sciences were not overlooked. They have, however, sometimes seemed to be outside the field of "archaeometry", at least as this was defined through the work of the Oxford Laboratory, with its bias towards the physical sciences.

The 1969 Conference mentioned earlier well reflects the position where, not least through the continued efforts of our colleagues in the Oxford Research Laboratory, a coherent professionalism developed. A highly significant step in this direction (and one initiated by the Royal Society and the British Academy) was the decision, accomplished in 1977, to set up a Science-based Archaeology Committee, by which archaeological science could be funded through the Research Councils. It was decided to structure it as a committee within the framework of the Science and Engineering Research Council. The considerable success of this enterprise has recently been reviewed in a useful publication by Mark Pollard (1991). And so today we see the discipline firmly and securely based, with three established university chairs now devoted to archaeological science (in Oxford, Bradford, and Cambridge).

2. The future impact of archaeological science on archaeology

There can be no doubt of the significance of archaeological science for archaeology as a whole—at any rate in some senses. Chronological questions, which used to be at the nub of most archaeological discussions, can now, in large measure, be resolved by the application of radiometric methods for the older periods, and of tree-ring work in more recent times. To say this is, of course, to oversimplify somewhat. But the whole field of prehistory, for instance, has been transformed. So too have other aspects of the discipline.

It is remarkable, therefore, that archaeological science has had so little impact upon the conduct of archaeological excavation in the field. Remote sensing and survey methods certainly anticipate the excavation process. And all manner of 'post-excavation' analyses succeed it. But it is not inaccurate to say that for the great majority of field archaeologists, the actual praxis of digging has not been altered in any significant respect. Certainly most archaeologists will utilise sieving procedures and sometimes flotation procedures for the recovery of finer and lighter residues. And some now use computerised systems for recording data in the field. But otherwise the changes in excavation practice (for example, from Wheelerian grids or boxes to broadly open-plan work) have evolved quite logically and quite independently of any considerations deriving from the archaeological sciences.

Now this is not because there is no scope for appropriate new methods. I myself have excavated an eleven-metre stratigraphic sequence (in north Greece—effectively a tell mound), finding the succession of occupation floors, "destruction deposits", and considerable depth of "fill" intercut by "rubbish pits", which are the commonplace of all tell mounds and indeed of all urban sites also. But no archaeologist could claim that one has a clear understanding of precisely how these deposits were formed, or of what they represent. Dr. Marie-Agnès Courty, in her illuminating paper, offered us a glimpse of what might be gained by the consistent application of the technique of soil micromorphology to deeply stratified sites. Hitherto taphonomic issues have been debated mainly on palaeolithic sites (principally in caves and rock shelters). The palaeolithic archaeologist has become uneasy as to whether the materials under study are really the *in situ* product of human activity at all. Or are some of these deposits the result of non-human agencies —hyena dens and the like? In later prehistory such questions are less often relevant. But that is no reason to neglect the crucial relevance of taphonomy —of the understanding of site formation processes—to the proper interpretation of every archaeological site. The potential impact of soil micromorphological techniques to the practice of excavation is clearly very considerable. It may well be possible to give an accurate interpretation of the mode of formation of every half centimetre of soil in a stratigraphic succession. One can imagine, then, the wealth of information which a deeply stratified site could yield.

Is it too much to contemplate a vision of the future where archaeological science would be integrated fully within the sequence of prospection, excavation analysis and publication, with interpretations offered rapidly in the field, in such a way as actually to influence the course of the digging process? The following might be the sequence of events:

1. Satellite reconnaissance, with a pixel resolution of just one metre or less, allowing the techniques discussed by Ian Shennan to be deployed to full effect.

2. Ground survey, using tractor towed resistivity and ground radar survey methods of the kind indicated by Arnold Aspinall, along with magnetic techniques also, if a non-metallic tractor and engine were devised.

3. Tomographic interpretation of the data, so that the notional "peeling" of the stratigraphic sequence of the sites, without actually excavating, could first be accomplished.

4. Stratigraphic excavations of selected columns of material using soil micromorphology to investigate formation processes.

5. Area excavation of complete settlements following such stratigraphic elucidation, using computerised point plotting of artefacts, as well as screening and flotation recovery techniques for samples from each stratigraphic unit.

6. Rapid quantitative assessment of the artefact material from the site using measurement techniques of the kind outlined in his paper by Clive Orton.

7. Development of a chronology based in the first instance on radiocarbon and thermoluminescence determinations, backed up where possible by tree-ring measurements (as reviewed for us by Dr. Baillie) either on preserved wood, or on carbonised timbers, with the aim of providing a chronology measured in decades or even years rather than merely in centuries.

8. Reconstruction of the environment of the surrounding region through time, using the holistic approaches outline at the meeting by Professor Berglund.

9. Dietary reconstruction, taking into account (as advocated by Martin Jones) the entire food web, using data from bones, seeds, coprolites and preserved food residues, including lipid analysis of the kind so profitably explored by Richard Evershed *et al.*

10. Investigation of the ancestry and descent of the food plants and animals recovered, focussing upon the DNA in seeds and animal bones and using the biomolecular methods reviewed by Robert Hedges.

11. Investigation of the ancestry and descent of the human individuals for

whom bone or tissue is preserved (using comparable DNA-based methods), and investigation also of the specific genetic relationships between them.

12. Investigation of complete trading systems, using characterisation techniques, such as lead isotope analysis, for the sourcing of traded goods (in the manner outlined by Noel Gale). The investigation would aim also to follow up production of the materials at the area of origin, and consumption on the sites where they were ultimately used.

13. Investigation of the technologies used in the production of artefacts, using the range of techniques summarised by Paul Craddock and by Michael Tite for metallurgical and ceramic studies.

This sequence is, of course, a very incomplete one, deliberately referring only to the methods reviewed in the course of the Symposium itself. In addition one would wish to lay particular emphasis on the rapid publication of the material and indeed of the post-excavation analyses. And one would wish also to see undertaken some interpretation of why the observed changes took place. Here some attempt at the computer modelling of the culture system would be appropriate—simulation studies constitutes one of the more significant fields omitted from the programme of the Symposium.

It should be noted that the emphasis on post-excavation work would lie very much with the study of whole systems: the environmental reconstruction and the dietary reconstruction would benefit from the holistic approaches indicated by Berglund and Jones. The trading and technological-production studies would again consider the entire system in the manner indicated by Gale, and again by Craddock and Tite.

Perhaps the day is not far off that certain excavation projects will be conducted primarily by archaeological scientists seeking material relevant to their specialism.

3. A cautionary word

Sometimes archaeologists and, I am afraid, archaeological scientists, rather readily take the view that the conclusions offered by the application of the methods of the natural sciences carry with them more weight than do those deriving from archaeology as such.

It is pertinent, then, to remember that the findings of archaeological science have been reversed just as often. One very striking case was offered at the present Symposium. In 1923, the petrologist H.H. Thomas identified the 'bluestones' at Stonehenge as consisting of spotted dolerite, using the standard petrological technique of the microscopic examination of a thin section of the material. He showed that the only relevant source of this material was in the Prescelly Mountains of Wales, and concluded that the bluestones had been transported thence by human agency during the neolithic period (Thomas 1923).

Some ten years ago this view was questioned by Dr. Kellaway, who argued that the bluestones could have been transported to the Salisbury Plain by glacial action. His proposals attracted much media attention but did not find widespread acceptance—mainly, as I recall, because the weight of geological opinion was against the extension of the glacial flow in question so far to the east.

It was fascinating, then, to hear the case for glacial action so persuasively put by Dr. Williams-Thorpe. But although I was impressed by the coherence of her arguments, it does seem a strange stroke of fate that should lead an ice sheet to uproot so many bluestones from the Prescelly Mountains, and then proceed to deposit them in considerable quantity in so localised a part of the Salisbury Plain. Whatever the merits of the case, we see here archaeological science in conflict with archaeological science. Either in 1923 or in 1991 an erroneous conclusion has been offered.

A second famous case which comes to mind is that of Glozel. The late Glyn Daniel always considered the entire site and all its products to be monstrous fakes, and he had sound archaeological reasons for his suspicions (Daniel 1975). It was with some astonishment, then, that one contemplated the thermoluminescence dates offered by the Oxford Laboratory, by Dr. Mejdahl in Copenhagen and by Dr. McKerrell in Edinburgh, all suggesting that the site was of very considerable antiquity (McKerrell *et al.* 1974). At Professor Daniel's request I read his paper to the annual Archaeometry conference in Oxford in 1974 (Renfrew 1975). And well I remember the confidence with which the assembled archaeological scientists dismissed his evaluation of the position. But I have not, for many years, met a reputable scholar (whether archaeologist or scientist) who would maintain that the Glozel finds were other than fakes. Glyn Daniel was right and the archaeological scientists were wrong. Yet what is even more disquieting is that there has been no subsequent publication to show precisely where the thermoluminescence measurements went astray, or what was wrong with them. So far Emile Fradin, the discoverer of the site and for long the proprietor of the site museum, has had the last laugh.

Another justly celebrated case of scientific fallibility is offered by Willard Libby's comparison of the Egyptian historical dates for certain organic samples from ancient Egypt and the radiocarbon dates for the same specimens. The historical dates were systematically older than the radiocarbon dates. Did Libby suggest that the radiocarbon dates might be in error? Not a bit of it. He concluded "This plot of the data suggests that the Egyptian historical dates beyond 4,000 years ago may be somewhat too old, perhaps five centuries too old at 5,000 years ago ... it is noteworthy that the earliest astronomical fix is at 4,000 years ago, that all older dates have errors and that these errors are more or less cumulative with time before 4,000 years ago". (Libby 1963, 279).

Later it was discovered that fluctuations in the radiocarbon time scale necessitated the calibration of radiocarbon dates by means of dendrochronology. The Egyptian historical dates were found to be right, and the radiocarbon dates once calibrated fell into line with them.

At about the time of the first Royal Society/British Academy meeting in 1969 there occurred the first international conference on the volcanology and archaeology of Thera, that remarkable island in the Aegean destroyed by a volcanic eruption more than three thousand years ago. At that conference the consensus of scientific opinion was with Professor Spyridon Marinatos that the eruption of Thera was responsible for the destruction of the Minoan palaces of Crete around 1450 BC. By the time of the second congress in 1978, it was felt that the date of the eruption was somewhat earlier, perhaps around 1500 BC, and that it preceded by some decades the palace destructions. Yet at the third conference, held two years ago, whose proceedings are being published this very day (Hardy 1991), the radiocarbon evidence was being interpreted to support a date for the eruption of 1628 BC, obtained from the study of the Irish dendrochronological sequence. Nor is the matter yet settled, for the ice core dates from Greenland would appear to contradict the tree ring dates from which they differ by some twenty years.

Such controversies, when uncharitably drawn in this way to the attention of archaeological scientists, sometimes cause vexation. Indeed, to speak too loudly of Glozel is still considered bad form in some quarters. But in reality they should be as much a cause for satisfaction as for embarrassment. For is it not, these days, a defining characteristic of real science that it is testable? If we follow a refutationist definition of this kind, in the tradition of Sir Karl Popper, we should not be surprised if we encounter a few refutations! That archaeological science should sometimes give the wrong answers, and that these can later be shown to be indeed erroneous, must be counted one of the subject's greatest strengths. It is a sign of the growing maturity of the discipline that these reverses can be contemplated with equanimity (or at least near-equanimity). Archaeological science has certainly now come of age, and can take in its stride such differences of opinion as these as a characteristic feature of scientific progress.

References

Allibone, T.E. (editor) 1970a: *The Impact of the Natural Sciences on Archaeology* (London, British Academy).

Allibone, T.E. (editor) 1970b: The impact of the natural sciences on archaeology. *Philosophical Transactions of the Royal Society of London, Series A* 269, 1–185.

Daniel, G. 1975: Editorial. *Antiquity* 49, 2–4.

Hardy, D.A. (editor) 1991: *Thera and the Aegean World III, vol. 3.* (London, Thera Foundation).

Libby, W.F. 1949: *Radiocarbon Dating* (Chicago, University of Chicago).

Libby, W.F. 1963: The accuracy of radiocarbon dates. *Science* 140, 278–9.

McKerrell, H., Mejdahl, V., Francois, H. and Portal, G. 1974: Thermoluminiscence and Glozel. *Antiquity* 48, 265–72.

Pollard, A.M. 1991: *Report of the Coordinator for Science-based Archaeology 1987–90* (Swindon, Science and Engineering Research Council).

Renfrew, C. 1975: Glozel and the Two Cultures. *Antiquity* 49, 219–22.

Thomas, H.H. 1923: The source of the stones of Stonehenge. *Antiquaries Journal* 3, 239–60.

Zeuner, F.E. 1946: *Dating the Past* (London, Methuen).

Proceedings of the British Academy, **77**, 295

APPENDIX

List of Poster Presentations on Dating Techniques

Dendrochronology: precision and potential
(Archaeology and Prehistory, Sheffield University)

Application of U-series dating methods to archaeology
(Harwell Laboratory, AEA Technology)

The concordance dating of a Holocene Mexican stalagmite
(Archaeological Sciences, Liverpool University)

Recent advances in the U-series dating of contaminated secondary carbonates
(Archaeological Sciences, Liverpool University)

ESR dating and the evolution of modern humans
(Godwin Laboratory, Cambridge University and the Natural History Museum, London)

Luminescence dating of coastal sediments
(Durham University)

TL dating of vitrified hillforts
(Scottish Universities Research and Reactor Centre and Paisley College)

The dating laboratories of the British Museum

Oxford University Radiocarbon Accelerator Unit
(Research Laboratory for Archaeology, Oxford University)

Optical dating
(Research Laboratory for Archaeology, Oxford University)

Archaeological applications of magnetic remanence
(Geological Sciences, Polytechnic South West and Clark Consultancy, Guildford)

Magnetic dating
(Archaeological Sciences, Liverpool University)

Dating and the Palaeolithic of Pakistan
(Universities of Sussex, Sheffield and Southampton)